The underworld

The underworld
Duncan Campbell

BBC Books

This book is published to accompany the
television series entitled *The underworld*
which was first broadcast in 1994

Published by BBC Books,
a division of BBC Enterprises Limited,
Woodlands, 80 Wood Lane
London W12 0TT

First Published 1994

ISBN 0 563 36793 8

Set in 9 on $11\frac{1}{2}$ pt Times by Selwood Systems
Midsomer Norton
Printed and bound by Clays Ltd, St Ives plc
Cover also printed by Clays Ltd, St Ives plc

BBC Books would like to thank the following for providing photographs and for
permission to reproduce copyright material. While every effort has been made to trace
and acknowledge all copyright holders, we would like to apologise should there have
been any errors or omissions.

Barnaby's Picture Library 16; Camera Press 207; Hulton Deutsch 30, 52 (above), 71
(main pic), 74, 132–3 (main pic), 132 (inset right), 196, 205, 252; Kobal Collection 25;
London News Service 152; James Morton 24; Popperfoto 44, 52 (inset), 64, 80 (left),
90 (below), 126; Press Association 33, 39, 133 (inset left), 237 (inset); Rex Features
86 (below), 164, 166, 170, 212, 229, 240, 251 (both); Scottish Daily Record 110, 124;
Sport & General 137; Syndication International 55, 71 (inset), 80 (centre) 85, 88, 94
(left), 106, 117 (both), 132 (inset left), 133 (inset right) 145, 149, 176, 183, 191 (both),
234 (both), 237 (main pic), 246 (above left) 257; Topham Picture Source 80 (right),
90 (above), 95, 246 (below).

CONTENTS

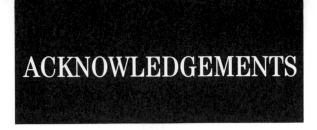

ACKNOWLEDGEMENTS

Many people helped with this book. I am very much indebted to the members of *The underworld* team at the BBC responsible for the many original interviews with the main players in the history of gangland. In particular, I would like to thank Lorraine Heggessey, Andrew Weir, Louise Norman, Frank Simmonds, Jonathan Dent and Sarah Horsfall. I would also like to thank those who agreed to be interviewed, often recounting events for the first time and, in some cases, at great risk to themselves.

Others assisted with advice, information, interviews, research and in other ways. I would like to thank, in no particular order: Bobby King, Ralph Edney, Torquil Crichton, Clive Christie, Ray Baron, Alex Marnoch, Neil Darbyshire, Brian Hilliard, Wally Probyn, Kathy Bailey, Veronica Forcella, John Masterson, Andy Malone, John Hodgman, Brendan Gibb-Gray, Rosanna Lusardi, Jim Dickinson, Pat Kavanagh, Sheila Ableman, Deborah Taylor, David Cottingham, Linda Blakemore, and Ruby Crystal. Tessa Clarke edited the book with great diligence.

I would also like to thank the staffs of Colindale Newspaper Library, the Guardian Library, the Mitchell Library and the Herald-Evening Times Library in Glasgow, the Bramshill Police Staff College Library and Camille Wolff of Grey House books.

I have referred to many books in the course of the research and their titles, for readers seeking greater detail, appear at the back of the book.

There will inevitably be omissions and errors. This is, in part, due to the fact that the hardest three words for villains, police officers and crime correspondents to say are: 'I don't know'. Also, many memories have become clouded by time and nostalgia. A plea of mitigation rather than a defence.

Now, as one Old Bailey judge likes to say to rambling defence barristers – get on with it.

CHRONOLOGY

23 December 1911 East End Vendetta trial.
27 November 1918 Billie Carleton dies of supposed drug overdose.
19 November 1922 Frattelanza Club fight.
18 January 1923 Cortesi brothers sentenced for Frattelanza fight with Sabinis.
18 April 1925 'Brilliant' Chang deported.
8 February 1931 Eddie Manning dies in prison.
24 October 1933 Kray twins born.
18 January 1934 Charlie Richardson born.
24 January 1936 Body of 'Red Max' Kassel found.
8 June 1936 'The Battle of Lewes' between racetrack gangs.
4 October 1936 Jack Spot leads attack on Blackshirts' march in East End.
10 January 1940 Ruby Sparks escapes from Dartmoor Prison.
1 May 1941 Murder of 'Little Hubby' Distleman in Soho.
31 October 1941 'Babe' Mancini hanged for murder of 'Little Hubby' Distleman.
5 December 1945 Kidnapping of Irene Coleman.
31 December 1945 Ghost Squad formed.
29 April 1947 Alec d'Antiquis shot dead by armed robbers.
9 July 1947 Billy Hill claims London gangland take-over in the 'battle that never was' against the Whites.
19 September 1947 Charles Jenkins and Chris Geraghty hanged for d'Antiquis killing.
3 September 1950 Sunday People expose Messinas.
19 March 1951 Alfredo Messina arrested.
21 May 1952 Eastcastle Street Mail Van robbery: £287 000 stolen from ambushed mail van, biggest robbery of its time.
2 November 1952 PC Sidney Miles shot. Christopher Craig and Derek Bentley arrested for his murder.
24 September 1953 Maples store burgled.
21 September 1954 KLM Bullion raid.
21 October 1954 People reporter Duncan Webb attacked.
11 August 1955 The 'fight that never was': Jack Spot and Albert Dimes' battle in Soho.
31 August 1955 Carmelo and Eugenio Messina arrested.
2 May 1956 Jack Spot attacked by Frankie Fraser and others.
25 June 1956 Tommy Smithson murdered.
21 July 1957 Jack Spot's Highball club burned down.
14 December 1958 Ronald Marwood stabs PC Raymond Summers to death.

8 May 1959 Ronald Marwood hanged.
16 August 1959 Street Offences Act changes face of prostitution.
7 February 1960 Pen Club shootings.
28 May 1960 Peter Scott/Gulston steals Sophia Loren's jewels.
11 October 1962 John Gaul fined £25 000 for living off immoral earnings.
11 July 1963 Harry Challenor plants half brick on Donald Rooum.
8 August 1963 Great Train Robbery.
15 April 1964 Great Train Robbers convicted and gaoled for up to thirty years.
12 June 1964 Jack 'The Rat' Duval beaten.
18 June 1964 Lucien Harris beaten.
12 July 1964 'Peer and Gangster' story published in *Daily Mirror.*
2 January 1965 Ginger Marks murdered.
20 April 1965 Reg Kray marries Frances Shea.
29 June 1965 Thomas Waldeck murdered.
8 July 1965 Ronnie Biggs escapes from Wandsworth Prison.
24 July 1965 Freddie Mills found dead in car.
7 March 1966 Mr Smith's: Dickie Hart killed in gangland fight.
9 March 1966 George Cornell killed in Blind Beggar.
2 May 1966 John Bradbury sentenced to death for Waldeck murder.
12 August 1966 Three policemen shot dead in Shepherds Bush.
11 November 1966 Harry Roberts caught for murder of three policemen.
12 December 1966 Harry Roberts, John Duddy, Jack Witney gaoled for life for murder of three policemen; Frank 'The Mad Axeman' Mitchell escapes from Dartmoor.
24 December 1966 Frank Mitchell killed.
4 April 1967 Richardson gang 'torture' trial starts at Old Bailey.
28 October 1967 Jack 'The Hat' McVitie murdered.
25 January 1968 Charlie Wilson recaptured.
8 May 1968 Ron and Reg Kray arrested.
7 January 1969 Krays trial starts at the Old Bailey.
8 March 1969 Ron and Reg Kray gaoled for life.
26 March 1969 Ralli Brothers robbery.
29 November 1969 *The Times'* allegations on police corruption.
9 February 1970 Ilford bank robbery: £237 000 stolen from Barclays Bank, Ilford, at that time the largest daylight bank robbery since the war.
7 May 1970 David Knight killed in fight.
5 March 1971 Vic Kelaher arrested by Customs.
22 April 1971 Car bomb placed under Jimmy Tibbs' car.
23 August 1971 Fred Sewell murders Supt Gerald Robinson in Blackpool.
25 August 1971 Dixons arrested.
18 February 1972 Trial of Bernie Silver.
27 February 1972 Commander Ken Drury exposed by *Sunday People.*

17 April 1972 Robert Mark becomes Commissioner of the Metropolitan police.

10 August 1972 Wembley Barclays Bank robbery.

5 November 1972 *Sunday Times* exposé of Drugs Squad.

23 December 1972 Bertie Smalls arrested.

March 1973 Bertie Smalls becomes a supergrass.

5 June 1973 'Chris' Krishnarma arrested. Later given what was then longest ever cannabis sentence of ten years.

31 December 1973 Bernie Silver arrested.

1 February 1974 Ronnie Biggs arrested in Rio de Janeiro.

25 April 1974 Jimmy Humphreys, pornographer, gaoled for eight years for attacking wife's lover.

11 June 1974 Maurice 'King Squealer' O'Mahoney arrested.

4 September 1974 Alfred 'Italian Tony' Zomparelli murdered at Golden Goose, Soho.

1/2 November 1974 Terence Eve murdered.

19 December 1974 Bernie Silver gaoled for six years on vice charges.

4 January 1975 George Brett and son Terry murdered.

24 April 1975 Bank of America robbery in Mayfair.

8 July 1975 Bernie Silver gaoled for Smithson murder.

12 January 1976 Barbara Gaul murdered by hitmen.

28 February 1976 Members of Scotland Yard's Obscene Publications Squad arrested.

24 June 1976 Edgeler brothers gaoled for Barbara Gaul murder.

18 October 1976 Bernie Silver's murder conviction quashed on appeal.

8 November 1976 'Dirty Squad' trial opens.

26 March 1977 Operation Julie LSD raids: 120 arrested.

7 July 1977 Kenneth Drury gaoled for eight years.

23 September 1977 George Davis arrested on Bank of Cyprus robbery.

8 March 1978 Operation Julie team gaoled.

19 October 1979 Customs officer Peter Bennett shot dead.

17 January 1980 George Piggott gaoled for murder of Alfred Zomparelli.

24 March 1980 £3.5 million silver bullion hijacked on way to Tilbury Docks.

4 April 1980 Charlie Radcliffe arrested on Operation Yashmak.

23 May 1980 Charlie Richardson escapes.

19 November 1980 Ronnie Knight cleared of murder of Zomparelli; Leonard 'Teddy Bear' Watkins gaoled for life for murder of Peter Bennett.

28 November 1980 Henry MacKenny and Terence Pinfold convicted of contract killings and gaoled for life.

3 December 1980 Colin 'Duke' Osbourne found dead in Hackney.

18 January 1981 Charlie Richardson recaptured.

24 March 1981 Ronnie Biggs kidnapped and taken to Barbados.

27 June 1982 Nicky Gerrard murdered.

28 January 1983 David Martin captured.

11 October 1983 David Martin gaoled for twenty-five years for attempted murder and robbery.

26 November 1983 £26 million Brink's-Mat robbery at Heathrow.

10 October 1984 Glasgow's Ice Cream war trial.

2 December 1984 Brian Robinson and Micky McAvoy convicted of Brink's-Mat robbery.

26 January 1985 DC John Fordham murdered in West Kingsdown, Kent.

10 June 1985 Johnny Knight and Terry Perkins gaoled for twenty-two years for Security Express robbery.

13 October 1986 Supergrass Dave Smith cuts his own throat.

12 July 1987 Knightsbridge Safe Deposit Centre robbed.

25 July 1988 Howard Marks arrested in Palma.

18 February 1989 Police informer Alan 'Chalky' White murdered in Gloucestershire.

13 April 1989 Jimmy Farrell and Terry Dewsnap shot dead on North Harrow post office robbery.

28 July 1989 Freddie Foreman returned from Spain to England.

4 August 1989 Train robbers Tommy Wisbey and Jimmy Hussey gaoled for cocaine dealing.

19 January 1990 Ron Cook murdered by Linda 'Black Widow' Calvey.

23 April 1990 Charlie Wilson shot dead in Spain.

13 July 1990 Howard Marks pleads guilty to cannabis charge, gaoled for twenty-five years.

28 September 1990 Roy Adkins murdered in Amsterdam.

27 November 1990 Armed robber Kenny Baker shot dead during Securior raid in Woodhatch, Surrey.

28 April 1991 Police informer Dave Norris shot dead in Belvedere, south London.

11 March 1991 'Abbi' Abdullah murdered in Walworth betting shop.

3 August 1991 David Brindle and Stanley Silk shot dead in The Bell, Walworth.

17 August 1991 Arthur 'Fat Boy' Thompson jnr killed.

12 June 1992 Paul Ferris cleared of murder of Arthur Thompson jnr.

30 October 1992 Joey Pyle and Pete Gillett convicted of drug dealing.

26 November 1992 Frank Sims gaoled for amphetamine operation.

13 March 1993 Arthur J. Thompson dies.

1 June 1993 James Moody shot dead in Royal Hotel, Hackney.

INTRODUCTION

The Essex Gang liked to meet in public houses in Hampstead, discuss likely targets for their armed robberies and ponder on how they could expand their activities into Europe. They were conscious that informers could win large rewards for helping turn them in and they knew the penalties were severe. It was not long, in fact, before their leader, a name well known in the popular press, was caught and given the maximum sentence for his crimes.

This was 1739, the Essex Gang were a group of robbers and poachers, and Hampstead, or Hempstead, was a village just north of London. They had already embarked on smuggling trips across the English Channel to France and they knew that George II was offering pardons for whoever informed on them. Their leader, who was executed in 1739 on what is now York racecourse, was Dick Turpin.

More than 250 years later, we still read about the gangs and Essex has more than its fair share of professional villains. One group of bank robbers in the seventies used Hampstead – Kenwood House, in fact – to plot their heists. Informers still seek milder sentences for helping the Crown and, although the footpads and smugglers are not hanged any more, the names of the best known still exercise the sort of fascination that enabled Dick Turpin, who was not averse to holding old ladies over a fire to persuade them to part with their savings, to live on in legend.

As we enter the turn of another century, criminals may have moved into computer blackmail and Common Agricultural Policy fraud, they may deal in Ecstasy and krugerrands rather than game and guineas and they may escape in helicopters rather than on Black Bess. But the underworld which kings and sheriffs sought to crush, which detectives and Home Secretaries have harried and hounded, which has fascinated writers from John Gay and Charles Dickens to Graham Greene and P. D. James, has survived, its structures changed and its nets spread wider, but none the less as sturdy as ever.

In the United States, crime is reckoned to generate an income in excess of all the top 500 businesses and corporations added together. In the United Kingdom, the figure may be lower but it is growing all the time, representing the fastest expanding industry in the country. Profits from crimes ranging from car-theft and shoplifting to cocaine smuggling and extortion now run into billions of pounds every year. Crime spawns hundreds of thousands of jobs, on both sides of its razor-wire fence, whether for burglars or bank robbers, lawyers or policemen, or the growing army of security officers. It shows no signs of abating as punishments from the seventeenth century's hanging of forgers to today's short, sharp shocks and electronic tagging have been tried and seen to fail.

There are obvious ways in which the underworld has changed: through the motor car and the aeroplane, criminals have become more mobile and elusive; the introduction of drug laws from the twenties onwards has unwittingly helped to create the most lucrative of all black markets; the regular use of firearms by criminals and, in response, by the police has increased the number of fatalities.

But there are strands that run almost unchanging through the underworld's history. There have, for instance, always been groups of 'aliens' at whose doors the blame for much of our organized crime has been placed. Russians, Jews, Chinese, Italians, Maltese, Chinese again, Turkish Cypriots, Pakistanis, Jamaicans and Colombians have all at various times this century been seen as the leading players in protection rackets, gambling, drugs, racecourse violence, vice, heroin trafficking, armed robbery and crack dealing. Certainly, pockets of immigrant groups, excluded sometimes from the more traditional ways of making money, have profited from their initial anonymity and the protection offered by a close-knit community; but there has also always been an enduring British criminal tradition that has co-opted or imitated the new arrivals.

Although Great Train Robber Tommy Wisbey says later in the book that there is no such thing as 'the underworld – just known criminals', that elusive country, 'Gangland', does still exist today. It may not be as definable as in the days before the Second World War when the Sabinis and the Hoxton Mob could be traced to a few streets of east London or when the Glasgow gangs were as well organized as Rotary Club branches. Modern criminals have no great desire to court the sort of publicity that Billy Hill and Jack Spot, the Krays and Richardsons attracted. But there are still large and powerful extended families where the main income is not entered on a tax-return form;

and there are still plenty of clubs and pubs which provide the ambience for drug dealing and money laundering in the same way that the old spielers housed gaming parties and illegal drink-ups.

The underworld remains a man's world. There have been some remarkable women inhabitants, from the 'Queen of the Forty Elephants' and the 'Bobbed-Haired Bandit' in the thirties to the 'Queen of the Shoplifters' in the sixties and the 'Black Widow' in the nineties. But crime is not an equal opportunities employer and essentially this is a boy's game, with the most prominent role for women still being that of loyal mum or long-suffering 'widow'.

This book is about the twentieth-century underworld, the people who chose and choose to live outside the law, those who, in Henry Mayhew's phrase, 'will not work'. There are other types of criminals, of course: the corporate swindlers and City fraudsters who often make far, far larger illegal sums, robbing with the pen rather than the sword and taking far fewer personal risks. And there are other murderers more calculating, sadistic and brutal than those within the underworld. But this book is not about the likes of Robert Maxwell or the Guinness profiteers, nor the Dennis Nilsens, Ian Bradys or Peter Sutcliffes. We deal here with those who have chosen crime as a profession – the career criminals, the villains, the bandits, those who have decided to live outside the law – and the world which they inhabit.

Some are the iconic names of crime and detection: the Brilliant Chang and Darby Sabini, 'Mad Frankie' Fraser and Albert Dimes, the Great Train Robbers and the Brummagen Boys, Eddie 'the King of the Safecrackers' Chapman and 'Taters' Chatham, cannabis smuggler Howard Marks and cat burglar Peter Scott; and, from 'the other team', Slipper of the Yard and 'Nipper' Read. Some have never troubled the public consciousness. Some have ended their days watching satellite television on their patio in Puerto Banus; others will continue to give pleasure to Her Majesty behind the dripping walls of some Victorian institution until well into the next century, uncomforted by the old maxim they learned on their first job: 'If you can't do the time, don't do the crime.'

As one armed robber remarked, if you take into account the unprofitable years most criminals have spent behind bars, they could have made as much money working part-time on a building site as they did with all their stocking-masked heists. For the vast majority of prisoners, the romance of crime is illusory and the reality of gaol is one of insanitary boredom. But it is through gaol that the underworld hierarchy is established and its pecking order, as strict as anything *Debrett's* could devise, is maintained.

The illicit nature of crime allows for much exaggeration and glossing over of events and by definition, the most successful criminals are the ones who have never been caught. Consequently, there are events about which we can only speculate as to where the truth lies.

When Charles Dickens wrote *Oliver Twist* he was criticized by his contemporaries for glamorizing crime. Television programmes and films today face the same criticism. Certainly, many criminals are ruthless bullies, some on the edge of psychopathy, but, equally, some are charming rogues who prefer the risks and rewards of the underworld to what they see as the hypocrisies and tedium of the overworld. All are citizens of that underworld. This book is about them.

1
THE BEGINNINGS

The Racetrack Gangs, the Mobs and the Smash-and-Grabbers

Mr Justice Hilbery was in stern mood as he surveyed the sixteen prisoners in the dock of Lewes Assizes. 'You had armed yourselves with weapons which have been aptly described as villainous instruments to use upon any fellow human being,' he told them. 'You showed no mercy to your victim and you intended to show no mercy. Crimes of gang violence in this country will be met with no mercy.' He sentenced the wielders of hatchets and knuckledusters, truncheons and chisels, to a total of fifty-three years in gaol for the part they had played in the Battle of Lewes. Its date, June 1936, might not be in the same history books as another, more famous, Sussex battle but it marked a high-water mark of violence that was to have resonances for more than the next half century. Britain now had her own very public gangsters.

But the story of the modern underworld starts in the previous century, in fiction rather than in fact. For so powerful was the effect on the public consciousness of the criminal life portrayed in Charles Dickens' *Oliver Twist* that many of the imaginary haunts of the book's characters were razed to the ground. When the London street clearances of the 1840s and 1850s took place Saffron Hill, where Fagin instructed his apprentice pickpockets, and Jacob's Island, where Bill Sikes met his death, were symbolically cleansed. But the Victorians were to learn, as were their descendants up to the present day, that it takes more than a slum demolished or a short, sharp shock to trouble one of the most enduring features of the capital.

The Seven Curses of London, which James Greenwood published in 1869, suggested that as many as 20 000 criminals, emboldened by the end of transportation to Australia and the inadequacies of the police, were at large in London at the time. Indeed, the police had scant notion of how to counteract the growth of the smarter villain. There was little in the way of detective work and the Criminal Investigation Department was not formed until 1878. The first commissioner at Scotland Yard, Sir Richard Mayne, had been opposed to the notion of such an outfit because of public fears that the new police would be a body of spies.

One of the best-known criminal figures in east London in the early part of the twentieth century was Arthur Harding, who was born in 1886 and who, unlike many of his contemporaries, lived to tell his tale. He received his criminal baptism in 1902, at the age of sixteen, when he was sentenced to twelve months penal servitude for helping a man called 'One-eyed Charlie' steal a bale of rags worth 18s from a cart. After three months in Wormwood Scrubs, Harding was transferred to the first of the new Borstals. These establishments had been set up to cater to young offenders and initially strove to provide training for a trade along with physical exercise and the reading of improving literature. But if prisons were later to be seen as universities of crime, the new Borstals were to become elite boarding-schools, turning out the hardened little villains who became the underworld figures of the twentieth century. 'Borstal made me fitter, stronger, taller and when I went back to my associates I found I was something of a hero,' Harding told his biographer, Raphael Samuel. His progression was typical of the career criminal of the time. He became the 'captain' of a group of thieves and an active participant in protection rackets and armed robbery.

There were violent, if infrequent, skirmishes between rival gangs. Around 1907, Harding and his friends became involved in a running battle against a team led by Isaac 'Ikey' Bogard, better known as 'Darky the Coon'. Bogard was a 'shundicknick', a pimp, by trade but renowned as a hardman who affected an American accent and dressed like a cowboy in an open-necked shirt, leather chaps and Stetson, with a gun – still legal in those days – stuck nonchalantly in his belt. He had a number of ex-boxers in his ranks and had been gaoled for punching a policeman in the face, escaping to a roof-top and then pelting the pursuing officers with tiles.

Harding claimed that the feud had been sparked when a former associate of his, George King, joined up with Bogard and another gangster, Philip Shonck, who planned to kill him. Before he could do the deed, Shonck was shot by one of Harding's henchmen, Tommy Taylor. This led to a series of shoot-outs in the East End.

Acquiring firearms seemed not to be a problem: some were stolen from a lax Irish constabulary and imported and others were seized in raids on local gunsmiths. Although he was proud of his Irish police revolver and happy to 'glass' an adversary in the face, Harding apparently had his standards: 'As an Englishman, I would never use a knife.'

The culmination of the feud was the 'Vendetta Affair' of 23 December 1911, which began with an argument over a woman and ended in a showdown between Harding and Bogard in the Bluecoat Boy pub in Bishopsgate, east London. Each side was about a dozen strong. Bogard offered Harding a drink which Harding, true to form, threw in his face, following up with the glass. 'The Coon had a face like the map of England,' he recalled of the aftermath. When Bogard and King asked for police protection at Old Street police court a few days later, Harding's team tried to ambush them as they came out and Harding was arrested. Eight of the miscreants stood trial at the Old Bailey. The evidence was shaky and the Bluecoat Boy manager was too frightened even to stay in London; he moved out to run a club in Southend, which gradually became a popular resting place for villains who found the nearby capital too warm. Harding was gaoled for three years for causing an affray and possession of a firearm in a court of law.

The *Illustrated Police News* reported the trial under the heading: 'East End Vendetta. Gang of Ruffians Broken Up At Last.' Mr Justice Avory issued a suitably bench-like condemnation in his summing-up: 'I wish to say that the condition of things disclosed by the evidence – that a portion of London should be infested by a number of criminal ruffians armed with revolvers – ought not to be tolerated further and if the existing law is not strong enough to put a stop to it some remedial legislation is necessary.'

Harding went to gaol but returned to the area to become a well-known East End figure. Bogard fought in the First World war, won the Military Medal and ended up working for the former head of the Flying Squad, Fred 'Nutty' Sharpe, who had become a bookmaker in Wandsworth and always had a soft spot for villains – 'a colourful rascally lot, these "wide 'uns",' as he described them.

The police were less tolerant of some of the other more desperate robbers at work at that time, particularly after what became known as the Tottenham Outrage.

On 23 January 1909 two men arriving with the wages for Schnurmann's rubber factory in Tottenham, north London, were ambushed by two Latvian immigrants, Paul Hefeld, who was armed, and Jacob Lepidus. In the struggle and ensuing chase a policeman, PC William Tyler, and a ten-year-old schoolboy, Ralph Jocelyn, who had joined in the hue and cry, were shot dead and two people were injured. The robbers fled, commandeering a tram whose conductor was forced at gunpoint to drive, a milk-cart and a van before being cornered at a high fence by the banks of the River Ching. Unable to scale the fence, Hefeld encouraged Lepidus to flee and then shot himself in the head; he died in hospital nineteen days later. Lepidus took refuge in a cottage where he was surrounded by both police and the outraged – and armed – locals who fired haphazardly into the house. As the police entered the back of the cottage, Lepidus either shot himself or was killed by a fusillade from two police officers who fired blind into the room where he was hiding.

The motive for the robbery was thought to have been to finance arms deals to Russia, masterminded by Christian Salnish (also known as Jacob Fogel) who returned there at the time of the Revolution in 1917. The groups involved in such enterprises, many of them immigrants from eastern Europe, were regarded as suspicious in both criminal and political terms and seen as threatening the stability of the capital because of their easy access to guns. 'Flocks of aliens, mostly Russians, were arriving at Irongate Wharf at the foot of Tower Bridge and were being housed in the Docks area,' wrote 'Nutty' Sharpe in his memoirs. 'Russians in top-boots and leather leggings and little round fur hats, wild-looking people from the most outlandish parts of that great uncivilized land, a lot were desperadoes and went in for crime straight away.' They were blamed for robberies and shootings and the line between the professional crook and the committed anarchist became blurred, not least because of a tendency to lump them all together in the press and Parliament.

Gambling of one kind or another played a major part in the life of the underworld: street bookmaking was illegal (until 1960) and the police were obliged to arrest a certain number of bookies every week. Consequently, the senior ones would pay hard-up men to be arrested on their behalf rather than face gaol themselves. Bribery of the lowly paid police officers was routine, with fixed rates of a shilling a day for constables and so on, depending on rank. The charismatic Edward Emmanuel led the Jewish bookies of the day and also organized boxing bouts, often rigged ones. Boxing started to establish itself as a backdrop against which both criminals and policemen socialized, a role it still plays.

Few of the underworld in the early years of the century enjoyed a reputation outside their own circle but one who did was Eddie Guerin. Born in London in 1860, he emigrated to Chicago with his parents as a child and his international approach to crime was about a century ahead of its time. He was a bad boy. He fell foul of the American police and Pinkerton's private detectives in Pittsburgh and St Louis, Toronto and Ohio. But he clearly revelled in the role of the young tearaway: 'What a red-hot game it was,' he later enthused of his time in New York. On the run, he returned to England in 1887 and made for the Criterion bar in Piccadilly which was then the haunt of 'the boys' or 'the heads' as villains were known. (They did not become the 'faces' until after the Second World War.) He was gaoled for attempting to break into a post office and sent to Holloway prison, where he was one of its last male prisoners.

Guerin's celebrity in the London underworld came from the widely held belief that he had escaped from Devil's Island off the coast of French Guiana in a rowing boat and had had to eat his companions in order to survive. The true story was more prosaic: he never actually went to Devil's Island, which was no longer used as a penal colony. Instead he was sent, as punishment for carrying out a robbery of American Express in Paris in 1901, to two of its neighbouring Îles du Salut. Money was smuggled to him by friends who sent him copies of the *Illustrated London News* and *Scientific American* stuffed with banknotes and he was able to make good his escape through a combination of bribery and cunning.

Back in Britain in 1906 after his escape, he briefly tried to earn an honest living as a tailor in Leeds in Yorkshire before returning to London. By now the French authorities wanted him back and on 29 April 1906 he was arrested at one of his regular haunts, a French newsagent in Charlotte Street, where he was buying *Le Matin* in an effort to discover whether he was indeed a wanted man. His former sweetheart, a prostitute called 'Chicago May', had betrayed him. He was successful in an action to avoid extradition on the grounds that he had been born in England and was freed but was later shot outside Russell Square underground station by the angry May and her new beau, a drunken hoodlum called Charlie Smith or Cubine Jackson. Guerin managed to square his dislike of 'snitching' enough to give evidence against the pair at the Old Bailey and Smith – 'I'm Mr Smith of Nowhere,' he said, when asked to identify himself at the London Sessions – was gaoled for life and 'Chicago May' for fifteen years.

Good escape yarns have always won the admiration of the criminal fraternity and Guerin's notoriety gave him an entrée to the British underworld, many of whose members became his friends: the bank robber Walter Sheridan, the Bidwell brothers, who were regarded as the best forgers of Bank of England notes, and 'Moocher' Wigram, who had a reputation for planning some of the major jobs of the era. But Guerin drifted into petty crime and was gaoled in 1917 for trying to break into the Metropole hotel in Brighton. What hurt more was that, when he went to the American Bar in London's Savoy hotel after his release, he was asked to leave as an undesirable.

By 1928, Guerin was able to write nostalgically of the 'good crooks' and say how he and the Scotland Yard men with whom he would occasionally drink had little respect for the new breed of criminal who had 'no skills'. Touchingly, he believed he was one of a dying breed: 'No doubt education is playing its part. "Honesty is the best policy" is one of the fundamental principles of the compulsory learning with which the younger generation of today are brought up.'

The Great War had its impact on the underworld just as the Second World War would in its time. Charles Leitch, an inter-war Scotland Yard detective, noted in his memoirs that the 'battalions of crime have been further swollen by the "new criminal" who in most cases is a criminal *"malgré lui"* – one who is driven into crime against his will by the fatal urge of an economic situation which he does not pretend to understand.'

Leitch and his colleagues believed that these men were unafraid of battle and killing and bitter at the failure to find them a role in society after the hell of the trenches. The detective saw a new generation of villain, brought up in the time of post-war uncertainty and disillusionment: the 'Legion of the Lost', he called them, men who wanted not just *'panem* but a large measure of *circenses'*. These were to become the motor bandits and the confidence tricksters, the smash-and-grab artists and the cat burglars.

In the over-heated post-war atmosphere of the early twenties, the alien criminal took on a special aura: a gang of 'international coiners and anarchists', as the police described them, established themselves in Hampstead. They were led by a Frenchman called Bonnot, the Red Bandit, who was, according to Leitch, the first 'motor bandit'. White Russians fleeing the Revolution could not be deported, a loophole exploited by criminals. And there was more than a whiff of anti-Semitism around the attitude to the Jewish criminals of the time. In *Crooks of the Underworld*, published in 1929, 'Charles Gordon' talks about the managers of night clubs who, 'being of Jewish persuasion', advised people on how to carry out insurance frauds with their stolen jewels.

But it was on the racetracks in the 1920s and 1930s that the idea of organized crime and gang warfare was to have its modern birth. Street gambling was illegal and the large sums that bookies at racecourses could make drew a criminal element who offered what amounted to protection. Bookies would be charged for the chalk for their boards showing the odds, the stools on which they stood and the sponging down of their boards between races. They were also expected to dawdle about their work with clients so that the pickpockets could get to work. These 'dips' were described by Detective Superintendent Charles Vanstone as 'feral, shifty little men, they darted about all over the place'. The gangs also asked bookies to buy tickets in aid of the 'distressed wife' of any of the gang members unfortunate enough to be gaoled. It was simple enough to disrupt the pitches of bookmakers who would not co-operate.

Young lads worked for the gangs 'on the bucket', which meant they assisted in sponging down the boards. 'They [the bookies] could have done it themselves quite easily,' says Frankie Fraser, who did the job as an eight-year-old, 'but it was part of the ritual that they had to pay for this wonderful benefit.' He would take home 7s 6d at the end of the day and the sponge man would do much better. To a young Fraser, whose father worked honestly for £2 10s a week, it was clear that virtue was not its own reward: 'I thought to myself – this is the game to be in.'

Billy Kimber, a Birmingham-based bookie who had been born in south London, ran the Brummagem Boys and from around 1910 controlled the racecourses at Newbury, Epsom, Alexandra Park, Earls Park and Kempton Park. He had rivals, including a team from Leeds, one from the East End and the 'Italians'. Razor slashings were a regular occurrence and a bookie was killed at Sandown Park. One favourite weapon was a razor blade stitched into the peak of a cap.

In 1921 the Birmingham and Leeds mobs decided to take on the 'Italians' – Kimber hated all foreigners – on the last day of the Derby meeting at Epsom but the Birmingham Boys ambushed their Leeds allies by mistake, only realizing their error when a Leeds man shouted out, 'You have made a bloomer. We are Leeds men.' The pitched battle lasted ten minutes and twenty-three men were convicted of offences relating to it. The Home Secretary, Sir William Joynson-Hicks, responding to public expressions of outrage at the mayhem, announced that he intended to smash gangdom: 'It may be difficult to get rid of these gangs all at once but give me time.' He needed it.

The 'Italians' who enjoyed such a fearsome reputation were better known as the Sabinis. Darby (Charles), Joe, Fred, George and Harry Boy Sabini were an Italian immigrant family who launched their Bookmakers and Backers Racecourse Protection Society to challenge Kimber's hegemony on the tracks. They worked closely with the Jewish bookies and there were a series of pitched battles between the two gangs in the early twenties. The Sabinis operated from their base in Clerkenwell in east London, the Little Italy of the era. Darby, a former boxer who had worked as a bouncer at the boxing halls in nearby Hoxton, held the position of paterfamilias in the local community. He sorted out internal conflicts and defended the honour of the young Italian women, most notably, so the story went, that of a barmaid whose dress had been stripped from her by a local bully.

23

While most of his men were of Italian origin, Darby also worked with the Jewish bookmaker Alf Solomons, a local streetfighter called Georgie Sewell and the man who was later to take over some of his territory: Alf White. In the end, the Sabinis were more than a match for the Birmingham mob who, as Arthur Harding saw it, were 'all "rough house", they weren't as clever as the Darby Sabini lot'.

The Sabinis had a menacing reputation: 'Darby Sabini and his thugs used to stand sideways-on to let the bookmakers see the hammers in their pockets,' recalled Ex-Detective Chief Superintendent Edward Greeno of the Flying Squad, who described another Italian member of the gang as having a 'name like a mineral water'. He claimed to have driven Darby Sabini away from Ascot on one occasion after the gang leader had been knocked unconscious by the Hoxton Mob. He had followed him to the gents, where Sabini's lieutenants were 'twisting his ears, a painful but effective way of bringing a man out of a fist-induced coma'.

The Sabinis were not above co-operating with the police when it suited them, specifically in helping them to arrest members of the

Birmingham Mob so effectively that Kimber eventually decamped back to the Midlands. Sometimes the Sabinis would assist the constabulary by chalking the palms of their hands and slapping a known thief on the shoulder, thus identifying him to the racecourse police. One of the more colourful villains on the racetracks was known as 'The Policeman' because he posed as an undercover officer; when a victim had grabbed hold of a pickpocket, he would 'arrest' the culprit and take him off to 'the station' (railway rather than police).

The financial rewards were great, and at their peak in the thirties gangs reckoned to take upwards of £5000 a day from the courses. But some criminals looked down on them. They were suspicious of the close relationship they often had with the police and accused them of being bullies because they tended to hunt in packs of twenty or so. The Jockey Club asked the police for help, without great effect initially. It remained a violent world, one touched on by Graham Greene in *Brighton Rock*, and there were many aspiring 'Pinkies' about as legitimate work dried up during that decade.

Richard Attenborough as 'Pinkie' in *Brighton Rock*. Left: The Sabinis and the Cortesis. Darby Sabini is fifth from the right.

The Sabinis brooked no argument and defended their reputation fiercely. But there was dissension within the Italian criminal community, specifically between the Sabinis and the Cortesis (another Italian gang), after Harry Boy Sabini had been shot and wounded in the Frattelanza Club in Clerkenwell in November 1922.

Louisa Doralli, the daughter of the club's manager, told in the subsequent trial how she had noticed the arrival of the five members of the Cortesi gang: Gus, Paul and George Cortesi, Harry 'Frenchie' (which was another name by which the Cortesis were known) and Alexander Tomaso, known as Sandy Rice. She had grabbed 'Frenchie' as he pulled a revolver out of his pocket but he wrenched it free. 'I didn't think they would shoot at a woman,' she said. Gus Cortesi had then hit Darby Sabini with a lemonade bottle and fired at him, but the bullet went through the window. Harry 'Frenchie', who had shot and wounded Harry Sabini, went on the run and the *Daily Express* advised its readers how to spot him: 'He walks with a Charlie Chaplin step, the result of a combination of flat feet and knock knees but he is able to disguise not only his walk but his features.' Not for long.

At the trial, George and Paul Cortesi and Tomaso were cleared but two of the Cortesis, Gus and Harry 'Frenchie', were gaoled for three years. Inspector Grosse told the court that there had been a number of fights between the two gangs and that there was 'a feud the bottom of which was difficult to fathom'. In sentencing Gus and Harry, Mr Justice Darling remarked: 'I look upon this as part of a faction fight which has raged between you and other Italians in consequence of some difference which the police do not entirely understand. You appear to be two lawless bands – the Sabinis and the Cortesis. Sometimes you are employed together against the Birmingham people and sometimes you are employed against each other ... I do not think there is much to choose between you but the Sabinis are within the king's peace while in England and people must not be allowed to shoot them or at them.' He warned the 'Italian colony' that if such conduct continued those responsible would be turned out of the country with their wives and children.

In its reports on the case the *Empire News* discreetly referred to Darby as 'one of the most talked of men in London'. The Sabinis certainly made frequent appearances in court following similar feuds, often over the honour of women. On one memorable occasion the judge, Mr Justice Darling, who was proud of his linguistic abilities, addressed one of the Sabinis in Italian, which most of the gang did not understand, informed the jurors helpfully that the name derived from the Sabines and retold the story of the rape of the Sabine women.

The Sabinis were also victims of an anti-Italian feeling abroad in the thirties. In one Soho incident, thugs had entered a club asking, 'Are there any raddies here?' ('Raddies' was short for radicals, the name given to the Italian followers of Garibaldi.) The severe beating of an unfortunate Italian with 'life-preservers' (coshes) and chair legs followed. Pitched battles continued.

The most celebrated of the conflicts was the Battle of Lewes in June 1936, mentioned at the start of this chapter. A gang of around thirty Londoners, mainly from Hackney and Hoxton, attacked a Sabini-protected bookie, Alf Solomons, and his clerk, Mark Frater. The aggressors had realized that undercover police were present – 'It's no good here, there are too many top-hats [detectives],' said one – but chanced their luck anyway. Police reported later how they had followed the gang and had heard one of its members, James Spinks, shouting 'There they are, boys, get your tools ready.' Frater was lucky to be wearing his bowler hat which partly deflected a hatchet blow from Spinks, whom police regarded as a ringleader. Someone in the crowd shouted a warning of 'Here they are boys. Blow!' But a total of sixteen of the fighters were later gaoled by the solemn Mr Justice Hilbery. Not all the press saw it as a moment of great significance at the time: the *Daily Telegraph* gave it only a couple of paragraphs on its back page beside the stop-press news of the Lindbergh kidnap in America. But the after-effects were great, both for the Sabinis and in terms of the public's attitude to organized gangs.

The Sabinis' power was already waning. Darby unwisely sued for libel after an unflattering profile appeared in the press, but he lost and was declared bankrupt. In court he denied being the 'king of the Sabini gang,' saying, 'I am just a humble, peace-loving man.'

The Second World War was the final leveller. Some of the brothers were interned as enemy aliens. Harry Boy took over from Darby, who had moved to the South Coast of England, and recruited desperadoes from Sicily. Darby went briefly to gaol for receiving and while he was inside his beloved son was killed in action with the Royal Air Force. Darby died in Hove in 1950, a broken man. His funeral was not a gangland extravaganza, but crime correspondent Edward T. Hart reported that his old adversary, the detective Jack 'Charlie Artful' Capstick, who had founded the Ghost Squad at Scotland Yard in 1946, threw a red rose from his buttonhole on to the grave.

The White family from King's Cross gradually took over the racetracks and some of the streets with a casual brutality. As safe-cracker Eddie Chapman, later to emerge as one of the underworld's best-known characters, recalls, 'They had a team of little villains who would go and cut off anybody's head for about a tenner.'

The key development for the criminal between the two world wars had undoubtedly been the motor car, which made speedy escapes possible. The police response was the formation in 1919 of the Flying Squad, a mobile squad that initially used a covered wagon from the Great Western Railway for surveillance and two RAF vans, one to patrol north of the Thames and one south. The name came from a *Daily Mail* journalist W. G. T. Crook, who referred to a 'flying squad' of picked detectives. There were eighteen in the initial squad – later to acquire the nickname 'Sweeney' from the rhyming slang of Sweeney Todd, the Demon Barber, and distinguished by its swooping eagle emblem. It would never be short of potential prey and one of its earliest targets was the twenties' best-known smash-and-grabber, one 'Ruby' Sparks.

Born in Bermondsey in south-east London, with a bare-knuckle fighter for a father and a receiver of stolen goods as a mother, Sparks began his apprenticeship as a junior mail-train robber, hiding in a hamper with the mailbags and sprinting out later with the loot. He was supposedly nicknamed 'Ruby' after he had stolen real rubies from a maharaja but been assured by an incompetent receiver that they were artificial; Sparks casually handed them out to friends, losing himself thousands of pounds in the process. He was also known as 'Rubberface' because of his habit of contorting his features whenever police tried to take a mug shot.

He first became a cat burglar but in about 1923 teamed up, famously, with the 'Bobbed-Haired Bandit', a young, middle-class woman called Lilian Goldstein, who drove a Mercedes and wowed the popular prints, one of which described her thus: 'She is often dressed in a red beret and motoring coat of the same colour, or in an all-green motoring outfit, and she is believed to be the brains behind recent country-house raids which have resulted in losses running into several thousands of pounds.' Goldstein came from a respectable Wembley family and was a dressmaker before she fell for one of the 'wide men' as a teenager and, according to the police, earned money by travelling round Hyde Park with clients in the backs of taxis. She had had a brief gaol sentence and a period of working as a saleswoman in London before meeting the dashing Sparks and acting as his driver. They worked together on smash-and-grabs and robberies for half a dozen years until they were arrested.

It could be a messy business. Sparks reckoned he had a 'handful of diamonds for each scar' and would carry bulldog clips in a clean handkerchief to keep the cuts he received on smash-and-grabs together until Goldstein could stitch them up. He also took advantage of the louche young men who liked to slum it in the West End: 'Upper crust teddy boys ... prepared to betray the whereabouts of their own mother's tiara for the price of a night at Quo Vadis.'

Even the police were in awe of Goldstein's driving skills. 'Nutty' Sharpe recalled: 'She could whiz that great long tourer about with the skill of an artist ... her trouble was that she ought to have been a boy.' The Bobbed-Haired one, for her part, objected when Sparks' friends greeted her as 'Hi, doll'.

They could not escape the law for ever and, although Goldstein was cleared of her part in the robberies, Sparks received a three-year term in 1927. His escape from Strangeways in 1927 was accompanied by a rhyming farewell note:

'The cage is empty
The bird is flown
I'm gone to a place
Where I'm better known.'

More sentences were to follow. He did not sit placidly in gaol and was a leading figure in the 1932 Dartmoor prison mutiny.

On 10 February 1939, he was gaoled for five years. Sparks escaped from Dartmoor on 10 January 1940 with two fellow convicts, no mean feat then or now, and remained at large for five months. There was a poignant reunion with the Bobbed-Haired Bandit in whose Wembley Park home he hid. He had become involved with more ruthless, young gangsters and was slowing down. Goldstein was sentenced to six months for harbouring him but served only three weeks, as she was deemed to have acted only because of her long-term and 'womanly' attachment to Sparks: 'I can understand the human element in this case,' said the judge. 'He was an escaped convict to the rest of the world but that is not how she viewed him.' But they parted, however, and Sparks eventually married a respectable woman called Anne with whom he ran firstly an ice-cream business and then, at the end of the Second World War, the Penguin Club in Regent Street, complete with waitresses dressed as musical comedy sailorettes.

As for Lilian Goldstein, she bowed out with typical panache, telling Sparks: 'I've had enough of this bandit queen lark.' Elsewhere in the underworld, there were very different larks afoot.

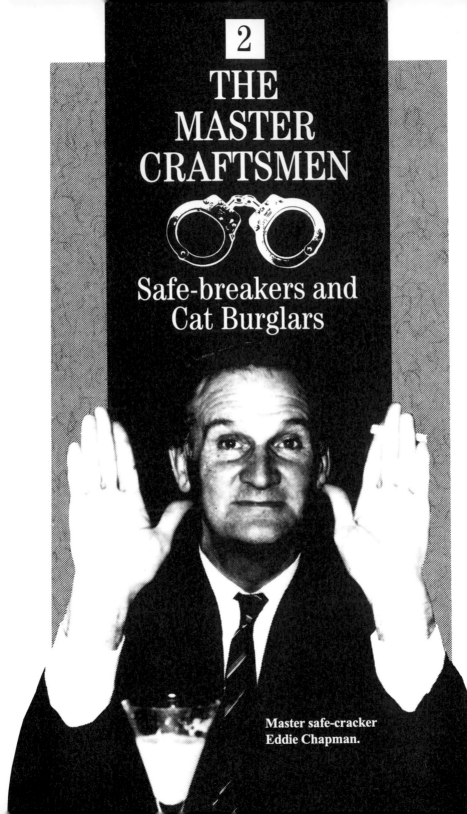

2

THE MASTER CRAFTSMEN

Safe-breakers and Cat Burglars

Master safe-cracker
Eddie Chapman.

'*T*here was a hell of depression hitting the country but we lived like multi-millionaires,' says Eddie Chapman. 'We used to motor down to Brighton in a drop-head Ford Sedan which cost £120 brand new. They did 90 miles an hour and we used to smash them up and just buy another one.' He had met two chorus girls from a show called *Panama Hattie*. 'The one thing we had was money. Whenever we ran out, we used to go out and blow another safe. Life was a bit fast and furious then.'

Alongside the racetrack gangs of the twenties and thirties had developed a new breed – the artisan criminals, the master craftsmen, the specialists with their own skills and techniques. Foremost amongst them was the safe-breaker, traditionally the brain surgeon of criminal society. He was by now so prolific that security firms were having to invent ever more elaborate ways of trying to combat him: spinning safes, sinking safes that dropped underground, sliding safes with spring-loaded money boxes, even the Trusty Alarm Box 'which growls like an angry mastiff if any unauthorized person picks it up'. The cracksmen were undeterred.

In the 1930s Chapman came into this arena. A young man from a small mining village outside Newcastle, Chapman had been an apprentice in the shipbuilding trade before lying about his age and joining the Guards. He found protecting the Tower of London a tedious job and on his first leave headed for the West End. A Marble Arch prostitute introduced him to a new world: 'I met a lot of small-time villains and did one or two things with them. I bought a civilian suit and I never went back.' But the military came back for him and he was sentenced to 112 days in the glasshouse. After his release he drifted back to his new friends, and soon to prison in Lewes where he met his partner-to-be, Jimmy Hunt. Hunt took him on his first serious job, a break-in of Fyffe's banana factory, where he learned how to rip the backs off safes with screwdrivers.

Chapman and Hunt became more daring. On one occasion they knocked a hole through the wall of a furriers in broad daylight, pretending they were watermen who had come to repair the mains. They stole to order – lipsticks, fur stoles, yeast tablets, whatever the customer ordered.

The thirties were innocent times and when an American crook arrived on the scene in an underworld club the locals were amazed at his ideas on crime: 'He was sounding off about "Don't you guys ever do any heists?" We said, "What's that?" He said, "Just knock on the door and hold a fucking gun there and they'll fall apart." We said no, we never carry guns. There was an unwritten rule.' But the American did ask, more pertinently, if they blew up safes and, having learned of the rather primitive methods then used, suggested that they explore the possibilities offered by gelignite.

Chapman and Hunt set off to Wales to find the explosive in the quarries and mines there and stole 400 detonators and two packets of gelignite. They practised in the countryside and, having brought down a mighty tree, decided they were ready to blow up safes. Their journey began at Edgware Road underground station, which was relieved of its takings, and they travelled onwards and upwards from there: 'Every week we were knocking something out. The papers got hold of it and every time there was a job it was on the BBC – "There's been another attack by the gelignite gang."' A specially formed police squad initially thought an American gang was at work because of the traces of chewing gum used to fix the explosive. The press speculated that the IRA could be involved.

Odeon cinemas were a popular target. Chapman would hide in the gents, perched above a cubicle, until the cinema was closed and then break into the manager's office and set to work on the safes. On one occasion, robbing the Odeon at Swiss Cottage, he miscalculated the timing on one of the two safes and was bowled over and injured. After he had recovered himself, he stuffed the money into a bag and made his escape. On the underground he realized that the office cleaners who were staring at this dishevelment were noting the suspicious words 'Odeon Cinema' on the bag on his knee.

The safe-breaking method was basic: 'It was simply a matter of filling the keyhole up with gelignite.' One trick was to hang a typewriter on the handle of the safe so that when the blast weakened the lock the extra weight would open the door before too much damage was caused. After overdoing the amount of explosive on a few occasions, he decided to keep a methodical list of how much had been used each time and its subsequent effect. 'Each safe used to boast it was "in-built explosive-free",' says Chapman. 'This wasn't true. We had a few failures but not many. Most of the errors were to do with using too much explosive.' The French letter now came into its own as something for the safe-breaker's weekend: it would be filled with gelignite and water, knotted and then poked through a lock. The condom kept the explosive together, preventing it from dropping into the safe.

The attractions of the life were obvious. For a while in the thirties Chapman lived in a hotel by the Burlington Arcade: 'We were kids. We had a suitcase full of silver, half crowns, sixpences, shillings and every time I went out I'd say take a handful. We over-tipped everyone.' It was a time when Fats Waller and the Four Flash Devils were playing at The Nest, when Lady Mountbatten would arrive with a black escort and a bottle of whisky was 12s 6d. The police knew what he was up to but could never catch him in the act: 'They started to come round the clubs and pubs we were using. Fabian [Superintendent Robert Fabian, the Scotland Yard detective] used to walk in and say, "I know you've had it off, you bastard, buy me a drink." '

'Fabian of the Yard'.

When other criminals complained at the additional police activity generated by all the safe-breaking, Chapman moved up to Scotland, having read about a record dividend being paid at a Co-operative store in Edinburgh. With a couple of accomplices, he drove north with gelignite and tools stashed in golf bags; their cover story was that they were off to a tournament. In the store, they found a half-ton Chubb safe in the office, and a difficult job was made more so when the look-out failed to spot a lurking policeman. One accomplice was caught in the Co-op itself, crashing into the pyramids of fresh fruit and tins as the policeman summoned help by 'playing his flute' (blowing his whistle). Chapman leapt aboard a slow train in his getaway and the team eventually drove south. They made it to Newcastle Corner where they were spotted by police and arrested. Two of the Yard's big names, Edward Greeno and Fabian, arrived on the scene but the local magistrate ruled that the robbers should stand trial in Scotland first and Chapman was granted bail. He raised bail for his confederates by breaking into another Odeon cinema.

Back in London, at Smokey Joe's club, he was warned that the Yard were looking for him and retreated to the Regent Palace Hotel: 'Written on the menu was "Come to sunny Jersey". I thought – that's a good idea.' And off he went with some accomplices.

The robbers' cover story in Jersey was that they were in the film business. The eventual plan was to head for South America. But their attempts to lie low were blown when one of the team sent some perfume to a new girlfriend he had met tea-dancing in Bournemouth. The faithless doxy told her brother, who was in the CID, and the hunt moved to Jersey. When his waiter's hand started shaking badly as he poured the wine, Chapman realized that the hotel must be under surveillance and fled along the beach. He told a local landlady he was just 'off the boats' and needed a bed for the night. He then broke into a handy cinema and stole £1200, planning to ship out to Dieppe at dawn. But he was hardly in bed when the police burst in shouting: 'Come on you bastard, put the bracelets on.' He confessed that he had just broken into a safe so the local police insisted that he stay and stand trial. He was gaoled for two years.

But the war intervened. The Germans invaded the Channel Islands in 1940 and found the disconsolate Chapman in gaol. They recruited him as a German agent in 1941 but, once free, he informed the British authorities of his new role and became a double agent. In recognition of this service, the outstanding charges against him were withdrawn, sparing him a possible sentence of twenty years for more than forty cracked safes. His story was later filmed as *Triple Cross*, starring Christopher Plummer, Romy Schneider and Trevor Howard.

'The deal was that any money I made with the Germans I kept,' says Chapman. 'I was working under British Intelligence and they behaved like a lot of Boy Scouts.' Chapman followed the motto of Do-Your-Best and kept safe-breaking, with jabs of cocaine before a big job to ease the pain of a bad back and give him the two hours he needed to operate: 'It was murder. If there had been a man-hunt, I would never have got away.'

Finally, after serving a total of only around four years for all his time safe-cracking, Chapman packed in crime and started a health farm – he had always kept in trim with boxers, believing a good criminal is a fit criminal. Amongst those who were to patronize his legitimate venture were boxers John Conteh and Frank Bruno. Chapman and his businesswoman wife, Betty, had invested wisely in other ways, buying a castle in Ireland and a yacht and sending their daughter to a good school.

If Chapman was the champion in the safe-blowing division, the most famous house-breaker of the post-Second-World-War period, and burglar to the gentry – 'His crime sheet read like *Debrett's*,' according to Chapman – was George 'Taters' Chatham. But Chatham lacked Chapman's ability to remain at large and was arrested so often he was rumoured to have his own room, 'Chatham's cell', in Chelmsford gaol. His first conviction was in 1931 and he spent a total of thirty-five years inside.

Chatham specialized in robbing the rich and famous and titled. He would break into a house and, if it did not live up to his expectations, he would try the one next door. Mr 'Teasy Weasy' the hairdresser and Madame Prunier the restaurateur were two of his victims. With the proceeds, he ran a 12-cylinder Lagonda and a sports Mercedes. He had a certain sense of honour: on one occasion he had stolen an eternity ring and a fur coat from Lady Rothermere, wife of the chairman of Associated Newspapers. He was approached by one of the family's editors and asked if he could recover the items, which he duly did, complaining only at the cheap quality of the coat which he said he would have never dreamed of giving to any of his girlfriends.

On one of his profitable expeditions his only accomplice was the London smog, a pea-souper so dense that people could not see more than a few feet in front of them. Using the cover provided by nature he broke into houses around Hyde Park, leaping from balcony to balcony and gaining meteorological recognition in the newspapers as the cat burglar who had 'made hay while the sun wasn't shining'. In December 1938 he was gaoled for six years.

One of Chatham's most famous heists, in April 1948, was that of the Wellington swords from the Victoria and Albert Museum, into which he broke via a window 12 metres (40 feet) up by tying two ladders together. It was a simple job: 'I smashed the glass, took the swords and was away.' He removed the stones, sold some and gave others to his girlfriend. He had no regrets: 'I was sort of besotted by them and thought I had to have them. I was a rebel against authority and I had no respect for the police. If I could outwit them in any way, I would.' He rationalized the burglaries thus: 'They were usually very, very rich people, millionaires. Some of them regarded it as a nice thing to talk about at dinner parties.' He once attempted to break into Raine Spencer's house but inadvertently walked off the roof and fell four floors. He was in hospital for six weeks but was determined, like a rider thrown by a horse, to get back on the roofs. In plaster, bandages and great pain he broke in and was in the process of putting the jewellery in his pocket when the maid walked in and alarmed her employers with her scream.

Chatham's tools were a screwdriver, gloves and a tiny torch, and he preferred to break in while everyone was at home at a dinner party so that there would be no alarms and the jewellery would be on the premises. Belgravia, Mayfair and Regent's Park formed his golden triangle. He picked his targets carefully, spending time in the public library examining reference books like *Who's Who* and *Burke's Peerage*, and glossy magazines like the *Tatler* and *Country Life* which acted as a sort of *Exchange & Mart* for thieves.

He also had his inside men. An ex-captain in the Blues, who claimed to have escorted the young Princess Elizabeth and her sister, would tip him off as to where money and jewellery might be found and a Lloyds clerk 'borrowed' confidential reports on insured premises, smuggling them out for Chatham to examine in a lunch-hour.

But while Chapman had accumulated his money and spent little time inside, Chatham gambled his loot as fast as he acquired it, reckoning to have stolen and spent several million pounds. In his sixties he was still stealing furs and jumping red lights to escape pursuing police cars. At seventy-six he was arrested for shoplifting. 'What have I got? A lot of sad memories. And thirty years inside.'

The inheritor of Chatham's mantle in the mid-fifties to late seventies was Peter Gulston, now Scott, an Irishman who had been burgling since he was a teenager but who took it up seriously after dissipating an inheritance and spending six months in gaol in Belfast. At his trial a policeman described him as a 'natural thief' which he took as a compliment. Scott's mainland career started when he was working in London as a doorman at a club and a 'suave, trench-coated guy' approached him with an offer of openings. He moved speedily into the first division of burglars. Although he was informed by a London criminal that he could never be 'one of the chaps' because he was Irish, his combination of charm and aggression secured him a permanent niche in the underworld.

It was not only the money that motivated him: 'Fear is a very private form of excitement and it's sexual in its context.' He soon moved into the homes of the rich, buying a new suit so that he felt properly dressed. He recalls an early job: 'The butler was laying a majestic table laden with food and silverware and I felt a bit like a missionary seeing my flock for the first time. I realized this was my life's work, persecuting the rich and the opulent.' He knew he had a talent for his chosen career: 'As soon as Lester Piggott throws a leg over a horse, you can see the magic. As soon as I climbed up a drainpipe, my confederates could see the magic.'

His informants included chauffeurs from Knightsbridge who let him know the addresses of the wealthy and when functions were being held. Scott was modest about his skills: 'The term "cat burglar" has been romanticized. You're really only a dishonest window cleaner. I actually watch window cleaners doing much more dangerous things than I've ever done.' Although he had given the fur trade 'the benefit of my degeneracy' for a number of years, he was principally a jewel thief, moving on to antiques, silverware and paintings. Mayfair was his private oyster and the pearls were real. He learned where the rich hid their jewels; one in soiled sanitary towels, others in the airing cupboard.

He lived on his wits. During one break-in 'a titled lady had come to the top of the stairs and I shouted up "Everything's all right, madam" and she went off to bed, assuming I was the butler.' (An earlier, notorious burglar had the almost endearing trademark of reassuringly remarking, when he heard the burgled resident stirring upstairs, 'It's only me"!') Scott took a number of bad falls, nearly impaling himself in Bond Street and falling through a canopy in Viceroy Court. His career was the subject of a film called *He Who Rides the Tiger* starring Tom Bell and Judi Dench, but Scott was in Dartmoor when they were filming and made little money from it.

His other connection to the film world came when he robbed Sophia Loren at the Norwegian Barn, in the Edgewarebury County Club, when she was making a film in England. He had read that she would be paid in jewels and thought he would have some for himself. On 28 May 1960, he drove into a garage in the area with a press card in the window of his stolen 2.4 Jaguar, pretending to be a journalist, and was tipped off as to her whereabouts by the petrol pump attendant. He spotted Ms Loren putting empty Chianti bottles in a bin and remembers her as 'an attractive peasant girl'. He broke in and removed a briefcase with cash and jewels and he recalls that the robbery was listed as the largest jewel theft in the world, worth around £200 000. On television subsequently, Ms Loren told the thief that she had put a curse on him as she came from old gypsy stock, a curse that Scott ruefully admits was successful, since he proceeded to lose all the money in the casinos. But he defends his calling.

'The police don't get terribly excited about people who burgle prefabs in Catford, who don't have the ear of the Home Secretary. All my victims were very prestigious people – the only people who end up with vast amounts of money or jewellery are very greedy predatory people and it's been one of the great privileges of my life to persecute them. I almost feel as though I was an agent of God bringing retribution to the self-satisfied. I used to go to Ascot quite frequently and you'd meet them all in their top hats and their finery, prats chattering in monosyllables. I had an endemic hatred for them. I don't think I was very greedy. I spent my life giving money to head waiters, tarts and the needy bookmakers. Of the two thieves on the cross with the Nazarene, I rather see myself as the one who didn't get into heaven.'

The solo professionals and the heavy gangsters did not mix too much. Gangsters, Scott believed, were parasites and predators to be avoided by the jobbing thief. On one occasion when a couple of gangsters wanted to join him on a raid because of his high success rate, he took them to a remote country mansion, placed them at the front of the building, went round the back and smashed a window to set off the alarm. Lights went on and the group sped away, relieved to have escaped. He asked the young gangsters to come again the next week but they had decided it was not the game for them.

The 'king of the cat burglars', Peter Scott or Gulston, with his wife Jackie, in 1969.

38

Scott has few regrets over his twelve and a half years inside. He was married to Jackie, a model, a 'great sport' but now lives alone in a council flat in Islington in north London. 'I have no money but I have retained my arrogance. I am not reformed, I just have no more time to offer them, no more of my life to give them behind bars, so I have stopped. There was no road to Damascus, no burning bush, I simply didn't fancy getting locked up again.' His last brush with the law was in 1985 when he was gaoled for four years on a theft charge. All told, he reckons to have stolen money and jewels worth about £30 million.

'I used to think I was one of the most attractive men in London. I was never short of beautiful women on my arm. It wasn't until I ended up in Regent's Park hitting tennis balls for a tenner an hour that I realized how totally unattractive I was. You almost become invisible in poverty. The number of people I've seen in recent years – the Rolls Royce slows when it sees me, and I can almost feel them thinking – "there's no mileage in talking to Peter now" – and it glides away. But I was only a very modest performer in the sin business. I have a suspicion that if the Nazarene is in residence he might remand me in custody for a while but he'll talk to me again.'

Scott, Chapman and Chatham were part of a long line of individual underworld entrepreneurs. There were others whose portraits would hang alongside them in a rogue's gallery of the first half of the twentieth century.

'Gentleman George' Smithson was one of the best known of the country-house burglars. He lived respectably in Kensington, where he consulted *Burke's Landed Gentry* and *Debrett's* to see who had property where. He arrived at his chosen targets by bicycle and mixed little with the traditional underworld. But despite his discretion he was gaoled three times between 1911 and 1929.

'Flannelfoot', the nickname of Edward Vicars, carried out hundreds of burglaries in the London suburbs in the thirties. He covered his feet with cloth so that he could move silently about a house, burgling it and then making his getaway on a stolen bicycle. He was so successful that a special squad was set up at Scotland Yard to trace his muffled footsteps. He was caught in 1937, credited with 135 burglaries that year, gaoled for five years and died in prison.

One of the most celebrated teams, who operated after the Second World War, consisted of Johnny 'No Legs' and Harry 'The Doctor' Bass. Their technique was more Ealing than stealing: the legless Johnny, an Italian by birth, would approach a jewellers at closing time in his electric chair. He would ask for assistance because he had lost the key to his tool-box. The jeweller would oblige by lending him his bunch of keys to try. At this stage 'the doctor', wearing 'an Anthony Eden' hat as one colleague described it and with a stethoscope round his neck, would arrive and ask for directions to Acacia Avenue. During the course of this conversation Johnny 'No Legs' would make an impression of the keys. They would then wait six weeks or so, checking that there was sufficient jewellery to be worth stealing. Bravingtons in Blackpool was their Waterloo. Jewellers had exchanged information and the police were waiting. Both were gaoled.

Another high-profile criminal of the forties was Bert Holliday, also known as 'the Gentleman Cracksman'. Four police forces hunted him but he was only caught when he was spotted in 1949 stealing a cheese from the Dumb Bell Inn in Taplow in Buckinghamshire. Although he came from a poor Elephant and Castle background, Holliday was a jewel thief in the Raffles mode. He posed as a retired jeweller, lived in a house called Jour de Fête on Friary Island in the Thames, rode to hounds and mixed in a southern county set. He also stole guns, antiques and petrol coupons. In his house the police found stolen goods that stretched back to 1932. Working sometimes with 'Poofy Len' Oades, Holliday was an expert climber and always carried a gun on his jobs. For a while he baffled the police. Four forces hunted him and men were drafted into hunt balls to try and spot 'Johnny the Gent' as their suspect came to be called. When he was finally arrested he was granted £2000 bail and disappeared for three days before shooting himself in a hotel in Virginia Water with a gun he concealed in a walking-stick. A suicide note expressed elegant regret that he would be unable to go fishing that day.

The thirties and forties were also the era of the conman. Many ruses were of touching simplicity, involving plausible rogues showing bogus newspaper cuttings that indicated they had inherited a fortune but needed a few quid to tide them over. The standard one required the conman to be possessed of a 'good' accent, an accomplice who would add authenticity to his story and a just-plausible hard-luck tale with the promise of easy riches for the victim. Many seemed to involve 'colonials' and one of the most successful in Britain was an Irishman, Fermoy-born Michael Corrigan or Cassidy, who worked under the name of Major Corrigan. He persuaded gullible souls to put money into Mexican oil concessions. In 1930, after promoting himself to chief inspector in Canada's North West Mounted Police and then general in the Mexican army, he was gaoled for five years. He bounced back as a supplier of aircraft to the Australian government, selling non-existent arms to the thirties French government.

Sir Richard Jackson, whose career spanned both the office of the Director of Public Prosecutions and the CID at Scotland Yard, bumped into Corrigan in the Carlton Bar after his release from jail. He recalled: 'He greeted me most affably, recalling that we last met "at the Old Bailey" as though it had been the Athenaeum.' Corrigan thrived in the forties, claiming a concession for exporting balsawood on behalf of the Guatemala government, selling 145 Piccadilly and bulk purchasing army surplus stores. Arrested for fraud in 1946, and facing a long sentence, he hanged himself with his tie in Brixton prison, leaving a library book called *Hangman's Tie* by his bed and a contrite note to his solicitors which said, 'I deserve everything for being such a greedy fool.'

The thirties and forties were an innocent time. Some people even fell for the cherishable 'Burn Up', in which the victim was shown a machine, not unlike the one that brought Frankenstein to life, which could reproduce money. All he had to do was provide the ready cash and it would then be doubled. Alas, in the midst of the transaction the machine would 'blow up' and the money would be 'lost'.

In the late thirties Eustace Hamilton Stewart Hargreaves, whom the press called 'The Biggest Spiv of All', profited from pre-war gullibility to con investors out of hundreds of thousands of pounds by selling a bogus liqueur which tasted revolting, and which he advised should be taken 'only in moderation because of its aphrodisiac qualities'. He was finally gaoled after the Second World War, in 1953, for eight years.

Crime was still very much a male pursuit, but a few women were joining the rackets. Margaret Dowse, known for her charm, worked with her boyfriend, Stanley Trinder. They would move to a town, find Dowse a job in a post office or shop, win the trust of the proprietors and eventually manoeuvre the situation for her to be allowed to take the cash to the bank. Then she would disappear and the couple would move on. By the time she was caught in 1960, Dowse was wanted in forty-one different towns, and selection boards for CID officers were asked: 'What would you do about Margaret Dowse?' Gaoled at Lewes Crown Court for five years for larceny, forgery and falsification of accounts, she asked for another thirty-seven offences to be taken into account. The police were shocked that a woman should be such a prolific criminal: 'She was scarcely an ornament to her sex,' remarked Sir Richard Jackson.

Most of the famous solo criminals were indeed men but one woman, Shirley Pitts, was to win the title of 'Queen of the Shoplifters' in the fifties. As a young girl in the forties she had already started perfecting her art and by the time she was in her twenties had a reputation for being one of the most skilled shoplifters in the country. She would organize the team which attacked Harrods, her favourite, and other major stores, using two or three accomplices to act suspiciously while the other went for the perfume counters. When the European Common Market was still only being discussed by politicians, she was organizing shoplifting expeditions to Paris and Geneva and Berlin. Gaoled three times, she escaped once while pregnant with one of her many children, who went on to respectable careers. When she died in 1992 she was buried in a blue Zandra Rhodes creation which friends said was stolen. A cortège of fifteen Daimlers cruised nearly twenty miles through London to her resting place in a Tooting cemetery where a trumpeter and guitarist played the 'Heaven, I'm in heaven . . .' lines from Irving Berlin's 'Cheek to Cheek'. There was a floral tribute in the shape of a Harrods shopping bag. Her epitaph was spelled out in flowers on her grave: 'Gone shopping'.

3
KINGS OF THE UNDERWORLD

From Billy and Spot to the Pen Club

Billy Hill, the 'boss
of the underworld'.

Frankie Fraser was typical of many of his colleagues in pretending to be mad to avoid the call-up for the Second World War. His most convincing move was to assault a doctor and leap out of a window in the Bradford hospital where he had been taken for assessment. Taken for further tests to the Royal Infirmary in Edinburgh, he was told that he would have the waves in his brain electronically examined: 'So I thought to myself "Let's kill the general! Let's kill the general!"' It must have worked. They said that, owing to my condition, I was discharged from the army.' Thus was born 'Mad' Frankie.

But if Fraser and many like him opted out of the war by pretending to be two mailbags short of a heist, the war was still to have an enormous effect on the underworld.

'War at any time is not calculated to foster a respect for life and property and a war to the death like the last one, in which the State perforce made great inroads on the liberty of the subject and the rights of property, was hardly the school in which one could expect respect for the law and the rights of others to flourish,' concluded Sir Harold Scott, Commissioner of the Metropolitan Police from 1945 to 1953, as he surveyed the steady climb of criminality. He believed that the introduction of widespread restrictions during the war, for reasons which were not always apparent to the average citizen, had bred a new lack of respect for law in general; evasions of petty rules were not regarded as 'crimes' in the old sense.

War had also uprooted hundreds of thousands of people, stability had been disrupted and children had grown up at a time of confusion and fear. There was the inevitable lack of respect for property, with the notion of 'to the victor the spoils' justifying what was essentially stealing and with looting in bombed cities seen as a minor peccadillo amidst the mighty evils of war. A large number of deserters who had neither identity cards nor ration books turned inevitably to villainy.

Rationing itself spawned crime, with ration books becoming a lucrative form of currency: in 1944, 100000 food ration books were stolen from the Romford food office in Essex, a haul reckoned to be worth £500000. The forging of clothing and petrol coupons was widespread. There were also extensive frauds in surplus vehicle deals and on the black market, currency fiddles and illicit sales of gun carriers, rifles, lorries, food and raw materials from army dumps. But more significant were the wilder reaches of crime encouraged by the war. Some servicemen had acquired a knowledge of explosives and commando techniques which was not always discarded with the khaki.

They joined the criminal who had either been in gaol for most of the war or who had dodged the call-up. Many career criminals, like Fraser, had feigned illness or mental instability.

The end of the conflict brought inter-gang rivalries into sharper focus. The White family from Islington in north London had emerged as the leading racetrack gang just prior to and during the war. The paterfamilias was 'Big Alf' White, the old confrère of the Sabinis and now a bookie whose star had waned somewhat after a bad beating at Haringey Greyhound Stadium in 1933. It was against the Whites that a young man, who was to emerge as one of the major figures in the post-war underworld, was to win his spurs.

Billy Hill, one of twenty-one children, was born in 1911 in Seven Dials off Leicester Square and grew up in Camden, north London. His father was a painter and decorator who had served time for assaulting the police and his mother was a receiver. One brother, Jimmy, was already a major pickpocket and many other members of the extended family were criminals. His brother-in-law, 'Brummy' Sparkes, was a well-known villain and sister Maggie, known as 'Baby Face,' or the 'Queen of the Forty Elephants', was an expert shoplifter. The latter nickname came about, according to her brother, because she hid her spoils on her person. (The *Daily Telegraph* crime correspondent of the forties and fifties, Stanley Firmin, had a different theory. He suggested that the 'Forty Elephants' came partly because of an association with the Elephant and Castle and partly because her fellow shoplifters were mainly large women: 'some being nearly six foot tall', and thus 'the Elephants'. Firmin claimed that these women would beat up young crooks who trespassed on their patch.) Maggie Hill had also made a name for herself by teasing a judge who gaoled her; she responded to his instruction of 'Take her down' by shouting out: 'You didn't say that last night when you were making love to me!' Eddie 'Devil's Island' Guerin was a family friend.

Compared in looks to Humphrey Bogart, Hill took a pride in his appearance and was a graduate of the birch. This brutal form of punishment involved a Home-Office-approved implement soaked in brine. It was administered by a prison officer whom the prisoner was not allowed to see, and attended by a doctor who would afterwards dress the wounds with medicated pads. The Cat, which was the other main form of official corporal punishment, was sometimes used so violently that a man's nipples would be torn off. A little leather singlet was provided to prevent this. As with the birch, there would be a large turn-out of officials to spectate.

Hill received his first sentence at fourteen and was to spend a total of seventeen years inside during his career. In the thirties he formed his own gang, the 'heavy mob' as they liked to be called, which competed with other gangs loosely known as the Elephant gang, the Angel gang and the Titanic gang. The Elephant gang had a reputation for carrying out serial shoplifting expeditions, shuttling the booty from expensive shops back to the Elephant and Castle. Hill's main money came from safe-breaking and smash-and-grabs at a time when security in shops and offices was still unsophisticated. He liked to give his team Runyonesque nicknames like 'Bear's Breath', 'Franny the Spaniel' (Franny Daniels), 'Horrible Harry' and 'Teddy Odd Legs' (Teddy Machin).

Seeking to establish himself as a major force in the underworld, Hill suggested in his autobiography *Boss of Britain's Underworld* that in 1947 he became the 'bandit king' of London by winning a historic showdown with the Whites. He claimed that he assembled 150 thieves and tearaways who were unhappy about the power wielded by the Whites who were taking protection money in the West End and charging a percentage to people using the illegal clubs. They included gangs from the Elephant and Castle, Kilburn, Paddington and even a contingent of gypsies from Essex. Hill recounted that the Whites, confronted by this show of strength, tacitly relinquished claims to the leadership of gangland. There was, indeed, a meeting of sorts but it seems to have been neither as large nor as epic as he recalled. Frankie Fraser, one of Hill's lieutenants, remembers only some of White's people being cut and Harry White hiding under a table in a club called the Nuthouse.

If the Whites had showed, Hill said, 'St Valentine's Day in Chicago would have looked like a Girl Guides' picnic.' However, it is more likely that the result of such a contest would have been a lot of striping and slashing, the favoured weapon of the time being the 'chiv' or knife. Hill claimed to have always slashed downwards, so that if his hand slipped he would not cut an artery, and he liked to leave his signature – a V for victory sign – on an enemy's cheek. He seems to have revelled in it: on one occasion he had been attacked by a man who shoved a broken glass in his face in a north London pub appropriately called the Butcher's Arms: 'I pulled the glass out of my face with one hand and the chiv out of my pocket with the other. Then I got to work doing a bit of hacking and carving. I don't know how many blokes I cut that night. I didn't care. When you get a jagged glass shoved into your face you don't bother about counting the blokes you chiv. You just hack away until your knife gets blunt or the others swallow it.'

Hill's smash-and-grab raids were a feature of London criminal life and he used to claim that he had so many villains anxious to work with him that he had to put them on a rota. He claimed, too, to have invented the 'run-out'. This method of stealing from jewellery shops used the most respectable looking of the thieves – one young 'screwsman' even had his hair waved to make him look like a toff who might be interested in an expensive engagement ring. Hill claimed that he used young blades from Eton and Dulwich College. The smart young man would go into a shop carrying *The Times* and a briefcase and ask to see some rings. Having won the confidence of the jeweller, he would then grab the rings and sprint out of the shop to the waiting getaway car.

Guns, mainly .45s, Lugers, Smith and Wessons and Colt revolvers, were easy to come by. Ex-servicemen had brought them back from the theatres of war and a post-war amnesty revealed no less than 30 000 in circulation. A revolver cost £5, an automatic £10.

Hill's lieutenants were a mixed crew. One, Bobby Ramsey, found God while in Dartmoor in the mid-fifties and would be seen calling on his Maker as he marched round the prison's football pitch. He beat up one cynic who thought it was a pose to fool the chaplain. (Pretending to have found God was a popular method of trying to obtain an early release, which some chaplains did little to discourage. One at Pentonville prison, in the days before radios and Sunday papers were allowed, ensured a full house in the chapel by reading out the football results in the Sunday morning service, between the hymns and the lessons.)

Not a man plagued by self-doubt, Hill claimed to have set up a business called Murder Inc. in 1952–53 which involved not murder, but merely 'warning' lovers away from unfaithful wives and collecting money from the husbands. His claim that around 300 such jobs were carried out seems fanciful to say the least.

The other major gangland figure of the fifties was Jack Comer, better known as Jack Spot. The 'Spot' nickname came, according to crime reporter Norman Lucas, from the fact that wherever Spot went there was trouble. He was born into a Polish Jewish immigrant family in 1912 and had won his awesome reputation by leading the attack on Oswald Moseley's fascist Blackshirts when they tried to march through the East End on 4 October 1936 threatening the Jewish traders in the area.

It was the Hill-Spot axis that was finally to supersede the Whites in terms of influence and power. Initially, the two men were friends and close colleagues. Spot even met Hill at the prison gates when he came out in 1949 and they and their partners had holidayed together in the south of France.

'Spotty' had fought briefly in the war, although he seems to have been at odds with the authorities for much of the time over discipline and was eventually discharged, like so many of his associates, on grounds of mental instability. Most of his family were killed in the Blitz and, after a violent argument with an anti-Semitic thug in a London spieler, he decamped to Leeds where he worked with émigré Poles who had established themselves in the underworld there and protected the Regal Gaming Club. At the end of the war, Spot returned to London and set about re-establishing himself in the criminal fraternity. He ran a successful illegal gambling club using the Aldgate Fruit Exchange as a front, complete with bogus staff whom he gleefully described as: 'All these geezers with respectable ties and tea-shop manners who acted as clerks [and] were on my payroll.' He reckoned to making £2000 a week from the chemin de fer, faro and rummy tables and boasted that 'Monte [Carlo] would look like a fun-fair compared with my spieler'.

He was also taking part in racetrack rackets and enforcing his position with selected attacks on associates of the Whites. His version of the fight for ascendancy with the Whites was that there was a pitched battle between the two gangs in a club off Piccadilly in January 1947. Each side had a different version of who started the slashing but Spot came out on top and claimed later: 'Coshes and knives were flashing about ... the King's Cross boys couldn't take it.' He claimed, without much evidence, that he could assemble 1000 fighting men armed with grenades, Sten guns and service revolvers to finish the job. However, there was to be no final confrontation. He told *Daily Sketch* readers, who were treated to his memoirs in 1955, that he was 'the king who kept his crown by being tougher than the other toughs'. (The *Sketch* cheerfully ran Spot's memoirs alongside stern editorials entitled 'Smoke Out The Rats' in which it said that gangland should be purged: 'We expect the police to clean up these vermin and to crush them for ever ... the jealous rats fighting it out on the streets and the alleys could in a short time make Soho a desert where no respectable citizen would risk his reputation or personal safety.')

Married to the beautiful Rita, a young Irish woman who had fallen for his undoubted charm and style, Spot played the part of the gang leader to perfection. Leonard 'Nipper' Read, the detective who made a name for himself tackling London's later gangs of the sixties, recalled Spot at the height of his power in the forties and early fifties: 'He dressed in beautifully cut suits and always wore a brown fedora and he had a religious way of progressing through the day. He would go to the barbers in Edgware Road station and they would shave him and when he felt immaculate he would walk down the Edgware Road, waving and saying good morning to people. He would go into the Bear Garden at the Cumberland Hotel and would sit there for the rest of the morning. People would come up and ask his advice about various matters and he would give it much in the way that Don Corleone did in *The Godfather*.'

Occasionally, Spot had to make his presence felt personally. In 1947, he beat up Johnny Warren, a member of the White's extended family, in a pub toilet in Soho. As he explained to writer Robert Murphy years later: 'I used to knock 'em out in the lavatory. That was my surgery. I used to go into the toilet and Bomp! Leave 'em in the piss.'

Spot hired young heavies for protection work and as body-guards, amongst them Joe Cannon, a west London hardman, who was later to spend many years in gaol for armed robbery. He made a niche for himself in British penal history by relieving himself over the desk of the governor of Brixton prison.

A familiar, cigar-smoking figure in Soho, Spot used the Mod-ernaires Club in Old Compton Street as one of his offices. When the telephone rang for him, he silenced the musicians' rehearsals of what he called their 'heeby-jeeby music' with an imperious wave of the hand. Spot liked people to do as he said. When pianist and trumpeter Denis Rose arrived two hours late for a gig, he told him he would never work in the West End again. The rest of the band played 'Please Don't Talk About Me When I'm Gone'.

One of the other main figures of the forties and fifties was Alberto Dimeo or Albert Dimes, an Italian-Scottish ex-borstal boy, RAF deserter, racing man and impetuous gambler. He was a respected figure in Soho and renowned for a sense of humour: he gave jazz club owner Ronnie Scott, with whose father he went racing, a magnum of champagne to open whenever the club started making money. It stands gathering dust at the club to this day.

Dimes had been charged with the murder on 1 May 1941 of Harry 'Little Hubby' Distleman, the doorman of the West End Bridge and Billiards Club – known to its regulars as the Old Cue Club – who had been stabbed to death on its Wardour Street premises. There had been a fight, probably over the barring of a man from another club a few nights earlier, and Antonio 'Baby' or 'Baby-face' Mancini, who managed the club downstairs, said he had slipped off his dinner-jacket and gone to investigate. He claimed that he had heard a voice shouting 'There's Babe! Let's get him!' and had stabbed Distleman in the chest in self-defence.

Distleman collapsed, crying, 'He has stabbed me in the heart. I am dying.' The *Daily Express* reported laconically: 'This is a crime Hitler did not commit ... It was just a good old-fashioned Soho crime.' The paper commented that 'Soho, well hit by the raids, chatted more over Hubby Distleman's death than of the night they hit the hospital on the corner. For they knew Hubby was just the victim of an internal war between gangs that have run through Soho even in the Blitz.' Mancini, Joseph Collette, and Dimes were charged with the killing and Mancini, whom detective Edward Greeno described as 'a highly-strung individual with a habit of assault-and-wounding' was convicted and hanged. Dimes and Collette were convicted of unlawful wounding. Greeno concluded: 'The hanging of Mancini put the fear of God into the racecourse riff-raff. Soho could now look forward to a nice quiet war.'

The rifts in the underworld were becoming apparent by the fifties and Hill, Spot and Dimes all had parts to play in the ensuing bloodshed. Hill had already written his 'Boss of the Underworld' story in the *People*, along with *People* reporter Duncan Webb, and Spot had penned his less fluent 'King of Soho' tale for the *Daily Sketch*. Frankie Fraser and the Hill team were becoming less impressed with Spot's tactics: 'He would terrorize a thief into giving him something, but he wouldn't go and thieve it himself,' says Fraser.

Hill tried to emigrate to Australia in 1955 but was not even allowed off the boat and returned to try and reclaim his position in a London where Spot had increasingly established himself. The two men drifted further apart and Spot had also fallen out with Dimes. According to Frankie Fraser, Dimes' deceptively easygoing manner – he would allow people to tease him about money they owed him – fooled Spot into thinking he was weak and had 'lost his bottle'. In 1955 the wily Hill was able to discredit Spot. He had found out that Spot had given evidence against three men in an assault case back in 1937. Although this was nearly twenty years earlier, Hill got hold of the depositions of the committal proceedings which showed Spot up as an informer and had copies made and pasted up in underworld

Jack 'Spot' Comer, Billy Hill's gangland rival, and his wife Rita. Inset: Albert Dimes who battled with Spot in 'the fight that never was'.

pubs. Spot was livid at this blow to his image, suggests Fraser, and thought that a fight with Dimes would improve his sinking status. He had already suffered the indignity of being arrested in 1953 for possession of a knuckleduster.

On 11 August 1955 Spot approached Dimes in Frith Street, in Soho, and stabbed him in the thigh and stomach. Dimes fled to a fruit shop on the corner of Old Compton Street where he knew he would find an industrial can-opener to use as a weapon. Spot pursued him with a potato knife but was waylaid by the shopkeeper, a woman friend of Dimes, who cracked him over the head with a set of scales. Dimes grabbed the knife and slashed Spot, who collapsed in a nearby barber shop. Spot was taken to the Middlesex Hospital. *Daily Express* reporter Frank MacGarry, who tried to enter the ward, asked one of Spot's associates what was being discussed: 'Peace, chum. Just peace,' came the reply, which MacGarry recorded in an article headlined 'The Drape-Suit Men Take Presents To Spot'. Dimes was treated in Charing Cross Hospital.

The fight itself was heralded as an outbreak of gang war. The *Daily Express* report set the scene: 'The hands of the clock above the Italian Espresso coffee bar pointed to 11.40. Mambo music was blaring from the juke-box ...' The spilt blood in the heart of the city seemed to authenticate the notion of a London gangland for a public that had resigned itself to celluloid gangsters with American accents. There was even a hint of pride in the reports. Britain had its own gangsters at last. The BBC News and Information Unit opened a 'gang warfare' file for the first time. 'The fight completely put the underworld, as they call it, right into focus and it hasn't stopped,' says Fraser.

Spot was tried for attacking Dimes and cleared – it became known as 'the Fight that Never Was' – thanks to the intervention of Parson Basil Andrews, an eighty-eight-year-old cleric who was down on his luck, having welshed on a number of betting debts, and who seemed to have wandered into the Old Bailey off the set of an Ealing comedy. Adjusting his dog collar, Andrews told the court that Dimes had been the aggressor and had attacked Spot first.

It later emerged that Andrews had been given £63 by one of Spot's associates, Morris 'Moishe Blue Boy/Blue Ball' Goldstein, to ignore the commandment about bearing false witness. Andrews admitted the deception and was then used as a major prosecution witness against Goldstein, Rita Comer (Mrs Spot) and two others: Peter MacDonough and Bernard 'The Yank' Schach. Andrews gave moving evidence: 'I was tempted and I fell.' Goldstein was gaoled for two years, Schach and MacDonough for a year and Mrs Comer, so striking a woman that even the detectives fancied her, was not gaoled. (Goldstein was a successful criminal and once bought himself a flash Mercedes; when he drove it home his mother, seeing the German-made vehicle, shouted at him: 'There's blood on the hands that made that car!')

The Hill-Spot feud rumbled on. In May 1956 Hill found that Spot was planning an attack on him and persuaded some of the latter's disloyal men to tip him off about their boss's movements so that he could get his revenge in first. Spot was well aware of what was now afoot and asked the police for help, which they felt unable to give. Fraser, on the run on a charge of grievous bodily harm at the time, was one of the hit squad, armed with a shillelagh. When he saw Spot and Rita and two of the Spot team, he shouted 'Right, it's on you, Jack!' and promptly set about him. 'He must have been practising his scream because it was louder than his wife's,' says Fraser of Spot's reaction. 'Hers was quite loud but his was even better. I just whacked him with the shillelagh a couple of times and someone else cut him and that was that.' Fraser said he would cheerfully have killed Spot because of his attack on Dimes. He had planned to humiliate him by cutting a noughts and crosses pattern on his face 'but unfortunately there wasn't that amount of time'.

Fraser and Bobby Warren were each gaoled for seven years for their part in the attack, despite Fraser's counsel's plea that he was 'a weaker vessel of mankind who has been used for a foul purpose'. 'Billy Boy' Blythe was sentenced to five years and two others, William 'Ginger' Dennis and Bert 'Battles' Rossi, to four. One of the accused, Tony Falco, giving evidence, complained to the prosecution: 'Would you like to speak less big words? I can't understand them.' During the trial Spot was described as 'a corner boy of the lowest ilk' and 'the man who prides himself as being the King of the Underworld – the scum of the earth'. Mr Justice Donovan told the jury: 'The civic value of the man Comer [Spot] is neither here nor there. If this sort of thing is allowed to spread it will not be safe for any of us to walk the streets.'

Hill waited outside the court, dressed in a grey slouch hat and brown linen suit, sitting on a bench marked 'Remembrance' in a nearby churchyard, his left-hand drive Buick parked ready for departure after the verdict. Spot, who had not given evidence against his assailants, said as he left the court, 'I ain't afraid of anyone but I want a quiet life now.' The reaction from the press was unsympathetic. Cassandra

Jack 'Spot' Comer (left) in Soho in 1956.

of the *Daily Mirror* referred to 'the scum of the earth flaunting their mob rule in London town'. Hill had made his point and the underworld joke of the time – 'Billy Hill's the boss – Jack Spot was very cut up about it' – marked the end of the Spot era.

But the battle was not yet over. When Tommy Falco was slashed outside the Astor Club the following year and required forty-seven stitches, he named Spot as his attacker. In fact, Falco was involved in a devious plot to have Spot gaoled in retaliation for what had happened to Fraser, Warren and Co. Falco had been slashed by Hill's side with instructions to inform the police that Spot had done it. 'It's a diabolical liberty,' were Spot's immortal words when he was arrested. This elaborate plan emerged during Spot's trial, when the appropriately nicknamed Victor 'Scarface' Russo gave evidence that Dimes and Hill had asked him if he would agree to have his face slashed for £1000 and say that Spot had done it. Russo, a Glasgow flyman down to his knuckle-bones, had taken half the money but he changed his mind about taking any further facial surgery. His evidence cleared Spot.

Spot moved into clubs but his first venture, the Highball in Bayswater, went up in flames shortly after it opened. He ran into heavy financial problems over misguided legal actions and was evicted from his West End flat. He slipped from view, living quietly in Ireland and London, where he was cared for by his loyal daughters and seen occasionally at boxing matches. He had the satisfaction of outliving Dimes, who died of cancer in 1972 and whose Kent funeral was attended by the actor Stanley Baker.

Others liked to claim a place in the criminal aristocracy. For instance, the *Daily Sketch* in 1959 carried a boast from a young man called Joseph Francis Oliva: 'I am the leader of a gang 400 strong. They call me King Oliva ... I am going to be the boss of the night clubs and run the night clubs round the West End. I have got to shift one or two big gang leaders to do it. But I have got a man behind me financing me.' He claimed he could raise his four hundred foot-soldiers with just fifteen or twenty telephone calls. But when he was later arrested for other, less spectacular, matters the 'King' abdicated and said he only made the claims for money. James Morton in *Gangland* suggests that a more genuine contender as the true godfather of the period could be Bert Marsh, known as 'Pasqualino Papa'. One of the old Italian community, he had been acquitted of one gangland murder but in general managed to avoid both the courts and the press and died a rich man.

The most notorious battles for ascendancy may have been fought on the streets but the underworld was attempting to acquire its big money elsewhere, not always successfully.

In the summer of 1948 the police were tipped off that a raid on a bonded warehouse at London Airport was being plotted. The plan was to drug the tea of the BOAC staff in charge of the warehouse and steal a million dollars worth of bullion and around £500 000 worth of other goods. On 24 July, seven masked men, armed with iron bars and bludgeons, broke in and found undercover police officers who had taken the place of the BOAC staff and were pretending to be drugged. The officers allowed themselves to be tied up and gagged with adhesive tape. One who did not seem drowsy enough was coshed into unconsciousness. But when the robbers were about to start opening the safe other policemen entered with the words: 'We are police of the Flying Squad. Stay where you are.'

There was then a wild fight between the two sides, immortalized as the Battle of Heathrow, and complicated by the fact that both sides had dressed up in BOAC uniforms. Eight gang members were arrested and charged, along with the airport loader who had tipped them off about the warehouse. There was a cherishable tale that one man did escape and thereafter became known as 'Handy Henry' because he had hidden under a police van, clinging to its axle all the way from the airport to Harlesden police station where he made his getaway. Spot claimed later that Teddy Machin also escaped and fell in a ditch where pursuing police failed to see him. Those arrested received sentences of from five to twelve years penal servitude. The loader, who co-operated with the police by identifying the gang, received only a bind-over. It later transpired that the plane due to deliver the haul had been held up by fog and had been unable to land.

But the symbolic robbery of the period was the Eastcastle Street mailbag heist in 1952, in which an estimated £287 000 was stolen. It was, as one crime reporter recorded, carried out with 'Montgomery-like thoroughness ... it went off as smoothly as any of our commando raids during the war'. Indeed, the actual raid on the van had been practised with precision on roads outside London, with the cover that the robbers were a film unit making a crime movie.

It was 4.17 a.m. on 21 May 1952 when a post office mail-van on its way from Paddington Station to St Martins-le-Grand general post office yard was held up in Eastcastle Street in the West End. When the van stopped at the lights, which had been tampered with, one car, a black Riley, blocked it in front and another, a green

Vauxhall, at the rear. Each car had four men in it. The men in the front car leapt out and attacked the post office men while those behind went to work on the back door of the van. One of the van crew, Henry Syms, was heavily coshed and two others hurt. Three of the robbers then drove the van, which had already had its alarm disconnected, to a yard in Augustus Street in Camden Town. There two other men helped transfer eighteeen mailbags – another thirteen had been abandoned – to a fruit and vegetable van already prepared with hidden panels. This van was driven to Spitalfields Market in east London and watched until it was felt that it would be safe to move it. The rest of the team sped off in their stolen cars to Covent Garden, where they dumped the vehicles and were picked up by other members of the gang.

From the start, it was clear that there had been inside information. It was also obvious that serious professionals were at work. The *Daily Mirror* speculated that those involved must be 'aged about twenty, probably ex-Borstal boys, expert motor-drivers'.

Ronald Howe, the head of the CID, took personal charge of the investigation with Detective Chief Superintendent Bill 'Cherub' Chapman of the Flying Squad and Superintendent Bob Lee running the operational side. The insurance assessors offered £25 000 for information leading to the recovery of the money. So seriously was the crime seen nationally that the Prime Minister, Sir Winston Churchill, asked for daily reports on the inquiry and the Postmaster-General, Earl de le Warr, had to give explanations to Parliament.

More than a thousand police officers were involved in the hunt, scores of villains were rounded up and 400 police cars carried out a sweep of arrests. None of the main robbers were ever caught but it was widely accepted that Billy Hill had organized the heist. *People* reporter Duncan Webb suggested that the job had been masterminded by a man to whom he gave the not very subtle pseudonym of 'Bill'. Hill himself could not resist bragging about the job in his memoirs, and told how a man who had disconnected the van's alarm by walking into St-Martins-le-Grand yard and tampering with the relevant wires in the targeted vehicle. The man was 'Taters' Chatham.

Frankie Fraser says that Hill was so anxious to avoid the sort of tip-off to the police that had scuppered the Heathrow robbery that he summoned his team on the eve of the heist, told them their roles and then allowed no one to leave, even to get their masks or their gloves. Hill had fixed up alibis for the gang, adamant that no one should stray outside the premises: 'Even if someone went to the toilet, someone stood outside. That's how thorough it was,' says Fraser.

The robbery was regarded by the police as the start of a new era, the beginning of 'project' crime. The message to the criminal fraternity was that crime was now big business, that planning and patience paid off.

Two years later, in 1954, a lorry belonging to KLM Dutch airlines stopped outside the KLM office in Jockey's Fields, Holborn, in central London. As its tailboard dropped a smaller van backed on to it, a man jumped from van to lorry, shouted 'Hold on, hold on a minute' and threw two boxes containing £45 000 of gold bullion into the van which then sped off. Hill was an obvious suspect. His warehouse – he was then in a legitimate business selling toys – was searched and every doll and teddy bear inspected, providing some comic relief: these were 'talking' dolls and bears which said 'Oooh' and 'Aaah' when picked up. Again, he was never charged but the word amongst his associates was that he had masterminded all three of these first, large post-war operations.

Hill had a faithful wife, much admired by his criminal friends, who only left him after twenty long-suffering years. He let her keep one of his Soho clubs and gave her a poodle called Chico as a going-away present. He embarked on a new relationship with Gypsy, a flamboyant woman on the edges of the underworld, and 'retired' in the late fifties, saying that he planned to go 'sunning myself in the Southern Atlantic or on the Riviera'. He moved to Marbella in the sixties then returned to England to run a club in Sunningdale, still with Gypsy until the mid-seventies. He died in 1984. Gypsy had her own brushes with the law: in 1957 she was acquitted of stabbing a man in the eye in the Miramar Club in Paddington.

Armed robberies were rare in the post-war years: there were nineteen, ten and nineteen in 1950, 1951 and 1952 respectively. Money was moved from bank to bank in brown vans or hired cars, some of whose drivers used to tip off criminals as to when and where they were going, even indicating by the use of the brake light whether or not the bank manager had handcuffed himself to the bag. As Frankie Fraser explains, it was necessary to beat up the inside man to make it realistic: 'You not only took his ignition key so that they couldn't follow, you took some of his blood.' (A sawn-off starting handle encased in rubber was a favourite weapon.) This was to persuade the police, who were inevitably looking for an inside man, that the recipient of such a beating could not have been involved. Robbers were still reluctant to use firearms.

Robert Fabian, one of the Yard's most famous detectives and no shrinking violet, had a helpful theory that all gunmen had grey eyes: 'Unless he is insane, the brown-eyed criminal does not carry a gun with intent to use it. He may think he does but the showdown proves him wrong. The man who shoots to kill has grey eyes.' Fatal shootings were rare, one of the reasons why those that happened received so much publicity.

On 13 February 1948, in Southgate, PC Nathaniel Edgar, patrolling with a colleague, was shot three times in the groin and thigh and died of his wounds. The man who killed him was a deserter named Donald Thomas. The hunt for Thomas is significant for students of police semiotics: in the press release the phrase 'a man believed to be able to help with their inquiries' was used for the first time. Thomas was found at a boarding-house in Clapham after photographs of his wife had been published in the newspapers and a landlady had recognized her. A Luger with eight rounds in its magazine and one in its breech was hidden under his pillow, and by his bed was a book called *Shooting to Live with the One-Hand Gun*. He was arrested after a short struggle.

A notorious killing a year earlier had involved Harry Jenkins, a member of a Bermondsey criminal family, who killed a motor cyclist called Alec d'Antiquis who had tried to stop him escaping from a hold-up at a pawnbroker's shop in Charlotte Street in London's West End. Jenkins was a self-confident young criminal, known as the 'King of Borstal'. At twenty-three, he knew all the tricks of the trade. He sent out for a lunch-time edition of an evening paper before the identification parade and shoved it in his jacket pocket; his idea was that a witness might spot it and reckon that he could hardly be the suspect if he had been out on the street so recently. He was nonetheless charged with his associates, Christopher Geraghty and Terence Rolt, and executed with Geraghty in Pentonville Prison in September 1947 after a six-day trial; Rolt was too young to hang. The shooting shocked even some members of the criminal fraternity. 'Most of the people in the underworld abhorred it as much as ordinary people,' says Eric Mason, a gangland figure. 'It wasn't the done thing.'

One shooting which was to be remembered decades later was that of PC Sidney Miles on 2 November 1952. Two young men, Christopher Craig and Derek Bentley, had been caught red-handed on the roof of a Croydon warehouse. Bentley was arrested and uttered the words 'Let him have it, Chris'. His family argued that he meant Craig should surrender the gun, but the police claimed it amounted to an instruction to fire. Craig shot Miles fatally but was too young to hang, a penalty given instead to the luckless Bentley. His execution at Wandsworth prison in January 1953 provoked angry demonstrations and was a major factor in the abolition of the death penalty. Craig served his sentence and re-emerged to live a quiet life as a plumber in the Home Counties. Bentley received a conditional posthumous pardon in 1993, after forty years of campaigning by his sister Iris.

While racetrack crimes had receded, the booming greyhound racing business offered openings. In December 1945 bookies paid out £100 000 in one night when a dog called Bald Truth won the last race at White City after starting at odds of eight to one. An intruder had hidden in an empty kennel beside the dogs that were due to run in the race and had fed all but the winner morsels of doped fish. The only clues were malted-milk tablets that the doper had eaten because there was no room to unwrap a sandwich. He was identified, but never charged, and dog-track security was sharply tightened.

The underworld was growing. Scots who had drifted to London during the war, and had access to gelignite in Highland quarries, were regarded as expert safe-blowers and the trade continued to be highly revered. An article in the weekly magazine *Weekend* in 1963 was even able to observe: 'Why is the British safe-breaker so good? One reason is that cracking a crib requires characteristics in which the British excel – skill, tenacity, stamina and patience.'

'Jump-ups' were another popular crime in the late forties. The style was to drive behind a lorry until its driver stopped for a cup of tea and then steal his load – hence the 'fell off the back of a lorry' tradition. More imaginative techniques developed: in the fifties, thieves would print a bogus numberplate identical to that of a targeted lorry and drive in front of the vehicle waving it. The driver would think his numberplate had fallen off and would stop and be robbed. Cigarettes were a popular haul. Eric Mason recalls that a team would know where a lorry was delivering and would wait until the driver was entering a shop. They would then grab cartons from the tailboard, sling them in a car and speed off.

'At Christmas time, you'd always look for a vanload of turkeys because you sold plenty, made a few quid and all your friends would get a turkey for Christmas so you'd make yourself a good fella.' The procedure was to take the stolen van to a 'slaughter', a warehouse either leased from or owned by a crooked farmer, where there would be a secure barn for unloading.

This period also saw the expansion of the Flying Squad. Within it was the Ghost Squad, formed on 1 January 1946 to infiltrate the gangs by using around thirty undercover officers who never revealed themselves or appeared in court. Its chief, Detective Inspector Jack Capstick, was told by the deputy commander of the CID, Percy Worth, that 'as far as the underworld is concerned, you will have no more material existence than ghosts'. But the Ghost Squad was disbanded four years later, amidst hints that some of the officers had taken their undercover role a little too literally. They claimed to have seized 780 villains in their brief history and recovered £300 000 in stolen goods. But their informers' bill of £20 000 was a high one.

Sporadic violent incidents involving known criminals continued. On 14 December 1958 there was a fight between two gangs, whom the police described as 'The Finsbury' and 'the Angel Mob', outside Grey's Dance Academy in Holloway, north London, a favourite haunt of the winkle-pickered wide boys of the time. A young police constable, Ray Summers, broke the fight up and was marching one of the leaders off when he was stabbed by a young man called Ronnie Marwood, who was hanged the following year at Pentonville prison despite a campaign for a reprieve. It was a forerunner of more violent times, encapsulated by a killing at the start of the new decade.

On 7 February 1960, Jimmy Nash, a member of the Nash family who were gradually moving into London clubland, walked into the Pen Club in Spitalfields, east London, with his girlfriend, Doreen Masters, and a couple of friends, Joey Pyle and John Read. The club, which was so named because it had been financed with the proceeds of a robbery on the Parker Pen Company, was owned by Billy Ambrose, an ex-boxer, and was a haunt of villains. A fracas started almost immediately and Ambrose, who was on home leave from a gaol sentence, was shot and wounded as he tried to intervene. But the target of the attack was a cheery Yorkshireman, Selwyn Cooney, who ran the Cabinet Club in the West End for Billy Hill. Cooney was shot twice in the head and fell over a television set with a bullet lodged fatally in his brain. There was a violent fight and the attackers fled, leaving the dead and wounded in their wake. The manager of the club, Fay Sadler, cleaned the place up and Cooney was carried out and laid on the pavement while an ambulance was called.

Views differ as to why he was shot. One suggestion is that he had been involved in an altercation with Nash's brother Ronnie about a car accident involving a woman friend called 'Blonde Vicky' James. Cooney was said to have sent her a bill for the damage to his Vauxhall Victor and to have taken the matter up in a club with Ronnie, even coming to blows. Boxer Jimmy Nash was seeking retribution on behalf of his brother, was the claim.

Jimmy Nash, who worked as a steeplejack and was known as the most peaceful of six Nash brothers, went briefly into hiding then turned himself in, accompanied by Manny Fryde, his astute and legendary legal representative, who announced that his client would say nothing and would not go on an identification parade. The police were given little help. Out of thirty-six people in the club, only four could remember seeing anything. Nash, wearing his lucky gold tie-pin, said that he had struck Cooney on the nose but denied having a gun. One witness retracted his evidence and there was a brilliant speech from defence counsel, Victor Durand QC. Nash was cleared of murder but convicted of grievous bodily harm and gaoled for five years. Pyle who was to re-emerge later, was gaoled for eighteen months for his part in the fight. There was a furious reaction to the verdict from Cooney's father. The *Sunday Pictorial* commented laconically: 'As far as the law is concerned, all that happened to Cooney is that he leaned on a bullet that happened to be passing.'

The Scotland Yard detective Bert Wickstead, who enjoyed the nicknames of 'The Old Grey Fox' and 'Gangbuster', believed that the murder of Cooney was an attempt to remove a man who had remained loyal to Billy Hill and who, after the latter's humiliating return from Australia, was still faithful. 'Hill had left a vacuum when he went into which tried to step all sorts of parties including the Nash family,' says Wickstead. But few members of the underworld give any credence to this neat theory.

The case was a watershed in that it led to the formation of the Criminal Intelligence Branch (first C11, now SO11) at Scotland Yard to co-ordinate information on known criminals involved in organized crime; the Cooney murder investigation had demonstrated that the police lacked basic key intelligence on gangland. Young CID officers were encouraged to attend courts where known gangland figures were appearing so that they would learn their faces.It was also the start of jury protection, whereby jurors in major trials are taken off to dine at lunch-time, protected from the public and potential nobblers.

The public gallery at Nash's trial was the criminal equivalent of the members' enclosure at Ascot. Wickstead recalls that, 'It was full of unsavoury characters. It's a great pity the devil couldn't have cast his net then because it would have saved London a hell of a lot of trouble.'

Indeed, trouble with a capital K was on its way.

4

GANGLAND

The Krays and Untimely Ends

**The Kray twins:
Ron (left) and Reg.**

While the Pen Club was writing itself into the history of the underworld, two young men were already making a name for themselves in another part of clubland. In 1954 the twenty-one-year-old Kray twins, Ronnie and Reggie, had taken over the running of the Regal billiard hall on the Mile End Road in the East End. They established their reputation when Ronnie cutlassed a Maltese gang that tried to extract protection money, and when both brothers beat up some docker heavies, one of whom had unwisely said to Ronnie, 'Here you are, sonny, you're just about old enough for a shandy.'

Most people in the neighbourhood already knew the twins well enough to know they were an altogether headier brew than lemonade shandy. Born into a close-knit family with gypsy, Irish and Jewish roots in October 1933, the sons of the feckless Charles and the fiercely protective Violet, they had established themselves as up-and-coming boxers. They often shared the billing at bouts, turning professional at the age of sixteen, and had been gaoled for assaulting a policeman before they were out of their teens. The fact that they were twins gave them an added aura, which their older brother Charlie believes made them a target for contemporaries who wanted to test themselves: 'It was like the Wild West – let's kill Billy the Kid and then we'll be Billy the Kid.'

The twins had already crossed more than cutlasses with the authorities and their National Service was divided between going AWOL, assaulting NCOs and kicking their heels in the glasshouse. They ended up in Shepton Mallet military prison, which unintentionally acted as a sort of Sandhurst for the training of the officer class of the underworld. Not for nothing did Ronnie eventually become known as 'The Colonel'. By the time they emerged they were ready for the action to which Ronnie's fascination with gangster movies was leading them.

They were noted early on by the older criminals and over the next few years were to receive assistance and advice from Jack Spot, who offered them a pitch at Epsom, from Billy Hill, now in semi-retirement, and from Tommy 'Scarface' Smithson, a loner involved in the vice trade, whose fearlessness the twins admired.

Clubs, both their own and others whose safety they guaranteed for a regular payment, were to be the stepping stones in their rise to fame. They acquired the one with which they were most widely associated in 1957. The Double R – 'a cowboy, lone plains drifter tribute' was how Charlie describes the name he says he invented – was a modest enough drinking spot in Bow Road, east London, for those on the edges of crime. The Glaswegian heavy, 'Big Pat' Connolly, and Tommy 'The Bear' Brown were employed as bouncers.

Ronnie was actually in gaol as the club was expanding, serving a three-year sentence for slashing and stabbing a young man called Terry Martin, who was a victim of a complex grudge-settling operation. Arrested by police with Martin's blood still fresh on his shirt, Ronnie explained: 'I've had a nose-bleed.' Even in the early days, he was starting to show signs of the unbalanced personality that was eventually to derail the twins. He used disproportionate violence to settle disputes, even shooting a man in the motor trade in the leg over a minor argument about payment. After starting his sentence in Wandsworth prison, Ronnie was moved to the gentler environs of Camp Hill gaol on the Isle of Wight. But the delusions from which he had started to suffer were worsening and he became violent. Once removed from the calming influence of his twin and unsettled by the death of his beloved Aunt Rose – who had told him so presciently when he was a small boy, 'Ronnie, love, you were born to hang' – he finally became dangerously irrational. He was eventually certified insane at Winchester prison and in February 1958 he was moved to Epsom's Long Grove hospital prison, the 'nuthouse' as he called it.

But he did not stay long. During a visit from Reggie and some friends, the twins swopped places and Ronnie escaped before the authorities realized the switch had taken place. The escape took him to a safe house in Walthamstow and then to a caravan in Suffolk, where he entertained himself by riding in an appropriately ramrod-straight fashion. Bored by country life, he would emerge periodically at the Double R after a decoy car had tested whether the police were watching for him. However, his mental health was deteriorating. He suffered frightening paranoid delusions, became suicidal and believed that relatives had become police informants or Russian spies. Harley Street psychiatrists were consulted and 'minders' tried to pacify him by indulging his whims but his worried family finally agreed that he was 'barmy' and in 1958 decided he should give himself up.

His period back inside seemed to have stabilized him slightly and he was eventually released in 1959 to find that Reggie, freed from his brother's erratic moods, had been able to consolidate the business. Ronnie bought himself a Dobermann Pinscher and entered the profession 'dog breeder' into his passport.

By now, however, the Krays were breeding something more powerful than big German dogs: what they saw as 'respect' and what others saw as fear. 'The Firm', as it was called, was being born. Amongst those recruited were the Scottish muscle of Ian Barrie and 'Scotch Jack' Dickson, an ex-marine from Leith, who had served with 45 Commando in Malaya; an admiring cousin, Ronnie Hart; financial advisers Leslie Payne and Freddy Gore; ex-boxer Billy Exley; Freddie 'The Mean Machine' Foreman and hardmen Connie Whitehead and Albert Donoghue. An impressive network of informers included young men who took Ronnie's fancy and were known as his 'spies'.

Albert Donoghue was one of the Krays' inner circle who had been recruited because of his reputation as a fearsome East End fighter, one who would battle for unofficial titles like 'King of the Teddy Boys'. 'To be told the twins were taking note of you was something to be proud of', he recalls. But he committed a minor indiscretion which offended Ronnie and was punished with a shot in his leg. He told curious police that he thought he had been hit by a firework – it was November – and his refusal to grass impressed the brothers who duly put him on a pension of £15 a week, with specific responsibility for looking after Reggie and collecting the various dues paid to the gang. 'I could eat and drink for nothing and I could get my clothes made to measure for next to nothing,' says Donoghue. 'If you needed a car, you just went to a car site and frightened the guvnor and pulled one off the front for a couple of weeks and run it into the ground.'

The twins' method of dealing with miscreants was straightforward: 'The guy would be kidded, made to feel easy. "All right? What you drinking?" That sort of thing. Then one would walk away from him this way and one that way. When everyone was out of the way they would just spring the guy. He would be done first with a weapon and then what you call "obliged". He would be seen to. Ronnie liked to be involved personally.' The twins delivered the punishments dispassionately: 'imagine you were fitting a new lock to your door, you'd be concentrating. They had the same sort of look. No horror or anything, just plain business. You're doing a little job.'

Bizarrely, some of those who felt as though they might have offended became upset if they were not singled out for punishment: 'It made them feel small, insignificant'. But those receiving major beatings could act strangely, too: 'one guy tried to get away from his kicking by crawling up the return slot on a jukebox, which is only so wide. He must have imagined in his head it was some sort of a door. He must have been terrified.' Sometimes violence was not necessary. 'Ronnie could just sit there and stare at a person for half an hour and that person would go away thoroughly cowed. That was how much fear they generated.' The members of the Firm knew enough not to get involved: to them, the relationship between the twins was like a marriage; outsiders did not interfere in its violent rows.

But it was Leslie 'The Brain' Payne who was to prove crucial in the transition of the Krays from East End tough guys to gang leaders. From Paddington in west London, Payne was ten years older than the twins and had drifted into crime at the end of his war service as a sergeant in Greece. He had bumped into the Krays when he was in the motor trade and their name had been taken in vain by someone seeking to avoid paying a debt. 'They seemed to grow fond of me,' he wrote in his memoirs. However, when they viciously beat someone up for him he realized that their affection had its disadvantages – and that it was better to have them as friends then enemies.

Payne introduced the twins to the 'long firm fraud', which was to provide much of their early cash. Long Firms or LFs were essentially corporate con tricks: a bogus company would be set up which would start buying the relevant goods; the first bills would be paid promptly and the confidence of the suppliers won. After a few months, a much larger order would be placed and the firm would disappear with the goods, leaving nothing but an empty warehouse and unpaid bills behind it.

The Krays needed the readies. They gradually acquired about thirty people on their payroll, each of whom was paid about £20 in cash. The money was generated by three long firm frauds, four clubs and a percentage of stolen property. Payne claimed that a subsidiary robbery team, with Freddie Foreman to the fore, also contributed. The Firm even had its formal 'board' meetings. The business side met at 11 a.m. on Monday mornings when the club managers handed over their profits – or what they thought the twins would accept as their profits. On Monday evenings the 'muscle' met in a pub to find out if anyone had been arrested or had run away. Reggie apparently thought that keeping formal ledgers with all transactions was a good idea; Payne told him that entering 'long firm' and its weekly income might not be the soundest business practice.

One regular earner was the Kentucky Club in Stepney, east London, smarter and more ambitious than the Krays' earlier efforts: black leather, red walls, *trompe l'oeil* windows, dance-band stage and a clientele that included actress Barbara Windsor, theatre director John Littlewood, trumpeter Eddie Calvert and actor Roger Moore. It was the beginning of a love affair, often reciprocated, with show business. Judy Garland might even have married Reg, claims Charlie, although that may now seem as fantastical as finding the end of the rainbow. At the Old Bailey trial that was to end their career, Ron told the judge offhandedly that if he had not been in court he would probably have been taking tea with Miss Garland.

Ronnie loved the club ambience and encouraged smokers to smoke harder so that the establishments would achieve a suitably fuggy atmosphere. In the meantime, Reg had developed his famous 'cigarette punch' whereby he would offer an intended victim a cigarette and, when the man accepted, would sock him hard, breaking his jaw; the secret of the trick was that the jaw was loosened when the cigarette was in the man's mouth and was therefore easier to break.

Payne recorded that Reggie often told his twin to relax and enjoy himself and that on one occasion Ronnie responded by treating the company to a manic version of 'Knees Up Mother Brown'. His favourite song of the time, which he would frequently request of singers in the various clubs, was 'Mac the Knife'.

Tales like these did the Krays' reputation no harm, nor did the pitched battles which Ronnie occasionally favoured, most notably against a bunch known as the Watney Street Mob who came off second best in a bloody clash with the Krays at the Hospital Tavern in 1959. But it was minor 'mistakes', not these public displays of violence, that took the Krays to court. Reggie was gaoled for eighteen months in 1960 along with a small-time crook called Danny Shay after a botched attempt at extracting protection money.

Esmeralda's Barn, a gambling club in Wilton Place, Knightsbridge, with a restaurant and, originally, a lesbian cellar bar, was their attempt in 1960 to move further upwards and westwards. According to one story, they acquired it in a roundabout way from the slum landlord Peter Rachman, who had passed it on in exchange for peace and quiet in his neck of the Notting Hill woods. (Payne suggested later that Rachman backed out of a possible joint venture when he realized what the Krays were like.) The twins loved the glamour of a West End club, particularly with a toff, Lord Effingham, whom they patronized – 'Effy, get the effing tea' – on the board. But Ronnie had no business sense and, while Reggie was serving his eighteen months, was granting credit and opening bottles of bubbly with abandon.

'They thought they were immune from prosecution and could actually walk on water,' says 'Nipper' Read, the detective who was to pursue them. He recalls the effect they had on people: 'If they drove down Commercial Road, everybody waved to them. If somebody had a drink with them, it was like having tea with Princess Margaret.'

He remembers his first sighting, in 1964, when working under-cover, of Ron Kray at the Grave Maurice, a Whitechapel pub which the twins frequented: 'There was a big American car and a guy stepped out with his hand in his pocket as though he had a gun there and sort of swept the street, making sure there was no one in sight and then gave a signal and the back door opened and out stepped Ronnie Kray. He was dressed like a 1930s Chicago gangster, with a long, long cashmere coat that reached to his ankles, tied in a loose belt at the waist. His hair was greased and parted and he wore his glasses. He looked like Al Capone without his fedora.' The style was important: 'Italian elegance with British bite, a Whitechapel translation of second-generation Mafia mufti,' as writer Iain Sinclair has since described it. Leslie Payne was not entirely convinced: 'They were fairly hygienic although they weren't very clever with their fingernails.'

Certainly, the twins had a presence which was particularly attractive in the austere fifties. 'Crooks are like everyone else,' says Read. 'They like to belong. The Krays called themselves the Firm and generated this feeling of fatherly protection or comfort to other crooks who felt that if they belonged to an organization of that kind, then they were subscribing to something worthwhile.'

At the time, it must have seemed that they were. More clubs were being tapped for protection money. The twins took over the Cambridge Rooms in Kingston, on the western outskirts of London, a venture mainly remembered now because a racehorse, Solway Cross, was raffled there for charity – the twins were great fund-raisers and did not mind people knowing this – and was won by the actor Ronald Fraser after a night of booze and bidding. Another club, Le Monde, in Chelsea, had become part of the portfolio. Payne suggests that in the mid-sixties the Firm was taking protection money from between a third and a half of all the illegal gaming clubs in London. Elsewhere they came briefly unstuck when the owner of the Hideaway Club, Hew McCowan, the son of a baronet, gave evidence against them in January 1965 on charges that they had demanded money with menaces. But one of the witnesses, Sidney Vaughan, had a change of heart after what was described as a 'visitation from God' that required him to recant his original story; and McCowan was undermined in court, partly because of the irrelevant introduction of his homosexuality.

The Krays' clubs included Esmeralda's Barn and the Kentucky Club where Reg (far left) and Ron (far right) are pictured with father Charles (front) and brother Charlie (second from right).

The case fell apart and the twins threw a rowdy celebration party. Later they took over the Hideaway Club, turning it into the El Morocco.

They also had dreams of larger empires. In 1964 they attempted to expand into Africa, attracted by tall tales from Ernest Shinwell, son of the Labour peer 'Manny'. The idea was to invest in a massive construction plan for 3000 houses and a shopping precinct in Enugu in Nigeria, where Ronnie enjoyed himself snacking on monkey meat and palm wine and briefly pondered the idea of bringing a Nigerian manservant home with him. But this scheme turned into fiasco. They had to rescue Leslie Payne from the local gaol, where he had been held under the charge of 'impersonating a company director', and withdraw. Further north, Tangier had become a popular watering-hole for the 'chaps'. Gypsy Hill ran a club called Churchills, a favourite haunt with both European and North African villains. Morocco became Ron's favourite country because of the young men there; he was already, remarkably for a criminal of that era, known as a homosexual.

Back in England, the twins' associations with the powerful were not without embarrassments. In 1964 Ron met Lord Boothby at the latter's Belgravia home to discuss a business deal which never went through and the meeting was recorded for posterity in photographs. Rumours spread and the *Sunday Mirror* of 12 July splashed with a tale of the 'Peer and a Gangster'. The *Daily Mirror* followed suit with a story about 'the picture we dare not print' and hints of Mayfair high jinks. Lord Boothby responded with a long letter in *The Times* in which he explained that Ron Kray had asked him to take part in a business venture, that he had been unaware that Ron was the 'king of the underworld', that he was not homosexual and 'I have not been to a Mayfair party of any kind for more than twenty years'. The *Mirror* contritely paid £40 000 damages.

Nearly thirty years later the Krays' biographer, John Pearson, suggested that Boothby had 'enjoyed the devil's own luck' in getting his apology and damages. Just after the twins were gaoled in 1969 Pearson was given a suitcase by Violet Kray which Ronnie wanted him to have. It contained friendly letters from Boothby, thanking Ronnie for a box of Corona cigars, for instance, and showing that he had known Ronnie for much longer than he claimed. There was also a photograph, taken at the Society Club in Jermyn Street in the West End, of Boothby with Ronnie, Billy Exley and other members of the Firm. In the centre of the photograph, as Pearson put it, 'was a teenage boy. On either side of him sat Ronnie Kray and Boothby, looking as if unable to decide which of them would eat him first.' Pearson suggests that the dishonest libel action not only cost the *Mirror* editor, Reg Payne, his job, but put the Krays 'off limits' to other journalists for a time: 'To confront the Krays might have raised awkward questions of their involvement with Boothby and to re-open that affair might have sparked off an uninviting scandal.'

The twins had also contacted Tom Driberg, the Labour Member of Parliament, who had been introduced to them by Joan Littlewood at the Kentucky Club in Stepney, east London, and who shared Ronnie's interest in young men. He became a regular attender at Ronnie's parties where, as Driberg's biographer, Francis Wheen, recorded, 'rough but compliant East End lads were served like so many canapés'. Driberg was persuaded to make representations to the Home Office on behalf of gaoled friends of the Krays and did not desert the twins, even after their incarceration, although he slightly played down his connection with them, saying he had a 'very slight acquaintance with them'.

In the mid-sixties the Krays were taking their role extremely seriously, even travelling in different cars, as members of the royal family use different planes, so that if one was killed the other would be able to carry on running the Firm. They also aspired to be mobsters on the scale of their celluloid heroes. Charlie Kray claims that a number of deals were done with the Mafia whereby the Krays helped dispose of stolen bearer bonds in the English banking system. But he also says that one of their largest transactions, the handling of $250 000 worth of 'hot' bonds that he had been sent to Paris to fetch, ended with them becoming literally too hot to handle. He burned the bonds in his mother's dustbin.

Payne was dispatched to conduct business with a criminal family in Montreal but the team was eventually deported back to England. Ron was briefly wined and dined in New York and came home entertaining grand notions of running a Mafia franchise in England. However, the indication is that the Krays, who provided entertainment and some forms of protection and escort services for visiting hoodlums and their show-business allies, were seen as small bananas by the American Mafia who regarded England as not worth the effort.

The Krays did, however, enjoy the company of the Mafia-connected George Raft, who tried to set up his Colony Club as a going concern in Britain but was banned from re-entry by the Home Secretary, Roy Jenkins, in 1967 on the grounds that his continued presence in the United Kingdom would not be conducive to the public good. The Colony Club closed two years later. Reg idolized Raft and would quote him admiringly in later life: 'He told me that his philosophy of life is that it is better to socialize every night rather than watch television and that's the way he keeps young.'

Had the Krays been content to take the considerable earnings that their protection racket brought them, both in London and increasingly in excursions into places like Birmingham and Leicester, and not sought an empire which they were ill-equipped to sustain, they might by now have been buffing up their tans on the south coast of Spain. But it was not to be. Cat burglar Peter Scott reckoned that the police initially did not bother prosecuting them and other gangsters because the gangs were mainly fighting amongst themselves: 'It wasn't until they moved into the elegant areas and saw themselves as [being] as good as the righteous that wrath descended on them. What happened in the sixties was that the gangsters failed to recognize the guidelines and started to push the perimeters out. Society blew the whistle and said enough is enough. They had one brandy too many and it went to their head.'

It was more than brandy the Krays were downing. Ronnie had a ferocious capacity for drink – everything from brown ale to bottles of gin would be dispatched in the long erratic nights of clubbing. In contrast, Reggie seemed to have settled down slightly and in 1965 married Frances Shea whom he had been courting in chivalrous fashion. The wedding was photographed by David Bailey who took the most iconic of the shots of the twins. But Frances left the marital home within eight weeks, dismayed by the otherworldly atmosphere of lurking menace and the constant presence of the Firm's foot-soldiers. She committed suicide in 1967, an event that Charlie Kray believed was pivotal in the final collapse of the twins: 'When that happened, Reg had a death wish, he really didn't care what happened to him.'

Reg Kray (right) weds Frances Shea in 1965, toasted by Ron.

The twins still hankered after a larger empire and unconditional respect. When George Cornell, or Myers, one of the outspoken henchmen of the rival south London Richardson family, made it clear that he had little of the latter for Ron, even calling him a 'fat poof' behind his back, action became inevitable. An additional factor may have been that Cornell was putting the squeeze on an East End warehouseman who was already paying the twins for protection, and indicated that he had no intention of backing off. Albert Donoghue is adamant that the 'poof' insult was not the reason for the death: 'Cornell was a loner and he had come over to our territory. It was an insult and Ronnie took it as an insult.' Two days after a shoot-out involving the Richardson gang in Mr Smith's night club in south London, in which Dickie Hart, an ally of the Krays, had died, Ron decided to cross a fresh boundary.

On 9 March 1966 Albie Woods, a bookmaker friend of Cornell, was killing only time when he agreed to spend an hour or so with him in the Blind Beggar on the Mile End Road. They had just been to visit a mutual friend, Jimmy Andrews, who was in hospital suffering from gunshot wounds. Cornell suggested a drink in what might have been seen as the heart of enemy territory. Woods noticed three men walk in, have a drink then leave. Shortly after two men entered. 'All of a sudden, George said "Look who's here." Then I realized that someone had stopped behind me. I saw a fellow taking aim at George. George was sneering at him. At that instant it was – BANG – the shot was fired and all I could see was a massive flame and smoke.'

Woods slid off his bar-stool and ducked behind the bar. There was a second shot: 'George was lying down beside me and I saw two pairs of legs walk across the middle of the bar, the next thing there's BANG BANG BANG BANG. I could hear the barmaid screaming. I put my arm underneath George's head and shouted "Get an ambulance quick."' Woods had no desire to be there when the police arrived so left Cornell with two men and went to phone Olive, Cornell's wife. 'I said "I have some bad news. George has been shot." She said "Who done it?" I said "I don't really know but you'll find him if you go to the hospital opposite the Blind Beggar."' Woods then drove to south London and eventually to Charlie Richardson's house, his blue mohair suit stained red with Cornell's blood. 'I told Charlie what had happened and he said "You'd better have a wash and brush up." He wasn't very pleased that George had been shot. A couple of news flashes came on. One said that a man had been shot in the Blind Beggar, another an hour later said he had been transferred to a hospital in Maida Vale. Then we got another flash which said he died.'

But Woods says he was unable to identify the two men and that even when the police finally persuaded him to attend an identification parade and asked him if he could tap the gunman on the shoulder, he was unable to assist: 'The police looked at me and I know they didn't believe me. If looks could kill, I would have been dead there and then. I don't think George would have wanted me to pick them out anyway. They say that those that live by the sword, die by the sword.'

One of the Krays' firm, Eric Mason, a Portland Borstal old boy and reputedly the last man to have received the Cat in a British prison, recalls the night of the murder. He had been driving home with his girlfriend, a dancer at the Pigalle in Piccadilly, when news of the killing came on the car radio. 'She said to me, "You've gone very quiet. Was that something to do with what was said on the radio? That's where you and your friends drink, isn't it?"' After Mason returned to his flat there was a call from Reg Kray telling him to go to a safe house the twins had in Walthamstow.

'I looked up at the flat and I saw Ronnie Kray's silhouette in the window. He came to the door and it was as if he had just returned from holiday,' said Mason later. 'He said "I've got some right good news for you." And I said "Oh, yeah, what's that?" So he said: "Here you are, have a gin and tonic." He had an ironing board and there was a bottle of gin on it. He had his jacket off, he was in his shirtsleeves and braces. He said, "I've just put a couple of bullets in that Cornell's head, I took his fucking head off." I went – "Phew ..."'

'He said, "You'd have been well pleased, if you'd have been there." So I said, "Yeah, I heard something on the radio." And he said, "Anyway, that mob know now that we don't mess about with mugs like them." I sat there and I was thinking to myself – any minute now the law could arrive and we are nicked. And Ronnie, it was as if he had said, "I've just run over a cat." There was absolutely no emotion whatsoever.'

Ronnie had good reason to be calm. None of the witnesses could remember seeing anything and the police inquiry ground to a halt. The Krays seemed genuinely untouchable. In any case, a few months later they had other cod to fry.

Frank Mitchell, known as the 'mad axeman' and famed for his brute strength and awesome lack of fear, was sprung from Dartmoor by the twins on 12 December 1966. It was suggested that the Krays wanted him as a counterweight to the Richardson gang's own unguided missile, 'Mad' Frankie Fraser. Charlie Kray denies this: 'The twins had all the respect or fear; they didn't need Frankie Mitchell.' Anyway, by the time of his escape, the Richardsons had been weakened by a bloody battle at Mr Smith's club and Mitchell was now regarded as something of an inconvenience. But the twins had promised Mitchell that they would help and he gradually put pressure on them to honour their word as he became increasingly impatient at not being given an official release date.

The escape was not particularly complex. Mitchell was the beneficiary of a liberal regime at Dartmoor that allowed him enough laxity to spend lunch-time in the pub on the edge of the moor. He would emerge with a crate of beer which he was allowed to take back to prison – 'an incredible state of affairs', as the judge, Sir Frederick Lawton, later described it. The Krays had to do little more than provide a getaway car and a hide-out.

Tucked into his safe house Mitchell, a simple soul who had been classified subnormal as a child, was supplied with a striking woman from the West End club scene, Lisa Prescott, with whom he promptly fell in love. Letters written on his behalf by 'Mad' Teddy Smith, one of the Firm's brighter recruits, or Lennie Dunn, a bookstall owner who had arranged the hide-out, were signed with the Mitchell thumbprint and sent to *The Times* and the *Daily Mirror* suggesting he would return to gaol if he was told when his final release date would be: 'Sir, the reason for my absence from Dartmoor was to bring to the Notice of my unhappy plight to be truthful, I am asking for a possible Date of release. From the age of nine, I have not been completely free, always under some act or other. Sir, I ask you, where is the fairness in this. I am not a murderer or a sex maniac, nor do I think I am a danger to the public. I think that I have been more than punished for the wrongs I have done.'

Little did Mitchell know that a more final form of punishment awaited him. When the twins decided that he should return to gaol, Mitchell refused and took a gun from one of his minders. He had become a nuisance and, after being told that he was going to be taken to a fresh hiding place, he was escorted to a van and shot dead. Albert Donaghue who, with Teddy Smith, had helped Mitchell escape in the first place told later that the 'mad axeman' had been shot in the chest and head while the van moved down through Barking.

As Albert Donoghue says: 'He wanted to circulate and he said that if the twins won't organise it, I'll go to them. This was relayed back and that was it. He signed his death warrant.' Mitchell was dissuaded from taking a jungle knife with him and told that Lisa could not come with them in case they ran into the police and because of Ronnie's attitude to women. He was accompanied to a waiting van by Donoghue, Alfie Gerrard (now dead) and three others and he sat on the right wheel casing. As the passenger door was shut and the engine turned on, the first shots rang out.

'Two guns just opened up,' says Donoghue, who witnessed two Kray henchman carry it out. 'BAH – BAH – BAH – BAH. Mitchell's on his knees and I can see them hitting him. He just fell back. As he started groaning, one of them went BANG BANG BANG around the heart. You could see his shirt jumping. Quiet. He starts groaning again. We're coming back onto the main road. As we do a left into the tunnel, he starts groaning again. The gun went under his ear and BANG that was the last one. Now we're on the main road so I said right, stop here. Common sense told me I should be next and I was waiting for a bullet.' He lived to tell the tale: 'I had a big old Crombie overcoat on and I had to walk along with it wide open to get rid of this smell of cordite and gunpowder ... They must have taken the body to pieces.' He returned to carry out a 'wet and dry' clean up of the flat where Mitchell had been hidden, taking care to wipe the fingerprints off the headboard of the bed which, Lisa had helpfully informed them, Mitchell used to grip.

The 'mission accomplished' code phoned through to the Krays was supposedly along the lines of 'the geezer's gone' or 'the dog is dead'. His body has never been found. Less attention was paid to what happened to Teddy Smith who also disappeared shortly afterwards.

Frank Mitchell's death was to become the Turin Shroud of the underworld, surrounded by myth and speculation: Ron claimed in his version of events that 'Mitchell wasn't mad, he wasn't an axeman and one day he will reappear and the world will know the truth'. Two years later, Reg dismissed the idea of the resurrection of Mitchell as 'sad to say, ridiculous' but provided a new scenario which suggested that he had been shot by 'an ex-boxer and three Greeks ... [he was] so strong that he was still alive after being shot three times'. 'Scotch Jack' Dickson says that Mitchell was probably cremated, although it had been put about that he was in the cement holding up the Box flyover in east London.

There was no investigation into the death since, as far as the police knew, Mitchell was still alive and on the run. The twins, fuelled perhaps by their apparent invulnerability, carried out another murder in October the following year. The victim was a big, stroppy, hard-drinking, pill-popping villain called Jack 'the Hat' (which covered his premature baldness) McVitie, who had crossed the twins. (He had also blotted his social copy-book by turning up at one of their clubs on a hot day dressed in his hat, Bermuda shorts and a machete.) The theory behind the murder has traditionally been that Ron, having 'got his button' by killing Cornell, egged his brother on to prove himself in the same way. McVitie was the chosen victim because he not only owed the twins money, which he had been too casual about repaying, but he had also been heard making threats against them when in his cups. He had supposedly been given the money to kill Leslie Payne, about whom the twins were already suspicious, and had clearly not carried out the job.

One of the Krays' men, Tony Lambrianou, was present at the McVitie killing and has a different explanation: 'The idea that there was a pressure on Reggie to kill somebody was a total fallacy.' McVitie, whom Lambrianou describes as a Jekyll and Hyde character, had offended the Krays by misbehaving violently and upsetting women guests in the Regency club, run by an underworld family called the Barrys, when out of his head on amphetamines. 'How far could they let him go? There might just be a time when they couldn't turn a blind eye any more. It meant people losing respect for them. There was no intention to murder anyone that night.'

Earlier in the evening, Lambrianou and his brother Chris had gone to meet some other associates, the Mills brothers, at a pub called the Carpenters Arms in Bethnal Green, east London. They had instructions to bring McVitie for a meeting with the twins. As Lambrianou tells it, it was just another Saturday in the pub when they set off in their Zodiac two-tone Mark II to the Stoke Newington flat in north London where Ronnie and Reggie were waiting. 'Reggie started to shoot him in the head but the gun failed to go off. There was a bit of talk from McVitie – "What have I done?" – and Reg told him, "You know what you've done, Jack." Jack sat down on the sofa and said, "I'm sorry, it won't happen again," but they had heard it all before. All of a sudden, Jack stood up and walked to the window and he punched the pane out. It was said that he tried to dive for it but, in fact, he punched it out of sheer frustration that he had been set up. There was a carving knife, a normal carving knife, and the next thing, it was over. I didn't actually see it because I turned away. It was said that Reggie pinned him to the floor with the knife through

Gangland murder victims. Left to right: George Cornell, Jack 'The Hat' McVitie and Frank 'The Mad Axeman' Mitchell.

the throat but that never happened. McVitie had been stabbed three times and I think the first stab killed him.'

Tony Lambrianou says that Kray did not intend to kill McVitie at first. 'He said to him "I've had enough of you, you fucking cunt, now fuck off and never let me see you again." McVitie could have avoided the aggravation but we're talking about a man who couldn't let go. I would have done exactly the same as Reggie that night, he couldn't let it get any further.' There were strangers in the room, he says, which Reg would have been smart enough to see as a potential problem if the murder had been premeditated. Lambrianou and his brother were detailed to clean up and get rid of the body, which was wrapped in an eiderdown. The body would not fit in the boot of the car so it was put in the back seat and the car was driven through the Blackwall tunnel and left beside a church. There it was picked up and disposed of in a pre-dug grave. The car was crushed into a 90cm×90cm (3ft×3ft) cube which was referred to afterwards as 'the Oxo'.

Donoghue shares the popular view on why McVitie died: 'When Ronnie got drunk, when he was heavy on pills, he would be screaming at Reg, "You cowardly bastard, I've done mine now it's time you, you skinny slag, about time you done yours." Simple as that.' According to Donoghue, there had been previous plans for Reggie to kill Joey Cannon, another heavy and former Jack Spot man. McVitie and Donoghue were given the job of taking the intended victim to a flat in Hackney.

'Before Cannon arrived, Reggie got this gun wrapped up in a bath towel to silence it and said "D'you reckon this will be all right?"' Reggie was to hide in one room while McVitie and Donoghue kept Cannon talking. In the event, when Cannon arrived, there was a staged scuffle and McVitie and Donoghue tipped him the wink to escape. 'When Reggie came out of the room, we said we'd had a scuffle and he'd gone. I think he was a little bit relieved.'

John Pearson in *Profession of Violence* says that Ron Kray enjoyed spreading rumours about what had happened to McVitie: that he had been fed to the pigs in Suffolk or to the furnaces of Bankside Power Station or buried in the foundation of a City block or in Epping Forest. When Pearson, invited to be the official biographer of the twins and still unaware of their activities, met Reggie shortly after the killing he noted he had a bandaged hand and asked politely how he had injured himself. 'Gardenin',' came the reply.

'Murder is a very gory scene, a terrible, terrible thing that you never forget,' says Lambrianou. As far as he was concerned, McVitie was a violent man who had once thrown a woman out of a car, had insulted the twins and who deserved a spot of discipline. 'It was too dangerous to leave him on the loose, he'd come back at you. It was just an unfortunate error.'

Eric Mason thought that the killing was slightly more than an inconvenient mistake. 'He was taken to his death as drunk as a sack. He should never have died that way. Reg Kray's got a lot of nice things about him but he did a lot of things in his life that, if he'd thought about them, he wouldn't have done. He was very much under the influence of his brother who is, without a doubt, a psychopath.'

As the blood flowed, even the twins themselves were seen by some of the firm as expendable and there was talk of Reggicide and Ronnicide in the ranks, as Albert Donoghue recounts: 'We knew it couldn't last. The Colonel was going crazy.' After the Cornell murder and the rumour that Cornell's brother was seeking revenge, Ronnie decided a change of tactics was in order: 'He said, "there's too much shooting going on". So he bought four axes, gave us each an axe to go and track him down. It would make a "change of pattern" is how they put it. That's crazy, isn't it?'

It proved to Donoghue that the twins were not really equipped to run the show: 'Ronnie should have just been brought out like a pit bull dog. They couldn't organize a piss-up in a brewery. They should have been lieutenants or sergeants with someone else organizing.'

Another strange death some two years earlier was also linked, without evidence, to Ronnie Kray. Freddie Mills, a former world light heavyweight boxing champion and one of the most popular of British post-war sportsmen, had been found dead in his car on 24 July 1965 near the Freddie Mills Nite Spot in Soho. There was a Belgian .22 rifle by his side. Originally the death was treated as murder and it was suggested that Ronnie Kray had had him killed because he owed the twins money and because the killing would establish Ronnie as untouchable. But this was speculation and after the owner of the rifle was traced and said he had loaned the boxer the gun so that he could go to a fancy-dress party as a cowboy it was accepted that Mills had died by his own hand.

Theories as to why Mills should kill himself have been legion: that he was gay and was about to face a charge for propositioning a man in a toilet; that he had enormous debts which he could not repay; that he had been depressed after the suicide of his friend, the crooner Michael Holliday; that he had a call-girl racket that was about to be exposed; and, most persistently, that he had been the man behind the Nude Prostitute or Jack the Stripper murders, which were never solved and which appeared to cease after his death. (The murders of Irene Lockwood, Helene Barthelemy and Mary Turner had been seen as different from other sex crimes. One or two of the women killed were known to criminals and some of the underworld were under suspicion.) The author Tony Van Den Berg came out with a fresh theory in 1993 that Mills might have been murdered by a Chinese gang seeking an entrée into clubland.

The prostitute murders were also linked to another odd underworld death of the time, that of Ginger Marks in January 1965. Marks, a minor crook, was shot apparently after being mistaken for another man on whom a contract had been taken out. His chief celebrity came from the outlandish ways in which his body was rumoured to have been disposed of after the murder: set in concrete and dumped in the Thames or slipped into a 'civilian's' coffin by a bent undertaker. Royston 'Little Legs' Smith, a dwarf actor who appeared in the Beatles' *Magical Mystery Tour* and who knew the Krays, claimed that Marks and 'Mad Teddy' Smith both ended up in cement-mixers.

Leonard 'Nipper' Read had been given the responsibility by Scotland Yard of nailing the twins after McVitie's death: 'The Krays were both idolized and feared. People either loved them or were terrified of them. Either way, no one was going to talk about them. And so I decided to go back to basics.' He set off after those who had drifted out of the Krays' circle.

He eventually struck gold with Leslie Payne, who had detached himself from the Firm and believed that the Krays had advanced plans to see him dead. McVitie had already been asked to do the job and Payne now believed that an American hitman called 'Junior', with a panther tattoo on his arm, had been hired. He made a 146-page statement to Read in the quiet of the library of a police section house in Marylebone. Payne would arrive from his Tulse Hill home every day and for three weeks told the tale. He was joined in his work by Freddy Gore, the other half of the Krays' financial team. The two were known as 'Laurel and Hardy'. Payne was granted immunity and Read used him to reassure other potential witnesses that it was safe to inform. Read believes his inquiry was hampered by the early leaking of his work by the 'mandarins' at Scotland Yard who liked to boast of corporate successes. He heard that there was a contract on his life and started looking under his car before setting off for work.

Read also tracked down Lisa Prescott, Mitchell's companion. Unfortunately she mistook the detectives for gangsters and tried to escape them by jumping out of the police car and into the Thames when they were taking her to Tintagel House, where the inquiry was based for security reasons; she had realized they were going in the opposite direction from Scotland Yard and therefore believed they must be impostors.

Albert Donoghue assisted the police after he had been told by the twins that he would have to take responsibility for the murder of Frank Mitchell. Donoghue had initially refused to co-operate with the authorities but, after his family had been threatened, he changed his mind and named Freddie Foreman as Mitchell's killer.

A shadowy American criminal called Alan Cooper, who had arrived on the scene at the time of the Krays' tentative relationship with the Mafia and had taken over Payne's role as adviser, was to act as a further plank in the ramp now being erected against the twins. His part would appear to have been that of *agent provocateur*, although it is hard to separate the fantasy from the reality in a man who once offered the Krays such handy hardware as a pigskin attaché case with a built-in hypodermic syringe, suitable for carrying out underworld hits.

The Krays themselves seem to have taken the news of the pursuit phlegmatically down at Fort Vallance. They bought two boa constrictors and named them Read and Gerrard after the two men tracking them: 'Nipper' and Chief Superintendent Fred Gerrard. But, early in the morning of 9 May 1968, as they lay in bed after a heavy night at the Astor Club, the police struck. Many of those arrested with them were offered deals if they co-operated.

It was clear that, with the Krays arrested and behind bars, tongues were being loosened. By the time the twins' trial started at the Old Bailey many of their old comrades had seen the writing on the wall and realized that it said 'co-operate or rot'. Billy Exley, who had helped run the long firm frauds, 'Scotch Jack' Dickson, and cousin Ronnie Hart who had enjoyed the high life with the twins, all agreed to help the police, earning the undying hatred of the brothers who still describe them as 'rats'. Hart later attempted suicide.

Lambrianou was one of those who did not cross over. 'I can look in the mirror and say I never pointed the finger or put them away.' He was puzzled that Donoghue should be one of the ones who did: 'He was the one that surprised me ... "Scotch Jack" Dickson has had to live with himself for what he did.'

Dickson retired from view after the trial and went into a ladies fashion business in the south of England. He has kept a low profile since his days with the Krays, emerging only to publicize his memoirs – but refusing to be photographed. (He is not to be confused with 'Scotch Jack' Buggy, a hot-tempered Glasgow heavy who operated in London at that time. Buggy was killed in 1967 and his bound body dumped in the sea, where it was found by two off-duty policemen on a fishing trip. Two men were charged with the murder years later but acquitted. Why he was shot has never been satisfactorily explained, although the most persistent rumour was that his death was connected in some way with Great Train Robbery money. The Krays inevitably came into the frame because Buggy was involved in protection racketeering.)

Neither Cornell nor McVitie, the men for whose murders the twins were gaoled for life, may have been, as Charlie Kray puts it, 'nice people' and both had suggested that they would get the Krays. But the second murder was last orders for the twins: 'When the McVitie thing happened,' Charlie says, 'I really knew it was the beginning of the end. You're waiting. At any moment they're going to come for you. It's a terrible feeling.' He denies that the twins operated through fear: 'The twins never asked anyone to do anything, if there were fights or whatever, they did it themselves.' The people who eventually gave evidence against them were 'the ones wanting to be gangsters, walking around being heavy with people. If people were nervous or frightened of the twins they must have had a guilt complex because if you haven't done anything wrong there's no need to be afraid of anybody.'

The Krays' trial opened at the Old Bailey on 7 January 1969 with eleven men in the dock. Court officials tried to hang numbered placards round the defendants' necks to identify them to the jury but the Firm objected strongly with Ronnie shouting 'This is not a cattle market' as he ripped his up. After Ronnie's barrister, John Platts-Mills QC, had remarked to the judge, Mr Justice Melford Stevenson, that the placards smacked of ancient colonial practices, the court relented and the jurors were given a plan of the dock with the names marked on it. The twins tried to tough it out but the testimony of more than twenty of their former associates was too detailed for them

Tony Lambrianou (left) and Reg Kray during their trial.

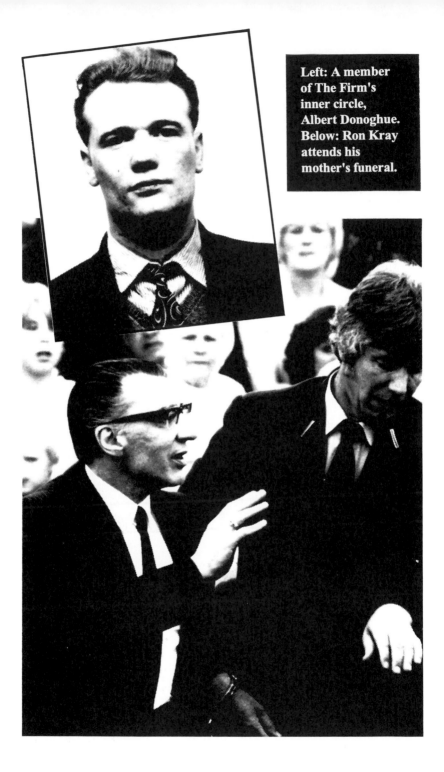

Left: A member
of The Firm's
inner circle,
Albert Donoghue.
Below: Ron Kray
attends his
mother's funeral.

to escape. Ron and Reg were duly convicted of the murders of Cornell and McVitie respectively and cleared, along with Foreman, of the killing of Mitchell. They were gaoled for life with a recommendation from the judge, whose country home was called 'Truncheons', that they serve at least thirty years. They were joined inside by brother Charlie, the Lambrianous, Freddie Foreman and Ian Barrie who were gaoled for their various roles in the mayhem. Donoghue was sentenced to two years for his part in Mitchell's death.

The Krays' melody has lingered on. They have become the royal family of the underworld, their slightest moves and moods catalogued, and there was a film of their lives in 1990. The premiere of *The Krays* was remarkable for the dozens of gangsterly dressed young men arriving by limousine, an effect only partially marred by the fact that close inspection showed that they had all hired the same vehicle which was doing a discreet circuit between the front of the Leicester Square cinema and a nearby pub.

The books pour out year after year. In 1990, in *Born Fighter*, Reg Kray announced that he had become a born-again Christian and wanted to be used as a 'vehicle for God ... I cannot become a saint overnight but I leave it all in God's hands'. His favourite reading had become Kahlil Gibran's *The Prophet* and he stunned prisoners in Parkhurst by saying grace before their Christmas dinner. He also castigated his fellow-inmates for reading pornography to satisfy their 'filthy, lustful desires' and attacked men who bullied gay prisoners. Contrition for the murder of McVitie was not part of his new religious baggage. He likened it to the killing of Argentinian troops in the Falklands War: 'I would sooner see the loss of the McVities of this world than the deaths of innocent young soldiers plucked from the joys of life by the bullets of war.'

Reg 'adopted' various young men inside. One of these new 'sons' was Pete Gillett, whom Reg met in Parkhurst and whose career as a singer he tried to promote. Gillett did make a couple of singles but they did not sell and despite proclamations of going straight – 'my life is now show business and watching out for Reg's best interests out here' – he was to find himself back in gaol in October 1992 on a major drug-dealing charge, disinherited by the Krays.

In 1991 a slim volume of the Philosophy and Poetry of Reg Kray entitled *Thoughts* was published in London. In the introduction the publishers, River First, informed readers: 'This book contains the thoughts, ideas and writings of Mr Reginald Kray. The main text was created over a nine-hour period which gives an insight into this man's

**Reg Kray keeping
fit in Parkhurst
prison.**

unique mind, hence textual and grammatical anomalies remain.' What followed was sixty pages of poems like:

'Puppy dog be my friend
I know you are loyal
And will stay with me till the end
I know I cannot ask for a better friend.'

Even Tony Lambrianou is puzzled that the Krays' mystique still hangs over parts of east London like old aftershave: 'I have met people who have got shrines to them in their homes.'

What is remarkable is that more than twenty years after Mr Reginald Kray and his brother Ronald were the most feared – or respected – criminals in London, there should still be such a market for anything to do with them. They are now a much more commercial enterprise, with everything from films (*The Krays*) and musicals (*England, England*) to boxer shorts and a £250 limited edition 'portfolio', than they ever were in the days of long firms and protection.

Perhaps the highest accolade they were to receive was when two Welsh brothers in their twenties, Leslie and Leighton Frayne, modelled themselves to such an extent on the Krays, even visiting their heroes inside, that they ended up being gaoled for eight years at Newport Crown Court in 1992 for robbery and conspiracy.

Ronnie still plays host at visiting time in Broadmoor, supping on alcohol-free lager, immaculately turned out from the toes of his polished shoes to his silver-sixpence cufflinks and as ramrod-straight as one would expect of a retired colonel. He married Kate Howard, who ran a strippogram firm, in 1989. Coverage of the wedding was on offer for £25 000 according to reports of the time. Mrs Kray subsequently published *Married to the Krays*, and *Murder, Madness and Marriage* in which she recorded that 'everyone who meets the Colonel is impressed by his charm and wit'.

Big brother Charlie, the mildest mannered of the trio, has not been in trouble since his sentence for being an accessory to the murder of McVitie. He moved to Spain where Ibiza and Benidorm are his favoured haunts, wrote two books on the family, dabbles in the music business and clubland and keeps trim beneath the Spanish sun.

Reg Kray concludes in his book that, 'My eventual aim is to be recognized first as a man and eventually as author, poet and philosopher.' A far cry from the dustier but more realizable dream of being Vallance Road's answer to Jimmy Cagney, to be 'top of the world, ma', that was to land the twins behind bars in the first place.

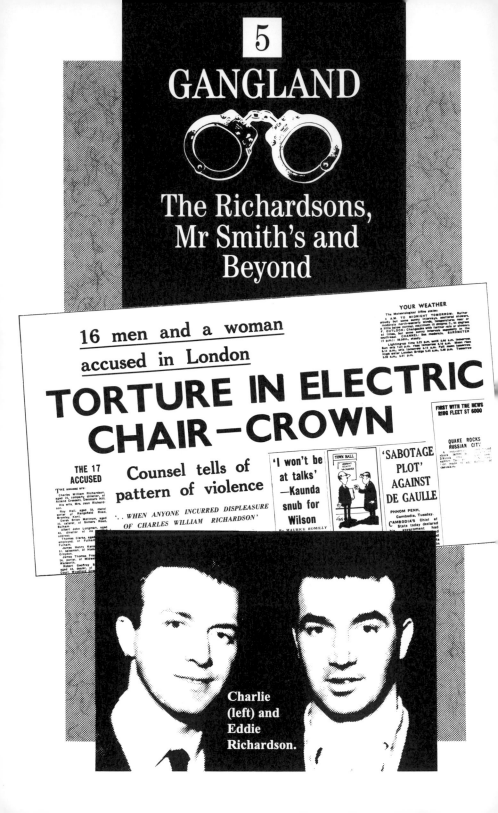

5

GANGLAND

The Richardsons, Mr Smith's and Beyond

16 men and a woman
accused in London

TORTURE IN ELECTRIC CHAIR — CROWN

THE 17 ACCUSED

Counsel tells of pattern of violence

'.. WHEN ANYONE INCURRED DISPLEASURE OF CHARLES WILLIAM RICHARDSON'

'I won't be at talks' —Kaunda snub for Wilson

'SABOTAGE PLOT' AGAINST DE GAULLE

Charlie (left) and Eddie Richardson.

While the Krays had been carving out their empire in east London, another little firm was quietly establishing itself south of the Thames. The Richardsons and the Krays were to clash, most spectacularly with the death of George Cornell, but their methods and style were very different.

'The Richardsons had more charisma than the Krays,' says Eric Mason, who had been at the sharp end of conflicts between the two gangs. 'You had to be tough and prove yourself to be with the Kray twins but the Richardsons were more interested if you had the ability to make money as well as being a tough guy.'

The two gangs had different approaches to people who crossed them, says Mason: 'A guy tucked the twins up over a gold deal and sent them a card from Honolulu saying, "I'm having a lovely time." The twins just wiped their mouths and laughed about it, whereas the Richardsons wouldn't allow anybody to tuck them up because they wanted the world to know – you don't mess us around.'

'Mad' Frankie Fraser, who had been courted by both Krays and Richardsons before joining the latter, was in no doubt which were the smarter team: 'Using racing terms, there would be no race, comparing the Richardsons with the Krays. The Richardsons were miles in front, brain power, everything.'

Charlie Richardson had been born in Twickenham in 1934, the son of Charlie, a former prizefighter and merchant seaman, and Eileen. The family moved soon after his birth to Camberwell and it was from this south London patch that he was later to build his empire, part legal – through his scrap business and foreign investments – and part illegal – through his frauds and gangsterism. It saw millions of pounds passing through his hands, an international business network and an office in Park Lane. Eventually, it also resulted in thousands of nights behind bars.

He was in trouble as a teenager and was sent away for the first time after he had stolen a car and eluded the police in a wild chase down the Old Kent Road before being collared. An extremely shrewd businessman, he turned his hand to making money as a peripatetic ice-cream salesman on his release from approved school and set up his first scrap-metal business before receiving the dreaded call to do his National Service.

Richardson had no greater desire to bull his boots and press his khaki than any of his predecessors in the underworld. His method of convincing the military authorities in Aldershot of this lack of enthusiasm was straightforward: 'Would you give away information

91

to the Russians?' he was asked by the officer conducting the initial interview. 'Fucking right I would, given half a chance.' Richardson then played mad, cutting up his uniform, giggling crazily, collapsing, making himself ill. Eventually he joined the regiment where he felt most at home: the prisoners serving in Shepton Mallet gaol where a contingent of men – the Krays, Frank Mitchell, the Nashes – who were later to become names in the underworld were embarking on their apprenticeship. His younger brother, Eddie, had meanwhile established himself on the outside, winning the local title of 'King of the Teds'.

The Richardsons, like the Krays, acquired an interest in clubs, starting with the Addington in Addington Square in south London, where they and their cohorts could drink after hours. It was a success. The restrictive licensing laws of the time were a boon to rough-and-ready clubs that could supply a drink in the mid-afternoon or the early hours of the morning. They opened another club, the Shirley Ann, with a local villain called John Bradbury.

One of the policemen sniffing around the clubs was a sergeant called Ken Drury, who was later to be gaoled for corruption. Richardson described his relations with the police thus: 'The most lucrative, powerful and extensive protection racket ever to exist was administered by the Metropolitan Police. As I got older and became involved in more and more dealings, legal or otherwise, I made regular payments to the police. It was a sort of taxation on crime ... Sometimes we would pay people to be "found" committing small crimes so that our friendly local protection racketeer in blue could have somebody to arrest and look like he had been busy.'

Johnny Bradbury, now living in Johannesburg, says that initially the police gave them no problems: 'We just could not put a foot wrong. It didn't matter what police station you went to. There was always someone that our local station knew who could contact someone and straighten things out.'

Clubs now played a major part in the Richardsons' lives, as they did for the Krays, and they won an extra set of spurs when, in the cheekily named Reform Club in the Elephant and Castle, they beat up the men who had beaten up a friend of theirs, Jimmy Brindle, the brother-in-law of Frankie Fraser. This was regarded as rough justice for people who had 'taken a liberty'. As Richardson later described the incident, it had a sound business spin-off to it: 'We worked together like a well-practised team until they lay unconscious at our feet in pools of blood and broken teeth.' It was 'big PR and our soaring reputation would protect us from challenges from ambitious competitors.'

But the police were already becoming aware of Charlie's activities and not all of them could be paid off. Although Richardson had been cleared of involvement in a shooting incident after witnesses failed to give evidence, he was gaoled for six months for a wholesale bacon theft. Facing further proceedings he fled to Canada with a girlfriend, Jean Goodman, who was to become his common-law wife. On his return, in 1961, he entered a new phase of his career: long firm frauds which he and Eddie operated with greater business acumen than did the Krays.

Being a smart operator, Richardson embarked on a variation of the theme in 1962 by setting fire to the warehouse buildings used in the frauds and claiming the insurance money. He would also tell the manufacturers of the goods that had gone up in flames that he was unable to pay them back because he was uninsured. The scheme made a six-figure profit and the Richardson business plan was on course. He had suffered personal tragedy at this time when his younger brother, Alan, was drowned in an accident on the Thames when the speedboat Charlie was piloting capsized.

On to the scene now came the various conmen and sharp operators whom Charlie saw as his way to a secure business future, but who were in the end to lead to his downfall. Jack 'the Rat' Duval, a portly conman known as 'The Prince of Fraud', seemed to offer the opportunities for investment that Richardson craved. Duval was a club-owner who had escaped from Russia in 1919 and been in the French Foreign Legion before joining the RAF in 1940. He was the archetypal wide boy and had flourished in the *laissez-faire* post-war business world before becoming what Richardson later described as 'a turd that floated down the Thames to my part of London'.

Duval's specialities in the early sixties included the importing of goods in rare supply, like silk stockings, and a travel company to take advantage of the new national desire to see 'the Continent', which was just becoming affordable. He also became chairman of a small bank, but came unstuck and 'did a runner'. When he did see Charlie again it was to be asked, 'Why aren't you a good boy?' and to be given a beating. He was learning, as others soon did, that it did not pay to cross Charlie. Duval apparently still did not digest the lesson. After taking money out of one of the companies in which they had a joint interest, he was summonsed on 12 June 1964 with one of his colleagues. They were both punished and a bloodied Duval went briefly into hiding. When Charlie discovered that he had passed dud cheques on him, he wanted a second appointment.

Unable to find Duval, he settled for Lucien Harris, an associate of Duval, an educated man who also worked as a crossword compiler. Richardson described him as having 'an accent and manner to go with his shop-window-dummy appearance and his fancy name'.

What happened to Harris was to form the corner-stone of the case that was eventually to derail the Richardson express. As far as Richardson was concerned, no more took place in confrontations like the one with Harris than the giving of a few right-handers to people who had taken a liberty or been out of order; their injuries did not even require an aspirin. According to Harris and the others who were to give evidence, what happened was far more brutal and sadistic.

Harris' account went thus: after his summons, he found himself in Richardson's office with Charlie and his associates – Roy Hall, whom Charlie had met when he tried to rob his own scrapyard, John Bradbury and brother Eddie. Charlie demanded to know where Duval was. Harris said he did not know and added that Richardson had been naïve to get involved with him in the first place. Richardson, who had been picking his fingernails with a knife, sent out for some scampi. When the food returned, Charlie shoved a piece of the hot scampi into Harris' eye.

Richardson ascribes this whole scene to imaginative script-writing: "Cleaning my nails with a knife? What an embarrassing and undignified scene when my nails were always clean and professionally manicured.' But what was to rivet the nation was the presence, always vigorously disputed by Richardson, of the Black Box.

This was a generator or old field telephone which was part of the scrap of the Richardson trade. Harris said he had to take off his shoes and socks and that wires were attached to his toes. Roy Hall, Richardson's long-time associate, was said to have turned the handle and Harris jumped convulsively from his seat. It was suggested that Hall was the Black Box man and was always the one who said, 'Shall I fetch the box?' The rest of Harris' clothes were taken off and further shocks administered. Orange juice was thrown over him, supposedly to make the shocks more painful. Harris said later: 'The leads were attached to my legs, my penis, the anus, the chest, the nostrils and the temples.' He was stabbed in the foot by Bradbury. Then, in what became a routine, a bottle of Scotch was ordered, Harris was allowed to clean up and Charlie even gave him £150 and a clean shirt.

Left: The Richardson's south London scrapyard and headquarters. Far left: John Bradbury.

'Our defence, our denial of these events was boring compared with their stories,' wrote Richardson in his memoirs. 'Such down-to-earth inanities seemed insignificant when the minds of the jury were so firmly imprinted with the image of a man with an electric torture-box attached to his wedding tackle.'

But Duval was still missing. Another man, Bunny Bridges, who might have known where he was, was brought in. Bradbury describes how Bridges was interrogated. Bridges had said that he did not know where Duval was so Charlie instructed Roy Hall and Bradbury to take him upstairs: 'We had what we called the torture box there, an old field telephone. We slung Bunny in a bath of water and then started putting the wires on his nipples and turning the handle and he was springing so high and screaming blue murder. We tied a piece of cloth round his mouth to keep him quiet. You could see he didn't know anything. We kept this up for about an hour and Charlie came running up and said "What are you two lunatics doing?"' Bridges suggested that Duval might be at his ex-wife's in Manchester and was given some petrol money to go and find him. James Taggart, who was accused of owing money and of being a police informer, was also brought in. He said he was stripped naked and given a beating, after which he had to mop up the blood with his underpants. Cyril Green claimed to have had a pot of boiling tea poured over him.

'You could honestly say that nine times out of ten they didn't know anything in the first place', says Bradbury. 'They really got tortured for fuck all.' But the troops did not revolt: 'you got orders, you do it. Otherwise you're liable to wind up on the torture box as well. You don't say no to Charlie.

'We could go and hit a bloke or put him on a torture box or break his toes with a pair of pliers or pull his teeth out, it didn't bother us. And there was no apparent reason for it', says Bradbury, who played a full part in the violence, often out of his head on purple hearts. 'The things we did, I can't believe it myself sometimes, it was unreal.'

One offender suffered a more basic punishment: 'I said to Charlie, "Have you got any pliers in your drawer?" He said "Yeah, what are you going to do?" I said "I'm going to break his fucking toes, he won't tell us what's going on." Charlie gave me the pliers and I got his toes and was bending them this way and that and just snapped them off. There was stuff in his drink so he didn't even feel the pain. So then I got annoyed and I took the knife and cut half his ear off.' The barely conscious victim was dumped near a hospital.

With hindsight, Bradbury is still puzzled at his own behaviour: 'it's different to putting a bloke on the torture box, it's just turning the handle, a big joke. But when you get a pair of pliers and break a bloke's toes and just sit there and don't feel a thing, that's when I knew I was going the other way.'

It was tiring work, remembers Bradbury: 'Charlie had a bar at the yard. Whether we had a policeman for a drink or whether someone was tortured, you can't sit there all night dying of thirst. We used to have a whisky or a brandy and a five minute smoke break and start again. It was like a factory on a tea break. You can't keep going on an empty stomach. We used to send round to the pie shop.

'A bloke could be lying on the floor like that time when we broke his toes and screaming and hollering and Charlie would just carry on with his fish and chips, talking to Frankie Fraser or me. After about fifteen minutes or so he'd say, "Right, carry on," and we'd get back to work again.'

There were also less ambitious but more traditional ways of keeping the money rolling in than big frauds. One involved a Heathrow parking fiddle which the Richardsons heard about. The attendants would adjust the time clocks that marked the parking tickets so that it would appear that the cars had been in the car park for less time than they really had. The extra money which was paid over for the tickets would be split between the members of the team who were involved in the racket and would amount to around £1000 a week. When the Richardsons became aware of the fiddle, they suggested that the team pay over £500 a week which, since they had little option, they agreed to do. This provided some handy readies while other businesses were being set up.

Brother Eddie's involvement with Atlantic Machines was proving much simpler. People were happy to have him and Frankie Fraser 'minding' their slot machines or, if not, were smart enough not to make a meal of it. Eddie was content to be making a comfortable living and enjoying a laddish life, playing for his Soho Rangers football team and mixing with show-business figures like the film star Stanley Baker.

The hardmen were cultivated by the up-and-coming gang leaders, who were as anxious to sign up star strikers as any post-war football manager. Fraser had been an obvious target and the young Kray twins had wooed him, taking his sister Eva to Dartmoor or Durham or wherever he was serving his sentence. But the Richardsons won his allegiance. It was a significant move and one that was to have

Soho Rangers football club: Frankie Fraser (far right, back row), Albert Dimes (second from right), actor Stanley Baker (far left) and Eddie Richardson (second left, front row).

echoes over the next thirty years. Fraser joining the Richardsons was, said one fellow-criminal, like China getting the atom bomb.

Fraser already had a reputation as one of the 'staunchest' of villains, a man who would never inform or buckle in gaol, and, despite being only five foot five inches, a package of controlled violence. His position in the underworld was regarded as the more remarkable because he did not come from a known criminal family: 'I'd come up from the ranks, literally fought my way up because I had no help from my family. My mother and father were dead straight so I had to make my own way. If you've got parents who have been to prison they can help you considerably with their contacts and guide you more sensibly.'

Charlie Richardson meanwhile had his eyes set on the money it seemed possible to make from mining in Africa, in particular the possibilities of exporting perlite from South Africa. It was the beginning of a remarkable phase of his life which was to lead to his involvement with the South African secret service, BOSS, and his glimpse of a fortune. In the mid-sixties he met Gordon Winter, a shadowy creature who combined work for South African intelligence with a job at the *Sunday Express*. Winter introduced Charlie to influential figures, not least of which was Winter's own wife, Jean La Grange, with whom Charlie fell in love.

It suited the South Africans to have a man in London who could burgle the offices of groups that were opposing apartheid. If the security services themselves were caught carrying out such burglaries their government would have been severely damaged; there was less of a risk if the job was done by professional criminals who could always claim they were just stealing equipment or money from an office. In Robert Parker's book on the Richardsons, *Rough Justice*, published in 1981, it is suggested that in March 1966 Charlie organized a break-in at the anti-apartheid movement's headquarters in Charlotte Street and the theft of files and papers that included names and addresses of members. The offices of the *Zimbabwe Review* and of Amnesty International were also burgled and it was only then that the possibility of politically motivated break-ins was taken seriously by the authorities.

Was Richardson also involved in political mischief in Britain? Robert Parker recalls interviewing Charlie in Benidorm. Richardson claimed that he knew of Downing Street shenanigans, of a former Labour minister involved in a sex scandal and a singer having an affair with a Labour politician's wife.

Meanwhile, in South Africa, the wheel was coming off the Richardson machine. There had been the murder of Thomas Waldeck, one of the brothers' associates, and the arrest of another, the violent John Bradbury, whose death sentence was later commuted to life imprisonment. In January 1966, after Bradbury's arrest, the *News of the World* wrote of 'Murder Incorporated' and how it was believed that a London-based organization of this name was behind the Waldbeck killing.

In London in the mid-sixties there had been violent scenes involving the cohorts of the Richardsons and the Krays. One of the Krays' men, Eric Mason, remembers, as well he might, one night in the Astor Club in Berkeley Square, a popular meeting-place for villains of the era; two gangs would occupy different parts of the club if they happened to be there at the same time. 'There was never any animosity. It was a kind of no-go area for villainy. At that time Jimmy Boyle [a Scottish hardman, later to turn prison reformer] was on the run and they were entertaining him at the bar.' There were some other Scots 'on the bevy' and one made a remark about Mason's friend's broken nose and asked him facetiously if he had got it falling off a bike: 'My friend knocked him out. All hell was let loose and so the Richardsons felt they had to make one against us for the discourtesy. So all of a sudden a few knives came out, axes and one thing and another.' Outside the club, Mason challenged the Richardson gang and said he would take on any two of them.

'I got in the car and somebody tried to stick a knife in me. We drove to Tottenham Court Road fighting all the way.' The Richardsons had a one-armed bandit workshop-cum-office there and Mason was bundled in and hit by Fraser with a chopper, so savagely that his hand was pinned to the top of his head. Fraser was then stabbed in the stomach and legs. A shotgun was held to his head. 'I woke up in hospital and I thought I was dead. I had 370 stitches and three fractures of the skull. After I'd been in a coma for a few days I woke up and I saw Ronnie Knight [the club-owner husband of actress Barbara Windsor]. I thought – this is me in heaven and the most unlikely angel was there at the end of the bed.' Revenge attacks were planned and the fire power required – 'enough to start a war' – was obtained, but Mason was arrested on a robbery charge before vengeance could be wreaked. The police approached him to give evidence against the Richardsons but he declined.

Then, in March 1966, there was a violent fight at Mr Smith's night club in Rushey Green, Catford, south London. Its full name was Mr Smith and the Witchdoctor and it provided food, drink, gaming and a dance floor. It was profitable but for the fact that some local heavies, led by the Haward brothers, Harry and Billy, were said to be extracting a tax from it in the form of free drinks all round for themselves and their associates. Eddie Richardson was asked to sort things out. On 7 March he went down to Mr Smith's with Frankie Fraser, Ronnie Jeffrey, Harry Rawlins, Jimmy Moody and Billy Stayton and found the other group, including Billy Haward, Billy Gardner, Peter Hennessey, Henry Botton and Richard 'Dickie' Hart, a south London thief known as 'the Catford Fart' by the Richardsons. By the end of the night Hart had been shot dead with a .45 automatic and two men, Eddie Richardson and Frankie Fraser, were badly injured.

One version of what happened is that when the Richardson-Fraser team was about to leave, the club manager asked if they would remove the other group. Eddie Richardson made the request, the Haward gang demurred and Richardson then challenged one of them, Peter Hennessey, who had called him a ponce, to a fight on the dance floor. Richardson forced him to the floor and asked him if he had had enough. Then, according to Fraser, 'Dickie' Hart pulled out a revolver and started firing. One man, Harry Rawlins, was hit in the shoulder. As Fraser described it: 'I said to Hart, "Let's get him out to an ambulance," and we got outside and the next thing you knew there was more gunfire and Hart was lying injured and I was shot in the leg.' Fraser's thighbone was broken by the shot. Hart was fatally wounded. Ronnie Jeffrey was shot in the groin. Billy Haward received serious head wounds. There was blood everywhere.

One of the men who helped the wounded to hospital was Jimmy 'Big Jim' Moody, an enormous man described by a friend as being like 'one filing cabinet piled on top of another' and with geisha girl tattoos on his arm. Years later he was to come to greater prominence, first when he escaped from Brixton prison with IRA man Gerard Tuite and later when he was shot dead in an East End pub.

George Barker, one of the officers who arrived on the scene, remembers finding Fraser: 'I stepped over a wall of a garden and there was a grunting noise. It was Frankie Fraser. I had accidentally trodden on his leg.' He stuffed a handkerchief into the gaping wound. Barker describes the mayhem: 'It was like a battle scene. There was a body lying in the gutter and we found a pistol and a big glass bar with a great lump of matted hair on it.' They covered these items of evidence with a dustbin lid and followed a trail of blood to where the wounded Fraser lay. 'Of course, all the combatants had left the scene. We weren't confronted with anyone other than Fraser and the dead body.' He was detailed to guard Fraser in hospital and recalls that his charge was entertained by the first portable colour television he had ever seen.

Billy Gardner, one of the Haward team, has his own memories of the incident. For a start, he says, they were not seeking money from Mr Smith's, which was regarded merely as a watering-hole: 'One day we heard that the Richardson mob were going to put some of their men in Mr Smith's. As Bill Haward and I were down at the Ark one evening, we got a phone call saying that they were there and they were going to smack Bill's bum. If they smack his bum, they've got to smack mine and all.' There were, he recalled, about fourteen or fifteen in the Richardson gang and Haward's team was outnumbered two or three to one, although Gardner says that there were only two 'danger men' (of whom Fraser was one) amongst the Richardsons.

'We sent out for some shooters and felt a bit safer. The atmosphere changed. It was all nice and cool and then all of a sudden the tension started to rise.' He recalls Eddie Richardson telling the Hawards to drink up and saying that they were no longer welcome, at which point Peter Hennessey invited Richardson on to the dance floor – but not to tango. Coats came off and a fist fight started but after five minutes 'all hell broke loose. Two or three geezers gave Bill a clump with a bayonet across the nut. Bill went to the gun in his waistband, got it caught in his braces, but let a couple go and all of a sudden it was off. I thought Bill was dead, the blood was pumping out.' Haward requested, 'If I die, just dump me somewhere and say a prayer for me.' He survived. Gardner helped Haward to a doctor who, although 'drunk as a sack' stitched the head wound up impressively and gave him some pills. The team then hid out in the area around the Elephant and Castle while the police search for the combatants continued.

Fraser was charged with Hart's killing on the basis of a statement from one of the Haward team, Henry Botton. He was acquitted of murder but convicted at the Old Bailey of affray in June 1966. The trial itself was the focus of allegations of attempted jury nobbling. One of the jurors had a bottle thrown through his window with a note attached suggesting that the jury, 'Bring them in guilty or else. A lot more where this came from. You're not alone amongst the twelve.' The apparent intention was to turn the jury the other way or implicate the police. Billy Haward was convicted of affray and gaoled for eight years, Henry Botton for five.

The Haward team disbanded after the battle. Hennessey was later murdered at a boxing match. Botton was shot at his front door – 'over a swindle he was doing with someone and they had the hump and when he opened the door – bosh – they gave it to him double-barrelled,' as one colleague recalls.

Two days after the Mr Smith's club shooting, George Cornell was shot dead in the Blind Beggar. The two events and the places where they happened were to become key signposts in the geography of gangland. The recognized reason for Cornell being killed is that he had insulted Ronnie Kray, calling him a 'fat poof'. Some contemporaries believe that taking him out might have been seen by the Krays as a stepping-stone into the Richardsons' territory. Some of the Richardsons believed that Ronnie Kray was taking advantage of the Richardson clan's disarray in South Africa and Mr Smith's.

The violence could have escalated into all-out gang warfare: shortly after the killing Roy Hall, a good friend of Cornell's and a member of the Richardson team, went round to the Krays' home in Vallance Road and shot the windows out. Violet Kray opened the window and told Hall that her boys were asleep and he should come round at a civilized hour. He departed.

But the police were now on the Richardsons' trail. Gerald McArthur, the Chief Constable of Hertfordshire, who was to be a leading figure in the investigation, says he was horrified by what he discovered. He had embarked on the inquiry after Taggart had approached him 'frightened for his life ... he was a man petrified, virtually shivering'. Taggart made a statement in which he said that he had had a dispute over money with another man, but was sorting it out when he was given a severe beating which had lasted five hours. The doctor who had seen him said that there was not an area of his body that was not damaged and that you could not put a 'penny piece' on any area of flesh that was not bruised. His head had swollen to twice its normal size. McArthur approached John Bliss, then the national co-ordinator of the Regional Crime Squads, and suggested that he contact other people who had fallen foul of the Richardsons. He says that another victim, Benny Coulson, 'really believed that in the end he was likely to die. They wrapped him in a sheet and were talking about taking him to the Thames at Vauxhall and dumping him in the river.' Coulson was told to say he had fallen from a moving car. He was given police protection but this was called off after he said it was an embarrassment in his area of Brixton. But the net was tightening around the Richardsons.

At 5 a.m. on the July morning that England was due to play West Germany in the 1966 World Cup Final, a team of sixty officers was briefed by McArthur. Seven hours later, eleven men were under arrest at West End Central police station. 'Charlie was in bed sound asleep,' said McArthur later. 'But he would insist on shaving before he came away. All the time I could see he was thinking to himself – how am I going to get away from this. I'm sure he still had somewhere in his mind that somehow or other he would beat it.'

The trial began on 4 April 1967, with twenty-six counts, some fraud charges having been dropped, against nine people: both Richardsons, Frank Fraser, Roy Hall, Tommy Clark, Jean Goodman, Alfred Berman, Jimmy Moody and Johnny Longman. A strange twist was that Charlie Richardson and Fraser thought they had come across the trial judge, Sir Frederick Lawton, two or three years earlier on Victoria station, when Fraser had 'recognized' him as the son of Governor Lawton of Wandsworth prison, under whom he had spent part of his unhappy sentence. Fraser had tried to have a pop at the 'judge' but had been dissuaded by Richardson. Sir Frederick said he had no recollection of the incident.

Prosecuting counsel Sebag Shaw opened the case thus: 'The

eight men in the dock are part of a gang of thugs under the leadership of Charles Richardson whose policy and practice over a number of years was to enforce his will and his intentions by violence and intimidation.

'This case is not about dishonesty and fraud, it is about violence and threats of violence, not, let me say at once, casual acts of violence committed in sudden anger or alarm but vicious and brutal violence systematically inflicted deliberately and cold-bloodedly and with utter and callous ruthlessness.'

As the trial unfolded in front of a fascinated and packed public gallery, the two versions of what had hapened diverged widely: Taggart claimed to have had a sustained beating and torturing. 'Somebody swore blind I pulled his teeth out,' says Fraser. 'In fairness, he gave me a good due as a dentist. Said it was absolutely painless, it was so fast.' The defence suggested that Taggart drove off afterwards and that the notorious Black Box never existed.

The judge, who had childhood memories of his father's prison occupation, believed the Richardson strategy was to have the case stopped in mid-trial because their chances of ensuring that it never started again were great. 'I thought I was seeing through this ploy and I refused every application,' he said later. The Richardsons were 'two dangerous villains'. Charlie, he believed, was a clever man and a very good businessman; he described Eddie as his brother's 'henchman'. Frank Fraser was 'an unbalanced character. He was just a hoodlum.'

Charlie Richardson was convicted and gaoled for twenty-five years. It was the highest ever sentence for grievous bodily harm and a double-barrelled shot across the bows of aspiring gangsters, according to the judge: 'I think the signal did go out to the criminal classes that this kind of activity was very dangerous indeed. The description of it as the torture trial was justified. Some very unpleasant things were done to the victims. They were given electric shocks. They were beaten. [The Richardsons] were conceited and of the opinion that they had such a stranglehold over street-traders and others in south London that no one would ever give evidence against them.'

His sentencing speech was a classic of the genre: 'One is ashamed to live in a society with men like you. There is no known penal system to cure you. You must be kept under lock and key. You terrorize those who cross your path and you terrorized them in a way which was vicious, sadistic and a disgrace to society. The only thing that will cure you is the passing of the years. It must be made clear to all those who set themselves up as gang leaders that they will be struck down by the law as you will be struck down.'

The police were commended publicly for their work on behalf of 'every law-abiding citizen in England'. McArthur approved the heavy sentence: 'It was a long period of torture for which there is no real section in the Acts of Parliament. They were getting bigger and bigger and more determined. In the end they could have developed very much as the Mafia developed except that the Mafia probably developed for better motives than Charles Richardson in that they were looking after their friends in Sicily who had been ill-treated by the government and were very poor.'

Richardson recalled: 'I wanted to say to everyone I could really sympathize with their need for a bit of colour and excitement. I could understand that they wanted a gangster mythology without relying on American imports. But not me, please, go to the Krays, they liked being gangsters.' He believed conviction was inevitable: 'After all the publicity and lies it would have been like having Caligula, Genghis Khan, Hitler and Stalin all in one box and taking the lid off to let them scuttle away.'

Richardson did not emerge permanently until 1984, after serving eighteen years, to be met by a Rolls-Royce and '100 lobster thermidors and a thousand bottles of champagne'. He wrote his autobiography, *My Manor*, went into the City, which he claimed was more dishonest than anything he had previously been involved in, and resumed his interest in Africa.

Fraser was gaoled for ten years, as were Eddie Richardson and Roy Hall. Fraser was to feature later in the 1969 Parkhurst riots which added another five years to his time inside. He was the ringleader and had checked whether other prisoners were agreeable to a riot, which had been long threatened but never put into effect. He received summary punishment from the prison officers, 'a thorough beating' as he put it, and needed sixty stitches in his head.

'Mad' Frankie was the bad boy of the prison system till the end. When he was moved from prison to prison he aggravated the officers by pretending, when the van stopped at traffic lights, that any nearby car containing young men was part of an escape plot, mouthing 'Not now! Not now!' to the bemused carload as though the escape was almost under way. He had spent around forty years in gaol by the time he reached his seventieth birthday in 1993. He had also been certified insane three times and been in Broadmoor and Cane Hill secure hospitals. 'I was brought up in the thirties era – James Cagney,

Humphrey Bogart, Edward G. Robinson – and prison seemed quite comfy in the films, they could all talk to each other through the bars.'

With the Richardsons gone and the Krays to follow them some two years later, what was left of the gangs of the era?

Few of the other 'families' were known beyond the prison grapevine or their local areas. But the Nashes, the Dixons, and the Tibbs were all at various stages given, rightly or wrongly, the title of London's major gangsters. The Nashes, an Islington family of brothers – Billy, Johnny, Jimmy, Ronnie, George and Roy, of course – had come to prominence over the Pen Club killing in 1960. In 1961 they were described by the now defunct *Sunday Pictorial* in a 'We Accuse' series as the 'wickedest brothers in England', in the wake of Jimmy's conviction in connection with the Pen Club fight.

Jimmy was said to be the quietest of the brothers, a teetotal, non-smoking boxer. At the time of his trial, his brother Johnny had eleven convictions, including ones for grievous bodily harm and carrying a gun; he was described as the 'Peacemaker' in that he was reputed to sort out gangland's warring factions. He was the 'chief hoodlum ... a whole menagerie of apes owe him their loyalty.' Roy had done time for manslaughter.

The Nash brothers holding wreaths to commemorate Ronald Marwood's death.

Billy was supposedly the brains of the family and wrote a piece for the *Pictorial*'s series in which he blamed the Street Offences Act of 1959 for 'moving the birds off the streets and into the clubs' and thus causing problems which had not previously existed in clubland. 'Me and my brothers would quit the rackets if we could,' he told readers. 'We have the toughest reputation in London. That means there are fools all over London who would like to take us and make their names.' The article was accompanied by a photograph of Billy holding a wreath in memory of Ronald Marwood, who had been hanged for killing a policeman and who had been hidden by the Nashes before giving himself up.

The Nashes' main interests were in clubs across London, including the Bagatelle and the Embassy in the West End. They did not court publicity in the way of the Krays, nor attract police attention like the Richardsons, and they never impinged on the public consciousness much beyond their brief flurry in the Sunday newspapers.

Even after the Nashes, the Krays and the Richardsons had slipped from prominence, one particular police officer was certain that there were organized gangs waiting to be busted. Says Bert 'Gangbuster' Wickstead: 'The first thing I did as a targeting was to look at the whole of the London scene to see who was creating mayhem where, why and what for. The first two targets were the Dixons [George and Alan], for the simple reason that they were marching around the East End boasting they had taken the place of the Krays: "You will now pay us protection, you will do this, you will do that." The Tibbs were the second because they were creating all sorts of mayhem in the East End, vans being blown up, they had to be looked after.'

George Dixon, who with one of his brothers, Alan, constituted the backbone of the Dixon gang, worked initially with the Krays. As a young boxer, he had been recruited by them after having a tussle with some of their henchmen in an East End drinking club. Dixon later told the *Sun* about their recruitment in the Regal Billiard Hall: 'The man I'd called "Eyebrows" beckoned me over. He growled: "I know you – you're one flash bastard." I said, "Yeah, I know." At that Ronnie Kray broke into a huge grin and laughed. Then he shook my hand. That was my welcome to the Krays.'

The Dixon brothers claimed to have taken over the Poplar and Limehouse areas and became used to what George Dixon referred to as 'the flash of yellow' – guns were kept wrapped in yellow dusters at that time. They took part in the Krays' Monday evening strategy meetings, with business being conducted in a different place every time as a security measure against other gangs and the police. They had their own equivalent of Leslie 'the Brain' Payne – Philip 'Little Caesar' Jacobs, who had been at school with the Krays and who ran three successful pubs. Jacobs liked to drive through the East End in a Rolls-Royce with a 'PJ' number plate and his Playboy-bunny girlfriend by his side.

George Dixon would carry out Ronnie Kray's orders: 'He'd look at me and then move his eyes to the person he wanted sorted.' The Krays repaid the favours. When George Dixon faced attempted murder and grievous bodily harm charges over a massive fight in a Stepney pub called Kate Hodders, the Krays saw to it that the case never came to trial.

But George claims that Ronnie tried to kill him on one occasion in 1966 in the Regency club, shoving a semi-automatic into his mouth and pulling the trigger before Reggie intervened. Luckily, the bullet jammed. George reported back to his brothers in Poplar and they suggested an all-out gang war against the Krays. Wiser counsels prevailed on both sides and Charlie Kray was sent as an emissary to say that Ronnie had felt that the young Dixons were becoming too arrogant. A meeting was arranged at which Ronnie handed George Dixon the bullet as a souvenir.

In July 1972 Jacobs and Alan and George Dixon were all gaoled after standing trial for a series of assaults, extortion and conspiracies. Prosecuting counsel Michael Corkery told the jury that the gang had promised, 'We have taken over where the Krays left off.' The sentences of twelve years for Jacobs and twelve and nine for George and Alan nipped whatever pretensions they might have had in the bud. Alan, who had worked as a singer in Jacobs' pubs, shouted from the dock 'Wickstead's reign is now going to be at an end' and told the policeman he deserved an Oscar for his performance. The mother of Leon Carlton, a club owner and one of the gang's members, shouted from the gallery: 'My poor baby. My son is as innocent as a new-born baby.'

As for the Tibbs, although there had certainly been violent clashes involving the family, few of their associates regarded them as running a 'gang' as such. Rather, they were seen as heavies who had become involved in an increasingly bitter feud. In 1968 Albert Nicholls had attacked George 'Bogey' Tibbs in The Steamship pub and in retribution Nicholls was attacked with a shotgun outside his minicab office. Johnny and Jimmy Tibbs were gaoled for two years for unlawful wounding. In November 1970 Robert Tibbs had his throat cut outside the Rose of Denmark pub but survived.

The most fearsome incident came when publican Leonard Kersey was said to have called the Tibbs 'dirty pikey (gypsy) bastards'. His wife, Diane, described what happened shortly afterwards: 'I saw the men hacking at somebody on the ground. Then I saw it was my husband. His face was falling apart.' The Tibbs had been victims themselves of attacks: Jimmy Tibbs' van and their café near their Canning Town scrapyard had been bombed in April 1971.

The last of the major 'gang' trials came in January 1973 when father James Tibbs, known as 'Old Man Tibbs', and three sons – John, Robert and the boxer Jimmy, a one-time middleweight British championship contender – were convicted with two other men, Michael Machin and Stanley Naylor, of a variety of offences including conspiracy to pervert the course of justice, possession of 600 rounds of ammunition, conspiracy to blackmail, wounding, attempted murder and assault on a police officer. Despite much evidence of the family's good works and the local people who appeared in the witness-box to affirm that the 'Tibbses are diamonds', they were gaoled for a total of fifty-eight years.

Prosecuting counsel Michael Corkery described the case as 'a sickening story of hatred, violence and severe personal injury on those they disagreed with and on whom they sought to impose their rule.' Charles Whitby QC, John Tibbs' counsel, told the court in mitigation that there was a tradition of great family solidarity among the people in east London: 'It is something the East End might teach the rest of the country about. But if it goes wrong and leads to vengeance and violence, then it goes badly wrong.'

A few hundred miles north, there were people who thought that they could probably teach the Londoners a thing or two about violence and vengeance.

6

GANGLAND

The Glasgow Teams

Jimmie Boyle,
former hardman
turned sculptor
and writer.

While London may have been the capital of the underworld, other cities in Britain had their own powerful and feared gangs. In Sheffield, in the twenties, two hardmen called George Mooney and Sam Garvin each led a battalion of young heavies who carried out minor acts of terrorism, robbed public houses, ran gambling clubs and generally behaved as they pleased. Mooney, of Irish extraction, was a pioneer of racetrack racketeering in the north and could teach his London counterparts a trick or two. Indeed, he had links for a while with the Sabinis while Garvin, a self-confident soul, dealt with the Brummagen Boys. Garvin, particularly, presented himself as the archetypal gang-leader: smartly dressed and glad-handing, organizing a high-profile collection for widows after a local mining disaster in classic 'charitable works' style. Meanwhile 'junior' gangs, led by younger tearaways armed with stool-legs, coshes and razors, were starting to impose themselves.

It was the Sky Edge tossing ring in Wadsley, a suburb of Sheffield, where games of illegal pitch-and-toss were fought over, that was the focus of the criminality, according to J. P. Bean's history of the Sheffield gangs. When Garvin led a splinter group away from Mooney in 1923, the chief constable of the time, Lieutenant-Colonel John Hall-Dalwood, expressed his concerns that the courts were not dealing harshly enough with such hoodlums.

Percy Sillitoe, later Sir Percy, arrived in Sheffield as Chief Constable of the East Riding in 1926. He was a larger than life character, born in 1888, educated at St Paul's School in London and sent out to South Africa as a young man to join first the British South African Police and then the Northern Rhodesian Police. His time in Africa was suitably exotic – hunting elephants, being nearly killed by a wounded lion near the Victoria Falls and being cured of rheumatic fever for £5 by a witchdoctor. His return to England as Chief Constable of Chesterfield must have seemed tame indeed. But he soon found the challenge he sought in Sheffield.

Sillitoe decided to tackle the problem of the Mooney and Garvin gangs head-on by drafting undercover officers into pubs that the gangs regularly robbed or abused by demanding free liquor and behaving riotously. 'I sent for both Sam Garvin and George Mooney and gave them a stern warning: "If any of my officers are put in the dock for hammering you, I shall be in the dock with them".' He was as good as his word. He made a point of attending any trials of the gang members and making a special plea for an exemplary sentence. The magistrates were now happy to oblige. 'If you stand up to [the gangs] and they realize you mean business they will soon knuckle under,' he told his officers.

Both Mooney and Garvin were eventually gaoled and Sillitoe sought them out after they had served their sentences. He describes his armistice meeting with Mooney thus: 'He stood and looked at my proffered hand for a long moment without saying a word. As I was about to withdraw it, he burst suddenly into tears, grasped it and said: "You are the first gentleman I ever had the privilege of shaking hands with, sir."' Mooney thereafter 'knuckled under' but Garvin was less amenable and Sillitoe claims he had to be harassed off the streets of Sheffield.

Sillitoe's version of events, however, should be taken with a twist of salt. J. P. Bean describes Sir Percy as an unashamed publicity seeker, who inflated his own role in tackling gangland. Some of the heroic incidents Sir Percy recounted were, says Bean, 'pure invention'.

Nevertheless, with the Glasgow gangs gaining a fearsome national reputation for breath-taking acts of violence and mayhem it is not surprising that it was soon a question of send-for-Sillitoe. He led the police there from 1931 until 1943. For an Englishman to head Scotland's largest and busiest force was seen as something of a national snub and it was made clear to Sillitoe on his arrival that the defensive senior officers felt they had little to learn from him. He disagreed, and there was a purge not dissimilar to the one that Sir Robert Mark was to bring to the Metropolitan Police some forty years later as Sillitoe attempted to attack the city's legendary heavies.

The Glasgow gangs achieved their public prominence in the twenties and thirties, partly because of the remarkable fictional best-seller, *No Mean City*, the Old Testament of Glasgow's gangland. But organized gangs had been operating there since the 1880s when the Penny Mob, so-called because they levied that sum on their members to pay for inevitable court fines, were active. Protection rackets were run at local racecourses probably well before they became established in the south of England.

The gangs were led first by 'chairmen' and then 'kings' and the prestige attached to the gang leader was enormous. The *People's Journal* of 1916 listed the Beehive Boys, the Bell On Boys, the Death Valley Boys, the Ging Gong and the Kelley Boys and warned readers of the 'hooligan menace' in their midst. The *Glasgow Herald* in the same era reported on the gang that shouted 'We are the Redskins' as they went into battle and the *Glasgow Evening Citizen* later listed the known gangs of the time as the Billy Boys, the Redskins, the Cowboys, the Beehives and the Calton Entry Mob. There was even the Baltic Fleet from Baltic Street.

There were other exotic names: the Hi-Hi in the north of the city, and the Ping Pong, the San Toy, the Village Boys and the Tim Malloys. Many demanded money from people as they left dance halls and theatres and, like their contemporaries in Sheffield, expected to drink free in the pubs. *No Mean City* paints a vivid picture of the time. Much of it was culled from actual incidents and put the fighting in a social context. The book's authors, Glasgow grocer A. McArthur and writer H. Kingsley Long, observed that 'battles and sex are the only free diversions in slum life'. Young men who wanted prestige in the slums of Britain's most overcrowded and insanitary city could achieve it with their fists in the ring, their feet on the dance floor or football pitch, or with a combination of feet and fists and razors on the streets of their neighbourhoods.

The arguments for and against the life are put by the main character, Johnnie Stark, the Razor King, and his hard-working, respectable younger brother Peter. 'Leave me my weapons and I'll finish far ahead of you,' says the gang leader. His brother retorts: 'A bliddy fine job being razor king – while it lasts. Wi' free holidays in Barlinnie an' aw! Christ! A great job for a gangster!' The Razor King, who would 'whirl his weapons like a drum major', was even given a set of razors as a wedding present. He eventually dies in battle.

Sillitoe believed that while many of the gangs were essentially young bucks flexing their muscles, many of them were run by professional criminals and 'older scoundrels' who were happy to employ the muscle for their own ends. Indeed, the 'fly men', the full-time villains, realized that the street kings, with their total fearlessness and the awesome reputations they carried along with their black-handled blades, had a valuable part to play in robberies. No one would dare inform on them or tackle them.

But the gangs themselves were not money-spinning operations as they were in London. They might bully their way to free drinks and the like but essentially the wars between them were about territory and pride rather than pound notes and commercial control. This did not stop fierce and bloody battles from taking place with hundreds on each side, yelled on by their 'queens' and their supporters.

Evidence of the violent scale of the battles can be gleaned from an *Evening Times* report in 1931 on a gang fight in Kerr Street, where the weapons left behind afterwards included 'the spear of a swordfish and a wicked-looking Gurkha knife ... a piece of copper tubing ... a

113

brass-headed poker ... a cudgel two feet long with a knob of wood as thick as the head of a drumstick ... a wooden baton ... an axe weighing a pound and half ... a steel file two feet long and a bayonet-like knife ... an iron rod three feet long with a hook at each end.'

By 1935 the *Sunday Express* was confirming that 'the gangsters have come to Britain. Glasgow, second city of the Empire, frankly acknowledges their reign of terror. A thousand young men – not forty are more than thirty-five – rule the poorer class districts. Their insignia of office are the broken bottle, the razor blade, the "cosh", the knife, and – newest and most effective of all – the bayonet.' There were comparisons then to Chicago – which Sillitoe visited in 1933 to compare notes with J. Edgar Hoover – and dark references to murders committed during gang fights. In truth, they seem to have been small in number, not more than one or two a year. Much more common were the savage and disfiguring woundings that the razors caused; the redeeming feature of this weapon of choice was that it did not cut as deeply or as dangerously as a knife which later Glasgow gangs were to favour. Razor slashings gave birth to the phrase the 'Glasgow smile' – a head butt was a 'Glasgow kiss' – and to music hall jokes like: 'Going past a hospital on your way home, pal? Get them to stitch – this!'

There were other criminal sidelines in the Glasgow underworld: good dancers could be legally hired by the dance halls but the practice of 'booking out', whereby a wealthy client would hire dancers of either sex for 'private tuition' was, in fact, genteel prostitution. The dancers had little choice: if they refused a booking, they would be sacked by the dance hall and lose the few pounds that kept alive their hope of a better life, away from the slums of a city which produced twenty-five of the country's forty most crowded districts.

There were smart gang leaders such as Peter Williamson, who was from a respectable family and had a reasonable education. He led the Beehives, one of the largest and most ferocious of the gangs, with a heavy named Harry McMenemy as his number two. The leader of the Parlour Boys, James 'Razzle' Dalzell, who was killed in 1924 at his own headquarters, was so self-consciously 'hard' that at gang festivities he would only dance with burly members of his gang because he considered it effeminate to dance with women. Bill Fullerton, leader of the Billy Boys of the era, described a wedding of a gang member: 'The bridegroom stood before the minister with a sword concealed in his morning dress. The best man had a gun in his pocket. I'll never forget the scene as they left the church. The gang waiting outside threw bottles instead of confetti.' Fullerton organized a famous drum-

and-flute-band march which led both Roman Catholics and Prot-
estants into a bloody battle from which one man escaped by hiding
in his bass drum.

Before the First World War the Redskins included some women
in their number, most famously Aggie Reid who earned the tribute
from Detective Inspector Douglas Grant that 'Aggie was a handful'.
Four officers were needed to arrest her. Some of the gang leaders took
particular pride in their smart appearance saying 'Watch the material,
Mac' to enraged constables who collared them. In general, the gangs
were not heavily motivated by religious animosity, but in the thirties
the Norman Conks, who were Roman Catholic, fought the Billy Boys,
who were Protestant, and the Rangers–Celtic football games of the
time became a focus for concentrated violence in which gang members
would participate. Grant noted: 'Neds have one characteristic in
common: a tendency to engage in senseless argument which not
infrequently ends in violence.'

Sillitoe realized that it was going to take more than a proffered
handshake to get the Clydeside 'Neds' to blub their gratitude and
pack in the game. His officers adopted a fairly brisk approach to
dealing with these hoodlums and were known as 'Sillitoe's Cossacks'
for their periodic heavy-handedness. After the war Sillitoe went on to
become head of MI5 in the Attlee administration.

The judiciary fought a losing battle against the violence which
continued regardless. In 1935 Lord Aitchison gaoled one gang fighter,
John McNamee, for fifteen years for culpable homicide 'in a dramatic
challenge to ruffianism in Glasgow', as the local press described it.
But it is fair to say that some of the most organized and pervasive
crime of the era was perpetuated by corrupt city councillors and
contractors, who became, during Sillitoe's time, the subject of a
police investigation that led to the arrest of many of the 'high heid
yins' who were so outspoken in their attacks on the more muscular
criminals.

The Second World War drew on the raw aggression of many
of the hardmen, recruiting them to Scottish regiments for whom they
became 'ladies from hell' on the battlefields of France and Italy and
North Africa. The most remarkable of all the criminals recruited to
fight in the war was Johnny Ramensky. Of Lithuanian extraction, he
had been born in Glenboig outside Glasgow in 1905 and had followed
his father into the mines in Lanarkshire. But thieving took him to
Polmont Borstal, near Falkirk, and he graduated to safe-cracking,
becoming one of the most expert in the field. Unbalanced perhaps by

the death of his young bride, Daisy, in 1934, he escaped from Peterhead prison and thereafter indulged, as his advocate Nicholas Fairbairn QC, was later to put it, 'a lifelong compulsion to break into whatever he was out of and out of whatever he was inside.'

So skilful with the gelignite was Ramensky that he was dropped behind enemy lines with the commandoes, a similar if more active role to that played by Eddie Chapman, his safe-breaking contemporary in England. His part was to break into German safes in captured headquarters, including Goering's, and release the papers and maps. When the Allies marched on Rome he was taken along to blow open the safes in foreign embassies. He cracked fourteen in a day. Having won the Military Medal for his endeavours, he returned to Scotland a hero but was unable to stop breaking into safes – Polar Ammon gelignite was his favourite explosive. His methods became more and more Desperate Dan and less and less steel-nerved pro. On one occasion he overdid the gelignite to such an extent that two patrolling policemen, unaware of his activities at that point, were literally blown off their feet.

At first, judges were lenient because he always pleaded guilty, never attacked his arresting officer except in self-defence, and had a fine war record, but the well of sympathy on the bench gradually dried up and the sentences became heavier. Ramensky never lost the affection of the general public and both the actor Roddy McMillan and the late Labour MP Norman Buchan wrote songs dedicated to him. But he was never able to re-organize his life as had Eddie Chapman. Released from gaol in 1964, he promptly broke into Woolworths in Paisley. He was caught for the last time, a white-haired soul of sixty-six, on the roof of a large store in Ayr. He died in gaol and was buried with gangland's equivalent of full military honours in St Francis Chapel in the Gorbals. The hardmen who survived the war returned home and the level of violent crime rose. In 1948 there were 253 robberies with violence in Glasgow and the increase in the attacks led to the formation of Glasgow's own Flying Squad in 1952.

By the sixties, the gangs were back in prominence. Some of the old names lingered on, but others sprouted like the pop groups of the era and enjoyed a comparable life expectancy. James Patrick, the pseudonymous author of *A Glasgow Gang Observed*, listed the names of hundreds. Patrick was a first-year teacher at an approved school who spent weekends in 1966–67 with one of his charges in order to observe the way gangs operated. While he acknowledged that he was

SMS 287H

Safe-cracker and gaol-breaker
Johnny Ramensky. Inset: In
uniform during the war in
which he won the
Military Medal.

merely getting a snapshot of their lives and had to avoid becoming involved in the violence himself, he was able to observe a tightly knit world with the sort of organization, structure and sense of loyalty that would have impressed Baden-Powell. By the time that Patrick published his exposé in 1973, two of the gang had been murdered and the book and its author's allegations and anonymity infuriated the city elders.

Amongst the best-known gangs of the late sixties were the Gorbals Cumbic and the Calton Tongs (who had supposedly taken their name originally from the *Terror of the Tongs* film), various Fleets, the Possilpark Uncle (after the television programme *The Man from UNCLE*). They now called themselves 'teams' not gangs, and had ever more exotic names, such as CODY (Come On Die Young or, possibly, Cowards Only Die Young). Some, like the YY Mods or the Young Young Mods, reflected their time. Patrick records that the gang to which he was co-opted dressed in the mod uniform of white cardigans, red polo necks, white trousers, red socks, and sandals. They rode on scooters with the 'infantry' in the rear. Some teams had girl members – the Drumchapel Bucks and the Lady Bucks are an example.

There were similar gangs in other major cities and towns; the Jacobites in Edinburgh favoured knives rather than the razors of their grandfathers and would celebrate to the tune of 'Bless Them All': 'Stab them aw, Stab them aw, The busies, the judges and aw.'

The Tongs were reckoned to be the biggest team in Glasgow with a rank structured along strict age lines: the YY Tongs or the Young Young Tongs were under eighteen, the Tiny Tongs were from ten to thirteen and there were even Toddler Tongs and Wee Tiny Tongs who could run errands or carry out thefts of cigarettes and clothes. Their tender years made them exempt from prosecution. One of Glasgow's best-known criminal solicitors, Joe Beltrami, recounts one trial where the junior sections of two gangs were represented: the Tiny Bison and the Woodhill Young Team. The Cumbies also had an under-age category. After a sheriff had described the activities of the teams as 'mental', the term was worn as a badge of honour by many gangs such as, in Edinburgh, Young Mental Drylaw.

Court reports of the early seventies contain many a 'stern warning from judge to gangs' and much 'gang law feared'. Lord Cameron was prompted to give one of the sternest of warnings at the end of the trial of members of the Barrowfield Spur on 5 June 1978: 'The streets of Glasgow are not going to be turned into a ring for ill-conditioned gladiators and their followers.'

A major underworld figure, although it was his later activities rather than his actions as a criminal that were to win him public attention, was Jimmy Boyle. Born in 1944, he was the son of a Glasgow hardman: one of his earliest childhood memories was waking to see a man entirely swathed in bandages with blood seeping through, either his father or one of his friends who had been the victim of a gang fight. Jimmy was in the Wild Young Cumbies, which was reckoned a heavier team than Big Cumbie, and in the Skulls, and was both a thief and a respected fighter. His weapons were a bayonet wrapped in a copy of the *Glasgow Herald* and a Walther automatic pistol.

As Boyle himself described the Gorbals gang life in his auto-biography, *A Sense of Freedom*, the dominant teams at the time were the two Cumbie gangs, the Beehive, the Stud, the Clatty Dozen and the Dixy. His work with knuckledusters gained him a teenage reputation that he did nothing to disavow. When he slashed another young gangster with a butcher's knife 'within days I was a force to be reckoned with and some kids were saying I was "mad as a brush". There was a sort of hero-worship about all of this ... I was intent on making a name for myself and the only way this could be achieved was by violence. There seemed to be plenty of rewards for the gamest guy and I was intending to be him.' Much of the gang warfare was still about face and territory rather than profit and protection, and bravado played a large part in it.

To escape pressure from the police, Boyle moved briefly to London, hanging around King's Cross and dropping purple hearts, but in 1963 was returned to face charges in Glasgow after he had assaulted a policeman for which he got six weeks in Wormwood Scrubs. He joined 'the Tallymen' who collected money for the loan-sharking operation led by Frank 'Tarzan' Wilson. The rate was five shillings (25p) in the pound. If the money was not repaid in a week, another 5s was added. Sir David McNee, later to become the Commissioner of the Metropolitan Police, was in the Glasgow Flying Squad at the time and took the unusual step of going round Gorbals pubs and addressing the drinkers on this pernicious system. In one pub he stood on a table and said he knew that people who were involved were present and called on others to inform on them: 'They listened in stony silence.' There were some results, however. A Glasgow solicitor was amongst those convicted of loan-sharking and the *Daily Express* reported 'McNee Hammers the Underworld', giving birth to the 'Hammer' nickname that was to follow him to London.

Boyle claims that non-payers were rarely beaten up and that the 'heavies' gradually took over the running of the businesses from the original moneylenders. He suggests that loan-sharking was the first hint of organized crime in Scotland. The main fights, he says, were with criminals who had borrowed money and refused to pay it back. He also worked as a bouncer – his ferocious reputation was an advantage here – and ran shebeens, basic affairs with one room in which drink was sold and another full of mattresses and prostitutes.

Boyle was arrested on a murder charge at the age of twenty but the charge was withdrawn and he did not stand trial. However, as he noted later, the fact that people thought he had done it did no harm to his reputation and so he did not discourage the idea. Ten days later he was attacked by two men and took out the eye of one of his assailants with a broken bottle. 'I felt much better after this, as though I had somehow "proved" myself.' Following another fight in a house in Govan, during which a near-scalping took place, he faced a fresh murder charge but again it was dropped. Again, despite the acquittal, he did not discourage the hint of his involvement which 'added to the myth which continued to grow around [the Tallymen]. Because we all came from different districts and within these districts each of us had reputations, there had never been this sort of gathering by guys in the criminal element in Glasgow before.'

He had met the Krays through Big Pat Connolly, who had acted as emissary for the twins' trip north, and noted the different approaches of the London and Glasgow gangs of the sixties: 'the majority [in London] lived very tough lives but concentrated on cash, whereas we in Scotland were more inclined to weigh things up from the physical side. The English guys realize this, of course, and recognize that Scotland produces good heavies and that is why they have so many in their firms.'

In 1967, when he was on the run after the death of 'Babs' Rooney, he headed for London again. Rooney had died in his Kinning Park home after a visit from Boyle and another man. There had been a heated argument which had ended with Boyle slashing Rooney's bare chest. Rooney was later found dead, although Boyle always claimed that he could not have killed him. In London Boyle was hidden by the Krays. But the police tracked him down and caught him in an East End pub called the British Lion after a car belonging to one of his associates had been spotted outside. Boyle had noticed how the pub had gradually filled up with what appeared to be workers from a local factory, all dressed in their overalls, and was puzzled when the barman unbolted a side door to reveal a large furniture van backing towards it. At a given signal the pub was swamped with police, many of them armed, and Boyle was returned to Scotland to stand trial. He was gaoled for life with a recommendation that he serve a minimum of fifteen years.

In prison, Boyle became a changed man after being involved in riots and receiving beatings so brutal that he would cover himself in his own excrement to avoid further attacks from the officers. Transferred to the Special Unit in Barlinnie, he came under the administration of one of the most enlightened penal projects in the country which sought to tackle the hardest of the criminals and confront them with their pasts and make them face their futures. Boyle responded by becoming a successful sculptor and writer.

His rehabilitation was not greeted with universal acclaim because a number of the Scottish tabloid newspapers were sceptical about his transformation and scathing about his new life when released in 1982, feeling that he had done insufficient penance for his violent past. Boyle opened a centre for drug addicts in Edinburgh and became a powerful spokesman on penal affairs. The television film of his life, *The Hard Man*, was a critical success. Sir David McNee, who had known Boyle in his younger Glasgow days, observed: 'I am told that he has put his violent past behind him; I certainly hope so and I wish him well.'

Lawyer Joe Beltrami reckoned that heavy duty characters like Boyle were peculiar to Glasgow: 'The "hard man" might well in earlier times have been regarded as a "bonny fechter" and admired – nowadays he is regarded as a hoodlum with a reputation for explosive reactions ... and a high pain threshold.'

But there was to be an outbreak of violence the consequences of which were horrific. In the early hours of 16 April 1984 petrol was thrown on a door in Bankend Street in Glasgow and a match lit. Six of the nine members of the Doyle family, the youngest only eighteen months old, died as a result of the ensuing fire. It was the bloodiest indication yet that the Glasgow Ice Cream Wars had finally spiralled out of control.

The notion of ice cream families fighting it out amongst themselves for pitches seemed faintly comical – film director Bill Forsyth used the wars as the basis for his film *Comfort and Joy* – but the reality was less jokey.

In *Frightener*, their book on the wars, Douglas Skelton and Lisa Brownlie write that they go back as far as 1978 when police took notice of the feuding over pitches in the Barlanark area. Police took the warring sides to Baillieston police station where a sort of truce was agreed. But by 1982 the Marchetti brothers were complaining that their drivers in Carntyne were being threatened. One woman who complained was Sadie Campbell, whose brother Tom was a Glasgow heavy in a gang called the Gauchos. When she stopped giving credit her van was attacked. Tom Campbell located one of the threateners who set two dogs on him. He stabbed one of the dogs through the heart and attacked the man. Shortly afterwards his sister's grocery van was blown up.

Campbell went into the ice cream trade in 1983 just after his thirtieth birthday and in 1984 he was arrested for the murder of the Doyle family. A policeman told him: 'You have spent your life creating the reputation of being a violent monster. Now that monster is going to turn around and bite you.'

In October that year Tom Campbell was sentenced to life imprisonment with the recommendation that he serve a minimum of twenty years. Co-defendant Joseph Steele was also convicted and gaoled for life. But the evidence against both men was disputed, Steele arguing that he would never say something as compromising as, 'It wisnae me that lit the match.' On home leave in April 1993 Steele absconded to London and superglued himself to the gates of Buckingham Palace to protest his innocence. He was taken back to gaol but escaped again and only gave himself up, on a pylon outside Barlinnie, after once again protesting his and Campbell's innocence.

After the exotically named gangs drifted from view in the eighties and the high-profile hardmen were locked away, it did not take long for a different type of 'team' to emerge with a new leader of its own.

Arthur Thompson had been born in Glasgow in the thirties and picked up his first offence for an assault when still in his teens. From then on his curriculum vitae reads like an application for a place in the British criminals' hall of fame: gaoled for extortion in 1953; gaoled for bank robbery in 1955; Glasgow ambassador for the Kray twins in the mid-sixties; mother-in-law killed in a car bomb meant for him in 1966; cleared of the murder of Arthur Welsh and James Goldie in 1966; wife Rita gaoled for three years for stabbing Mrs Welsh; manager of a gambling club; major protection racketeer; gaoled for a £3000 warehouse burglary in 1968; son Arthur gaoled for drug-dealing charges in 1985; shot in an attempted murder in 1988 (although Thompson and his family claimed at the time that he had been injured by a flying part from a drill); run over in 1990 and suffered broken leg.

In 1991 Arthur 'Fat Boy' Thompson junior, his son and heir, was murdered while on a 'training for freedom' weekend leave from Noranside prison in Forfar where he was serving his eleven-year drug sentence. He was gunned down outside his home at just after 11 p.m. with three .22 bullets, crying out 'I've been shot, hen' to his sister Tracey as she ran from the house.

But it was the double murder in 1992 which followed the Thompson killing that was to shock Glasgow. Joe 'Bananas' Hanlon, aged twenty-three, and Bobby Glover, aged thirty-one, both members of the Barlanark team, were killed in a car in Darleith Street, Shettleston, near the Cottage Bar, shot in the back of the neck and up the anus. Just thirty-six hours before his death Glover had written to the *Sun* claiming that he had nothing to do with the murder of Arthur Thompson junior. The two dead men were regarded as foot-soldiers in the Barlanark team and had already been warned by the police that they were in danger. At the time of their death, Detective Chief Superintendent John Fleming of the CID specialist services said: 'I had told them a year ago, "Unless you get out of this scene then the next time I see you will be in a mortuary."' They told him to 'get on his bike'. For a Glasgow which believed it should now be known as a European city of culture it was a blow. Its reputation for hardness, once worn like a lion rampant tattoo on the forearm, now seemed an embarrassment.

A young man called Paul Ferris was charged with Arthur junior's murder. He had been aware early on that he might be a suspect and had his lawyer take the unusual step of sending a fax to Glasgow's *Daily Record* making it clear that his client had 'no connection whatsoever with the murder of Arthur Thompson.' Arthur senior, whom Ferris had also been accused of attempting to kill, gave evidence at a long and lively trial and treated the jury to some colourful language. Questioned about one man whom he blamed for fitting up his son on heroin charges, he said that if he was a 'dog with AIDS' he would not want to know him. Asked if he was well known in Glasgow, he replied: 'I have more cousins than Hitler had an army – everybody claims to know me.'

One of the chief witnesses against Ferris was a supergrass from the north of England called Dennis Wilkinson or Woodman. He had been in Barlinnie prison with Ferris and claimed in evidence that, while there, he had heard him confess to the killing of 'Fat Boy' or

the 'Mars Bar Kid'. Wilkinson had helped to gaol twenty men for a total of ninety years and gave evidence for five days. The jury were clearly unimpressed and Ferris was cleared. There were some dark Glasgow jokes about his future such as: 'What's the difference between Elvis Presley and Paul Ferris? Paul Ferris is *definitely* dead.'

Arthur senior died of a heart attack in 1993 at the age of sixty-two and notice of the passing away of a 'treasured grandfather' was published in the *Glasgow Herald*. Even in the grave he did not escape action. There was a bomb scare at his funeral in Riddrie Park Cemetery on the edge of Glasgow.

Stories about Arthur were legion. His headquarters, two council houses knocked together, was known as Ponderosa, although some called it Southfork after the Dallas soap opera. His advocate, now Sir Nicholas Fairbairn, said he was 'the coolest godfather Glasgow had ever seen ... smooth, silken, slow and deadly' and expressed fears that, with his death, Glasgow would turn into a 'criminal Bosnia'. A smart man, witty and courteous, at the end of his days Arthur objected to his image to such an extent that he successfully sued *Scotland on Sunday* for remarks made about his criminal involvement and celebrated the four-figure settlement from the paper with Havana cigars all round: 'Why does nobody believe that I've retired?'

Grandfather and 'godfather' Arthur Thompson senior.

7

THE ROBBERS

From the Great Train Robbery to the Shoot-outs

Great Train Robber Roy James.

Sitting in a convoy of Land Rovers as they sped through the early hours of a Buckinghamshire dawn, one of the robbers fiddled with the radio to try and find the police wavelength. Over the airwaves came the voice of crooner Tony Bennett. He was singing a song called 'The Good Life'.

And for those next few magical days, during which the robbers could not sleep, it must have seemed that the good life had indeed arrived for them all. They had just stolen £2 500 000 from the Royal Mail night train on its way from Glasgow to Euston in London, and, in doing so, had carried out Britain's largest-ever robbery and written a chapter in British criminal history.

This was, of course, the Great Train Robbery, the high-water mark for British robbers and one that has endured in the memory even though robberies of more than ten times the value have been carried out since. It occupies a peculiar place in the British psyche, partly because of the daring of its conception and partly because of the strange paths since taken by some of its perpetrators: gaol, escape, flight, kidnap, drugs, murder, revenge.

It was always an ambitious job although one of the robbers, Tommy Wisbey, says now that it was only nine months from conception to execution, during which a team that could both handle the physical side of the heist and keep its collective mouth shut until it had taken place was assembled. The plan was, in many ways, quite simple. Fix a false signal so that the train stopped, disconnect the van with the money from the rest of the train, steal the mailbags by threatening the mail-workers, hide out in a nearby farmhouse until the initial hue and cry had died down and then quietly launder the stolen money.

The crew eventually assembled was a gallery of south and east London criminality: Buster Edwards, a thief, club-owner, former boxer and small-time fraudster; Gordon Goody, a massive man with a reputation as a robber and with 'Hello Ireland' and 'Dear Mother' tattooed on his biceps; Bruce Reynolds, the 'intellectual' of the group, officially an antique dealer, who enjoyed spending the proceeds of his crimes at the Ritz and the Savoy, driving an Aston Martin and holidaying in the south of France; Charlie Wilson, a bookie and well-known 'face'; Jimmy White, an ex-paratrooper who had worked with Reynolds; Bob Welch and Tommy Wisbey, who had an inside man on the railways with whose help they were carrying out some modest robberies on the Brighton line; Roger Cordrey, a train expert; Jimmy Hussey, a big man who had convictions for everything from pick-

127

pocketing and theft to attacking the police; two drivers – Roy James, who was involved in crime because he could not find the sponsorship that would enable him to move up a grade to Formula One motor racing, and Micky Ball; Ronnie Biggs, a carpenter by trade and small-time villain until the robbery, a friend of Reynolds and, more crucially, of a retired train-driver who was co-opted to drive the train the brief distance necessary; Bill Boal, a minor player who worked in aircraft components and whose job was to get rid of the money; Leonard Field, a florist whose brother was a heavy criminal; John Wheater, the public-school-educated solicitor whose function was to purchase the farm; and Brian Field, no relation to Leonard, a solicitor's clerk from Oxfordshire, whose job it was to help Wheater. And the ones who have never been caught.

Some of the team, like Wisbey, already had experience of train robbing. One of their stunts was to use a man made up to look like an invalid and seated in a wheelchair, who would be kept in the guard's van with his attendant. When the train stopped at a pre-determined spot, the guard would be attacked by the 'invalid' and his companion who would then make their escape down the line and into a waiting car. Another ploy was for Wisbey and his associates to travel as passengers and one of their number to pretend to have an epileptic fit. The van would be raided while the guard assisted. But the sums had been comparatively small.

Once the amalgamated team had decided to carry out the robbery, they looked for a place near enough to London for them to slip back into their normal haunts and yet not too close to any built-up area where people would notice what they were up to. Bridego Bridge near Linslade and Cheddington and between Leighton Buzzard and Tring was all they had hoped for: secluded, handy and with the added advantage of an army base nearby which would allow them to move heavy vans at odd times without necessarily arousing suspicion. Originally, the plan was to carry out the raid in June but it was thought there would be more money on the train in August because of the holiday fortnight.

Planning was meticulous. The team equipped themselves with blue overalls so that railwaymen would assume that they were working on the line if they were spotted before the robbery. Roy James, who had agreed to find out about uncoupling the engine from the train, posed as a schoolteacher who wanted to teach his pupils about trains and was able to discover some of the basics of the engine's mechanics.

And so at 3.03 a.m. on 8 August 1963 the false red signal was activated. 'It's coming down, chaps,' said Bruce Reynolds. 'This is the real thing.'

As the train stopped at Sears Crossing the fireman, David Whitby, went to the telephone at the side of the track to find out the reason for the delay. He saw Buster Edwards and asked him what was happening. Edwards grabbed him and hustled him down the bank to where two of the others were able to hold him. Whitby agreed not to resist with the remark, 'All right, mate, I'm on your side.'

The driver, Jack Mills, appeared at his cab and realized what was up. After a brief struggle he was coshed and collapsed bleeding. Who actually hit him has always been a subject of debate, the more so as it was this one act of violence that marred the operation in the eyes of many and certainly led to some of the years in the heavy sentences that were to follow. In Piers Paul Read's *The Train Robbers*, published fifteen years after the event and written with the sometimes mischievous co-operation of the robbers, it is stated that as 'Gordon (Goody) pinned [Jack Mills'] arms to his body, Buster (Edwards) hit Mills twice over the head with the cosh.' But Edwards denies this version. He says that the publishers would only do the book, for which all sides were rewarded, if the robbers would agree to say who had struck the blow. Edwards duly volunteered himself but says that the assailant was one of the men who was never caught. This is the view expounded, too, by Biggs who in 1993 was quoted in the *Sunday Express* as saying that the wielder of the cosh was a 'heavy villain' who was never caught. Tommy Wisbey says he does not know who struck the blow: 'In the mêlée it could have been anyone.' Truth was, after Jack Mills, a major casualty in the affair.

The robbers tried to get their ex-driver conspirator to move the train but he was unable to set it in motion because he could not 'get the vacuum'. The bleeding Mills was told to take over the controls, and shunted the train to its predetermined position for the robbery to proceed. Four of the gang burst into the coach where the post-office sorters were going through the mail. There was no resistance and the process of unloading the bags began. The robbers formed a chain down the embankment and whipped the sacks from hand to hand on to the lorry, taking 120 and leaving half a dozen behind.

Wisbey says that he and Wilson patched Mills up: 'He said "I think you're real gentlemen." We sat him on the grass verge and asked did he want a cigarette and, "Do you want any money, we'll leave it on the grass verge for you." ' Mills declined the offer. Then, leaving Mills and Whitby handcuffed together with the instruction 'Don't move for half an hour', the robbers set off in a convoy of Land Rovers and a lorry back to Leatherslade Farm.

Over the police radio came the response of the Buckinghamshire police: 'You won't believe this,' said one officer over the airwaves to his colleagues, 'but they've stolen a train.'

But the robbers were tuned to Tony Bennett. 'We were all singing "The Good Life",' says Wisbey. 'We got the prize. It was a feeling of elation. I think it would have been harder taking sweets off a baby.'

Back at the farm they started counting their haul and found they had around £1 200 000 in £5 notes and £1 300 000 in £1 and 10s notes. The money was divided up into shares of around £90 000 each. The plan was for the farm to be cleaned and all fingerprints and tell-tale signs to be removed. But the police were hovering already. The casual warning to Mills and Whitby that they were not to move 'for half an hour' had indicated to the police that their quarry was within a limited circumference and by 13 August they found the vehicles and the mailbags at the farm. Now, because of some simple errors at odds with the professionalism of the rest of the plot, the game was almost up.

Originally described in the press as the Cheddington Train Robbery, the heist soon took on the name that was to exemplify daring crime and the resulting media coverage made arrests imperative for the police. Flying Squad chief Tommy Butler was appointed to lead the inquiry from London after some toing and froing between police from the local and the capital's forces. He was a veteran of investigations into Jack Spot and Billy Hill and his full-time hobby – at fifty, he still lived with his mother – was catching crooks. Assisted by a remarkable number of casual clues left at the farm and in the vehicles, he was gradually trawling through known criminals currently on the job and arrests began.

Most of the gang were aware as soon as the enormity of the robbery became clear they were liable to be picked up for routine questioning on a 'round up the usual suspects' basis. They had been counting on the lack of any incriminating evidence either at the scene or at the farm and on the general reliability of the team in the pre-supergrass era. But their careful plans were gradually coming unstitched. Damning fingerprints had already been discovered: Roy James had fed the cats at the farm and his prints were found on their bowl. Hussey's gloves had shrunk in the heat and his exposed palm had left its print on the tail of the lorry. Edwards' prints were on the money-wrappers and those of Wisbey, Wilson, Daly and Welch were also traced. Goody's mother was raided, prompting him to write a whimsical letter to the police expressing his disappointment that he should be regarded as a suspect – 'more than I can stand'. For this reason, he told them, he would absent himself until the true villains were apprehended.

Wisbey had set off on holiday after treating his daughter Marilyn to an *Emergency Ward Ten* nurse's outfit. His mood was not helped by two friends with him who, completely unaware of what he had just done, insisted on telling hoteliers that they were, ho ho, the Great Train Robbers, about whom the papers were then full.

The round-up of the gang was speedy and largely successful. Within five weeks, five members of the gang had been arrested and another five had been identified and were wanted by the police. Thirteen men eventually stood trial on a total of ten charges, the main one, which all faced, being conspiracy to rob the train. Some of the robbers eluded the sweep, either initially or through subsequent escapes, but for the others, as they were driven to court, there was little light at the end of the tunnel.

Roger Cordrey, who had been found with £80 000 of the stolen money (which he returned), pleaded guilty. The trial of the others, in front of Mr Justice Edmund Davies, began on 20 January 1964 in the Aylesbury District Council Chamber which had been turned into a court-room for the purpose. It had the advantage of being close to the scene of the crime and investigation but, more importantly for the police, it made the chances of jury nobbling more remote than if it had been heard at the Old Bailey. None the less, according to some accounts, attempts were made to extract money from the robbers' wives by people who claimed they could fix the jurors.

The robbers made bold attempts to defend themselves. Wisbey, for instance, explained a palm-print found in the bathroom as being a result of him slipping there when he had been delivering a load of fruit to the farm. The trial received acres of coverage and the press benches were packed. 'All the people one knew were there,' observed journalist Peta Fordham, who wrote a book on the case, *The Robber's Tale* and who was married to Wilfrid Fordham, one of the defence barristers. Her descriptions of the main protagonists reflected some of the ambiguity about the crime felt by press and public alike: 'White is the most ordinary and engaging little man in the world ... Charlie Wilson, the sort of father you see by the hundred in France on Sunday

Scene of the Great Train Robbery. Insets, from left to right: Tommy Butler, who led the investigation, Buster Edwards, Charlie Wilson and Bruce Reynolds.

outings ... Goody, nerves of steel and the wolfish handsomeness of the pack leader ... Edwards, one of the keenest brains in the under-world.' She was to write that, 'the events were so vividly in the minds of the actors that they remember, like Henry V's men at Agincourt, with advantages what feats they did that day.' Piers Paul Read was to say in his version of events that 'politically one might describe the train robbers as Saxons still fighting the Normans'.

Mr Justice Edmund Davies took a slightly less breathless view of the defendants. Cordrey was the first to be sentenced and, having pleaded guilty and returned so much money, he might have expected a certain leniency. The judge told him that he was guilty of 'a crime which in its impudence and enormity is the first of its kind in this country. I propose to do all in my power to ensure that it is the last of its kind; for your outrageous conduct constitutes an intolerable menace to the well-being of society. Let us clear out of the way any romantic notions of daredevilry. This is nothing less than a sordid crime of violence inspired by vast greed. As to violence, anybody who has seen that nerve-shattered engine-driver can have no doubt of the terrifying effect on law-abiding citizens of a concerted assault by masked and armed robbers in lonely darkness. To deal with this case leniently would be a positively evil thing.'

While Cordrey must have realized by this stage that he was unlikely to be receiving just a stiff fine and probation, he must still have been shocked at the sentence that the judge announced: twenty years. Although the others had joked through their trials – Goody had drawn cartoons – they now appreciated the fate that awaited those of them who had played larger parts and pleaded not guilty. Their fears were justified. Bill Boal received a twenty-four-year sentence and the Fields twenty-five years each. The mother of Lennie Field shouted out her protest from the public gallery and Field, who was then aged thirty-one, shouted back: 'Don't worry, Mother. I'm still young.' The major players lined up to hear that they were to be gaoled for thirty years. Wilson did manage a final dark joke, kidding the others that he had received a single figure sentence.

The sentences stunned the men. 'We were thinking in terms of ten to eighteen,' says Wisbey, who eventually served twelve and a half. 'I thought the judge was off his head. It was like he was at a bingo hall – three oh – thirty.' One of the policemen cheerfully told him he would be in a wheelchair when he came out.

The robbers were distributed around maximum security gaols. Some measure of how seriously their prowess was taken can be gleaned from the fact that one northern chief constable speculated about the possibility that atomic weapons might be used to effect their escape and also raised the possibility of tanks coming through the streets of Durham to free them. The Chief Constable of Leicester, Robert Mark, was even summonsed to see the Home Secretary, Sir Frank Soskice, who suggested that the prevention of the escape of the robbers was a matter for the army rather than the police. Mark dissuaded him and was given a dozen new automatic rifles for his force.

But the authorities still had to follow the recipe for successful punishment: first catch your robber. Still on the run, Reynolds and Edwards waited until the Court of Appeal turned down their colleagues' pleas in the summer of 1964 before deciding to leave England. Mexico was the chosen destination and the escape route was via the south of France with the aid of false passports. Reynolds made it there first with his wife and booked Edwards and his wife into the Hilton Hotel. Reynolds, the most cosmopolitan of the robbers, was at ease in their retreat but it was not exactly Edwards' glass of Corona and his family missed home (as later portrayed in the film *Buster* in which Edwards was played by singer Phil Collins).

White, who had also fled, was recaptured and received an eighteen-year sentence, a stiff penalty but a large reduction from the trial sentences. Edwards decided to give himself up, having learned that Detective Superintendent Frank Williams would treat him fairly if he did so. Although Tommy Butler of the Flying Squad thought at first that the surrender must be a joke, Buster Edwards was taken back into custody on 19 September 1966. At his subsequent trial he was gaoled for fifteen years.

Wilson, whose reticence during the trial had earned him the title of the 'silent man', had meanwhile escaped from Winson Green prison in Birmingham and made it, complete with beard and bogus passport, by ferry to Calais and eventually to Montreal. Here he was joined eventually by his family and by Reynolds, who had found out that he could not make a living in Mexico. Reynolds was restless and moved on to the south of France. Wilson seemed to have blended successfully into Canadian life but on 25 January 1968 Tommy Butler and fifty Royal Canadian Mounted Police officers arrived at his door as he was about to take his daughter to school. He was soon on a plane back to England and a cell in Parkhurst.

Reynolds quit France and moved first to London and then to Torquay where on 8 November 1968, Tommy Butler, who had stayed on at the Yard to track the remaining train robbers, arrived on his doorstep with the words: 'Hello, Bruce, it's been a long time.' To which Reynolds, ever the Cavalier, replied: '*C'est la vie.*'

And then there was one. Ronnie Biggs had escaped from Wandsworth prison in July 1965 through the ingenious use of a rope ladder and a pantechnicon lorry with a specially constructed turret that had been parked outside the gaol. Two getaway cars waited nearby. Biggs made it first to Paris, where a plastic surgeon changed his features, and then to Australia, to Adelaide and then Melbourne, where he led a suburban life as Terry Cook, the carpenter. But when an illustrated article about the train robbers appeared in Australia a previous acquaintance recognized him, told the police and his photograph was broadcast on television. Biggs decided he had to move on again and sailed for Brazil, which had no extradition treaty with Britain. There he remains to this day.

In 1974 he was nearly hoisted back to England after a *Daily Express* journalist, Colin Mackenzie, had met up with him in Rio de Janeiro. The *Express* had tipped off the police about the meeting and Chief Superintendent Jack Slipper appeared at the hotel where the interview was due to take place with the standard 'It's been a long time' greeting. But Biggs did not come quietly. His Brazilian girlfriend, Raimunda, was pregnant and, as the father of a Brazilian child, Biggs was immune from deportation. In 1981 a ham-fisted attempt was made by three seedy English ex-soldiers to kidnap him and bring him back to England via Barbados. This also failed.

Bob Welch emerged in June 1976 as the last of those gaoled at Aylesbury to be released. Hussey and Wisbey were to be gaoled for cocaine dealing in 1989.

Jack Slipper is sanguine on the robbery: 'I have to respect them for some aspects of it and I admit it was bold and daring but they were no Robin Hoods and I've always been convinced that it was only by chance that there wasn't more violence.'

What happened to all the money has never been completely explained. Certainly, the robbers on the run found themselves having to pay out vast sums for false passports and escape routes. Those inside saw their 'investments' being frittered away by former friends who assured them that the businesses in which the money had been placed had failed. Later the robbers would emerge to find that some of the money-minders had acquired fine houses or even hotels.

The main lesson to be learned from their capture was that too many crooks – at least fifteen here – left too many clues. The underworld had known of the job for too long and the likely suspects

The Biggs game hunter: Jack Slipper.

were too easy to round up. Young up-and-coming robbers learned that there was safety in lack of numbers and, accordingly, the most successful teams of the sixties and early seventies were four-handed or five-handed and did not share too widely the knowledge of jobs which were planned.

The massive sentences handed out to the train robbers did little to deter the armed robber – some members of the underworld felt that they might as well be armed since they could hardly face a stiffer penalty than thirty years – and by the early seventies he was in his Balaclava-ed pomp. Robberies were happening every few days and the police seemed unable to catch any of the figures who sped off from banks and security vans in stolen cars.

Bank robbers were the new criminal aristocracy, 'the faces', admired by the young villains, fancied by the prettiest of the girls who enjoyed the clubs and the clothes and the racing weekends at Longchamps. They saw the Krays as old-fashioned and mocked them with the nicknames 'Gert and Daisy', chumps who had been caught because they stuck their necks out, dinosaurs who liked Matt Monroe while the new boys played The Doors and T Rex on their newly discovered car tape-decks as they slung their 'happy-bags' stuffed with sawn-off shotgun, masks and gloves into the back seat. They also realized that provincial robberies were easier to carry out because of laxer security arrangements and the distance from the knowing eyes of the London detective.

They were mainly from the London area and a large number were from around Hornsey Rise, 'Hungry Hill' as the young hoodlums liked to call it, and the patch that spanned Holloway and Finsbury Park, the Angel and Hoxton. They fancied themselves. A bunch of them were photographed posing moodily, by Don McCullin, one of their schoolmates who had gone straight, for an *Observer* colour supplement feature entitled 'Little Chicago'.

Eric Mason, who worked in the sixties and early seventies and served a total of seventeen years for robberies, initially met up with other robbers in the two main robbery centres of higher education: Dartmoor and Parkhurst. As a former safe-cracker, he realized early on that bank robbery was the coming thing: 'Peters weren't worth it. People weren't keeping money in them any more. You found it easier to pull up at a bank, one minute later you would walk out with everything that was on show.' Monday morning was a good time, when banks held large sums neatly packaged behind their counters waiting for the security to take them to the feeder banks.

'You'd walk in on a Monday morning, jump over the bank counter, two or three of you, hold the staff at bay with a shotgun, let one go in the air ... and take the bag that was waiting for Securicor plus all the night-safe bags plus the money in the tills. You were guaranteed twenty or thirty grand in every bank. It took you one minute.' Mason's timing was accurate and the press duly christened the team 'The Minute Men'.

The shotgun was used partly for show, according to Mason. 'We'd take the shot out of the shells and replace them with ordinary household rice. It would make a noise and the only stuff that would come out would be rice.' While this might have made matters safer all round, it had an unfortunate side-effect for Mason. When he was arrested in Cardiff, detectives realized that the same *modus operandi* had been used by robbers in Nottingham and London – four bank robberies had left enough rice to start a curry house chain splattered over tills and counters.

Mason reckoned that there was an almost psychological barrier against robbing banks and post offices: 'In the old days you had this thing, you don't do it because it's establishment. In the sixties, people began to realize that anything was fair game in the days of Profumo, people realized that politicians, people we looked up to, were fragile and people lost respect. People began to realize this was a big con. The barriers started coming down.'

The normal method for Mason and his colleagues was to smash the glass of the inside doors of the bank: 'That would be the first effect and we'd fire a shot into the roof. There'd be no opposition. The one thing you never did was lay a hand on anybody. I did once and it stuck with me for many years. We went into a place and a woman was standing by the wall absolutely petrified and I tried to reassure her by putting my hand on her and saying, "Just sit down, don't worry, luv, nothing will happen to you." The mere fact of me touching her absolutely broke her completely. She went into hysterics. I learned from that that you never touch anybody. You just cajole them into sitting on the floor and don't worry about things.'

Some robbers used ammonia sprays, after which security guards wore glass shields over their faces; the robbers merely switched tactics and carried black spray-paint cans to spray over the visors. But the really heavy-duty villains were discouraged.

The speciality of the Crash-Bang Gang, operating from 1969 to 1972, was to park about a hundred yards away so that their getaway car could not be blocked. The normal procedure then was for one or two quick changes of the stolen vehicles before a 'meet' to share out the spoils.

One reason for the high success rate of the robberies was that sophisticated alarm systems connected to police stations and video cameras, which would become regular features by the nineties, did not yet exist. There were few time-worked safes, it was still easy to recycle money through the system via bookies or casinos, and bullet-proof grilles had still to become standard.

Robbers were clearly not much affected by the recommended normal sentence of fifteen years for bank robbery laid down by the Court of Appeal in 1965, and the increasingly heavy sentences that followed. These double-figure sentences were very much a post-war phenomenon. Sir Frederick Lawton recalled: 'My father (former governor of Wandsworth prison) told me in his early days in the prison service that anybody who got a sentence of more than five years was looked on with pity, as it was regarded as a very cruel sentence indeed. In my early days at the Bar, the standard sentence for robbery with violence in the streets was twelve months imprisonment and twelve strokes of the Cat.' (Eric Mason, the recipient of such a beating in the presence of Governor Lawton: 'He was as bad as any prisoner I ever met. He took great pleasure in watching me be flogged.') Sir Frederick, who had gaoled Charlie Richardson for twenty-five years, also expressed the concerns of some members of the judiciary that the long sentences for armed robbery might lead robbers to kill a potential eyewitness as the difference between the sentences for murder and robbery was slight.

The issue was brought into grim focus on 12 August 1966 when three police officers in an unmarked police 'Q' car were shot dead after checking on a suspicious-looking vehicle with three men in it at Shepherd's Bush. One of the men, John Witney, was swiftly traced and after his alibi had crumbled named the other two as John Duddy and Harry Roberts, who was known as a robber of post offices. Duddy was caught in Glasgow but Roberts, a former soldier with decorations for service in dangerous terrain in the Far East, bought himself camping equipment and hid out in thick woodland in Hertfordshire. Home Secretary Roy Jenkins described the killings as 'a threat to the whole fabric of society'. An enormous manhunt was launched and Harry Roberts' face was everywhere, provoking a macabre football terraces taunt: 'Harry Roberts, he's our man, He shoots policemen, Bang Bang Bang.' Roberts was eventually caught on 11 November after a gypsy, who had been wrongly accused of stealing, pointed out smoke coming from a campfire in the forest near Bishop's Stortford.

All three men were gaoled for life. Duddy died in gaol. Witney, who had not fired the fatal shots and who said that Roberts' policy was 'leave no witnesses', was freed in 1992. Roberts remained in Dartmoor and told the *Guardian* in 1993: 'We shot them because they were going to nick us and we didn't want to go to gaol for fifteen years. We were professional criminals. We don't react the same way as ordinary people. The police aren't like real people to us. They're strangers, they're the enemy. And you don't feel remorse for killing a stranger. I do feel sorry for what we did to their families. I do. But it's like people I killed in Malaya when I was in the army. You don't feel remorse.'

Perhaps the paradigm of the robbery era was the Wembley bank job. This was planned at a meeting in the Thatched Barn Hotel in Boreham Wood, north of London, at which one of London's most active robbers, Bertie Smalls, selected the wines. It took place on 10 August 1972 and £138 000 was stolen. Six raiders blasted shots into the ceiling and then ran from the bank in single file carrying bags of money and looking so ponderous that one witness described it as 'like something out of a *Carry On* film'. The raid had been timed to coincide with the arrival of Security Express at the bank and a spokesman said, almost admiringly, that it was 'spot on'. The robbers were gone within 90 seconds.

Another typical job was the Ralli Brothers robbery in Hatton Garden in London on 26 March 1969. An inside man, Clem Eden, let in the robbers, led by Bertie Smalls, at 6.30 a.m. They then hid in the ladies' lavatory until the rest of the staff arrived, tying them all up, including their inside man. By threats, they overcame the two-key system whereby one staff member had one key and the combination number and the other had one key but no number. They met to share the spoils at the home of 'Vodka Johnny' Richards in Finchley in north London.

Some jobs required larger teams. Here is how bank robber Bobby King described the robbery of Barclays Bank in Ilford in February 1970: 'There were nine of us. The planning was five to six weeks. I had to go in the bank dressed in a suit looking like a travelling salesman writing a moody cheque out, mingling.' They had been tipped off about the run from a local Tesco supermarket by a friend of a friend of a relative of a security van driver, and knew that a red Mini arriving at the bank in advance of the delivery was an indication that big money was around: the Mini was meant to check out whether there were suspicious characters in the vicinity. King's colleagues, some dressed as painters, held up the driver, who dropped the bags and ran. The robbers piled into a white transit van and fled, turning right, left, right, left until they reached their next fleet of stolen cars for the second stage of the getaway.

Insiders were often crucial to some of the more spectacular heists. Never more so than at 6 p.m. on the evening of 24 April 1975 when eight smartly suited men entered the Bank of America in Mayfair and departed three hours and around £8 million later. The key to their success was a feckless young petty criminal and electrician called Stuart Buckley who was, amazingly enough, employed by the bank despite the fact that he had only just emerged from prison for handling stolen goods. Buckley's job had won him the attention of some more experienced criminals who discussed his access to the vaults in meetings in the Crooked Billet pub in Wimbledon. He took Leonard Wilde, known as 'King of the Twirlers' because of his expertise with keys and locks, Johnny the Boche, so-called because of his slightly Germanic appearance, and other members of the gang, posing as fellow-electricians, on conducted tours of the premises under his employers' noses. The bank's computer room, in the same building, was in use sometimes 24 hours a day and gave an excuse for movement at odd hours.

After Buckley had turned up the in-house muzak to give some added sound cover Wilde was shown the complex twin dials that opened up the vaults. Buckley even removed the lock from a back door to the bank so that the gang could have a key made to fit it.

On 26 October 1974 the gang made their first attempt to break through. They had discovered that the alarm worked much like an old-fashioned record-player, coming down on a disc which was immediately relayed through to the nearest police station; by removing the needle they were able to de-activate the alarm. But the other aspects of the robbery were less simple. The drills first started to overheat – they had to be cooled with ice-cold Cokes from the building's soft-drinks dispenser – and then snapped. Billy Gear, the look-out man, spotted computer workers but his shouted warnings could not be heard above the drilling so he disconnected the power. The attempt was a failure and the gang had to abandon the pieces of broken drill as they departed.

Amazingly enough this attempt, with its clear hints of inside involvement, did not alert the bank to the role of Buckley, who was actually asked to assist in strengthening the electronic security. It was while working in a false ceiling above the vault that he 'accidentally' shoved his electric screwdriver through the ceiling and, to his surprise, saw the manager and chief cashier carrying out a routine opening of the twin-locked vault, each with knowledge of one lock's combination number. Buckley, perched above them, was able to witness each man dialling the four key numbers per lock. This was, if the word can be used for such a break-in, dynamite for the robbers. But to ensure that Buckley had correctly observed the numbers he was asked to go back and hide out again, this time with a pocket spy-glass. Concealed with two bottles, one of orange juice and the other for him to urinate in, he was able to check and record the vital numbers.

As he left the bank on the day of the robbery, he flashed his car-lights twice to let the team know the coast was clear. The game was on. Ninety-four of the 550 safe-deposit boxes were broken into and cash, jewels, rare books and works of art were scooped out and split between the gang above a greengrocer's shop in Lambeth. They might have escaped with more had not a member of the computer bureau staff, who was working upstairs, come down to use the office telephone to make a dial-a-disc call. He was tied up along with his colleagues and the robbers decided to make a speedy departure, taking Sir Winston Churchill's old Mauser pistol, which he had used as a subaltern in the 21st Lancers during the cavalry charge at Omdurman in the Sudan, but leaving behind an Enid Blyton first edition and a Picasso.

The police, led by Detective Superintendent Bob Robinson, had been watching Buckley since the earlier aborted attempt and he was arrested the next day. His share of the loot was found in a wood in Brenchley in Kent. Others in the team were already under suspicion: Billy Gear, who had taken his son to the dentist before the robbery, had used his wife's car because he was late and it had been ticketed nearby by a traffic warden; Jimmy O'Loughlin had been seen entering his house with a heavy suitcase. Buckley decided to give evidence for the prosecution which resulted in a smaller sentence, a third of what the other main players received.

At the end of an often bad-tempered ninety-one day trial, Wilde was gaoled for twenty-three years, Billy Gear for eighteen years, Peter Colson for twenty-one, Jimmy O'Loughlin for seventeen, Micky Gervaise (later to become a supergrass) for eighteen months, Henry Jeffery for twelve years and Henry Taylor for three. O'Loughlin had escaped briefly by pretending to be a solicitor's clerk during an appearance in a magistrate's court. Mr Justice King Hamilton, no friend of the criminal he, said that between £2.5 million and £8 million had been stolen but only £485 982 recovered and said he was giving them stiff sentences so that 'what has been salted away will remain salted away as far as you are concerned'. He described Colson as 'slippery as quicksilver' and said he was 'beneath contempt' for making allegations about police corruption.

This was one of the Robbery Squad's successes. It had been brought under one command with the Flying Squad and Number 9 Regional Crime Squad in 1973 and during that year there had been twenty-six bank robberies compared with sixty-five the previous year. By the following year the figure had dropped to seventeen. In 1974 150 people were arrested for robberies going back to 1965, for sums totalling around £3 million, and twenty-seven of them were gaoled for a total of 315 years. But this was partly because the robbers were shifting their tactics. The rise of the robbers seemed unaffected. There were 380 robberies in 1972 in London and no fewer than 1772 ten years later.

So what made a bank robber? The authors of *Cops and Robbers*, John Ball, Lewis Chester and Roy Perrott suggested that, 'There was a marked gap between the status they could achieve in straight society and what their aspirations encouraged them to feel they deserved.' And they noted, too, the 'sense of the casual' in the approach to crime, with the robbers scoffing at what the public imagined went on – the Mr Big, the detailed planning and so on – when much of it was quite casually planned and executed, done at speed to avoid leakage from the growing number of informers.

John McVicar, an armed robber who became famous mainly through a daring escape from Durham gaol in 1968, had his own theory: 'The professional criminal wants respect, prestige and the recognition of those who subscribe to his own need of machismo. The field in which he tries to achieve this is one in which profit, crime and gangsterism overlap.' His mother put it more bluntly when she described her son and his friends' apparent fascination with prison life: 'I think you must all like it in there, you're always talking about it when you come out.'

McVicar was a bright war-baby who had drifted into crime as a boy and picked up sentences for riotous assault, robbery with violence and possession of offensive weapons and had spent time in Wandsworth, the 'Hate Factory'. In 1966 he and a group of Parkhurst prisoners engineered a court case in Winchester so that they could escape from the coach on the way back. Nine, including Roy Nash, tried to escape, but only two, including McVicar, succeeded and he was at large for the summer. In 1967 he was gaoled for fifteen years for firing at a police car after an attempted robbery.

His escape in October 1968 from Durham, accomplished with the assistance of the man who was the unofficial chairman of the prison escapologists society, Wally Probyn, brought him to prominence partly because Durham was such a difficult prison to break out of and partly because he was described in the press, American-fashion, as 'public enemy number one'. He remained on the run for two years before being recaptured in November 1970 after an informant, encouraged by a £10 000 reward, had tipped off the police. His own assessment in his autobiography paints a less glamorous picture perhaps than the one given him when Roger Daltrey played him in the film *McVicar*: 'As a criminal I have been a lamentable failure. Whatever money I earned by crime, I could have earned as a labourer in half the time I have spent in prison ... Money has always been a secondary goal; crime has always been directed to more powerful objectives.'

But McVicar has since been able to turn his reputation and an education he acquired inside, including a degree in sociology, to his advantage. He emerged to take a post-graduate degree at Leicester University and became something of a media pundit on

John McVicar.

crime, fashioning a successful career as a freelance journalist for the likes of *Esquire*, the *New Statesman* and the *Guardian*, clubbing at Groucho's and playing tennis to keep in trim.

For his part, Probyn was caught during the Durham escape but emerged to write *Angel Face*. He had had this nickname since his youth, which had been spent almost entirely in custody for petty offences. He had also escaped from Dartmoor and numerous young offenders' institutions and almost made it out of Parkhurst on the Isle of Wight with Harry Roberts, whom he reckoned did not really want to make the final jump: 'He was pitting his wits against the screws to find ways but it was only in theory; he didn't want to do it in practice.' Probyn went on to careers in the antique business and as a photographer. He settled in Hoxton with his rare fish collection and became a father in his fifties. He was portrayed by Adam Faith in the McVicar film but never really felt at home in the limelight and has never followed the gold-chain 'diamond geezer' school of ex-villains.

To a certain extent Probyn took on the mantle of another 'great escaper': the late Alfie Hinds, a safe-breaker and burglar whose spectacular escapes in the fifties captured the public imagination. A member of Mensa, Hinds protested his innocence of the 1953 break-in at Maples department store in Tottenham Court Road for which he was gaoled for twelve years. He used his escapes to publicize his claims of innocence and his time inside to become a barrack-room lawyer. He successfully sued Herbert Sparks, who had arrested him, when the detective wrote about his great cases and named Hinds. A libel jury awarded Hinds £1300.

One robber who came to prominence in the seventies was George Davis, who had been convicted of robbing the London Electricity Board offices in Ilford in March 1975. An enormous campaign, spearheaded by his wife Rose and friends and with the oft-graffitied slogan 'George Davis is Innocent OK' was launched to prove his innocence. Its most public activity was digging up the pitch at Headingley cricket ground in Leeds in the middle of the Ashes Test. He was pardoned and released but on 23 September 1977, grown flabby of mind and body, he took part in a raid on the Bank of Cyprus in Holloway, north London, and was caught in the act and gaoled. His behaviour created a general cynicism about miscarriage-of-justice campaigns for the next few years.

Many other 'faces' also lost out: Billy Tobin, one of the best-known bank-robbers of the seventies, was gaoled in September 1981. And not all the 'faces' survived: Adgie Pitts, brother of Shirley 'Queen of the Shoplifters' Pitts, died young in a car crash in the sixties. Two years earlier he had been the getaway driver in an attempted springing of another villain, Freddy Sampson, driving on the pavements through the streets of Tooting in a spiffy red Jaguar car.

Other robbers met more brutal, untimely ends. The Torso Murder case in 1977 involved two of the most controversial deaths: Billy Moseley was cut up into pieces and dumped in the Thames without his head and Micky Cornwall, who was known as 'the Laughing Bank Robber' because of a permanent grin, was shot in the head and buried in the traditional shallow grave in Hertfordshire. Reg Dudley, who had a long criminal record and had worked at the Krays' El Morocco club, and 'Fat Bob' Maynard were convicted of their murder after what was then the Old Bailey's longest murder trial.

It was claimed that Dudley and Maynard formed part of a gang called Legal and General which held sway in north London. In fact, this was a joke name given to them because they looked, on one occasion in a pub, like the two characters in a Legal and General television commercial. At their trial it was claimed that such traditional gangland motives as pursuit of loot, jealousy or informing had been involved. But the evidence against the two men was always shaky – supergrass Tony Wild later recanted his evidence against them – and few in the underworld believe that the right men were caught for the murders. In a macabre gesture that indicated that the wrong men had indeed been gaoled, Moseley's slowly defrosting head was left in a public lavatory in Islington shortly after the trial ended in June 1977.

Some robbers became prominent for reasons not entirely connected with their professions. On 2 May 1970 silver bullion worth £400 000 was stolen from a security van in Mountnessing in Essex. One of the men arrested for this was George Ince, who received a fifteen-year gaol sentence for the crime. But he became better known as the man wrongly accused of the murder of Muriel Patience at the Barn restaurant in Braintree, Essex. He had been picked out on an identity parade. Ince had the embarrassing alibi that he had been with Dolly, the wife of Charlie Kray, and he was eventually acquitted. The case became a *cause célèbre* for those seeking a change in the identification rules of evidence.

David Martin achieved possibly the highest profile of all the robbers who made a reputation for reasons other than their hauls or escapes. He was a remarkable character, much more complex than the image of the 'transvestite bank robber' with which he was later saddled. He was a risk-taker: he used to enjoy stealing unmarked police cars from outside police stations, zooming across the English Channel to France for the weekend and calling the police station from Charles de Gaulle airport in Paris to tell them where they could pick up their Rover. He was a small man and could pass for a woman when, in drag, he effected escapes. He had been to Borstal for assaulting an off-duty policeman, served a long sentence for cheque frauds and had been part of a team that used a dust-cart as a battering-ram, to escape from Brixton prison in 1974.

In August 1982 Martin had been spotted posing as a security man called David Demain in a West End building. Asked to empty his pockets by PC Nicholas Carr, he had opened fire and wounded the officer in the groin. 'Demain' was traced to Crawford Place in Paddington where police saw a woman at the entrance. The 'woman' turned out to be Martin who first pulled a semi-automatic pistol from his handbag and then a Smith and Wesson .38 revolver from his waistband. The police fired back and Martin was shot in the head and shoulder and captured. A search of his flat suggested his involvement in a series of robberies and thefts. But before he could come to trial, Martin, using a duplicate key, had managed to escape from Marlborough Street magistrates court where he was attending a remand hearing. The hunt was on. A tip-off led police to a yellow Mini in Earls Court on 14 January 1983.

The police, believing that Martin was a passenger in the car, opened fire. They hit their target five times and pistol-whipped him in the street as he spilled out of the Mini. It was the wrong man. The innocent passenger was a film technician called Stephen Waldorf, who was later paid £120 000 in compensation and departed to France to write a fictionalized account of the event. He felt no bitterness: 'I could never muster it. I hate wasting time hating people.'

A fortnight after the event, police had found out that Martin would be dining at the Milk Churn in Hampstead. They were plotting his movements through tapping the telephones of his friends. Just before they were about to pounce, Martin realized that a trap awaited him and ran for the underground station, sped down below, leapt on to the electrified line and headed for Belsize Park. There, in an alcove, Martin was found. He had a tiny penknife stuck to the roof of his mouth with chewing gum.

In October 1983 he was sentenced at the Old Bailey to twenty-five years. He had not expected such a heavy sentence and could not face the tedium and the fear of becoming a prisoner with 'the 100 yard stare'. He hanged himself in his cell. Even the policeman he had

The elusive
David Martin.

shot expressed his regrets. (Robbing in drag is not quite as popular as films might suggest, but bank robber Bobby King recalls an occasion when an attempt was made to approach a security van by using a robber who had been dressed in his girlfriend's clothes. The robber, a small but quick-tempered man, had to push a pram in which a sawn-off shotgun was hidden towards the security men and then hold them up. Unfortunately for the gang, the blagger in drag had to pass a building-site and was subjected to a few 'get yer tits out, darlin'' remarks from that direction. For a moment it appeared that he was about to lean into the pram and grab the gun to teach the builders a lesson. The other robbers panicked and intercepted him. The robbery was abandoned, thus jettisoning a few thousand pounds and a potential hammer-blow for the women's movement.)

Bank robberies still take place in the nineties and new methods of studying security systems are now learned in prison where inmates examine each other's depositions, which are passed around to prove to other prisoners that their owner is not in for something 'disreputable', like sex offences. Some of these will be statements from staff members of places that were robbed, detailing, among other things, how a security system is triggered. The bank robber is now more likely to be a loner, a chancer, than a member of a team of professional robbers.

One of the reasons for the decline in the robbery teams is that they found themselves facing not only the narksmen but the marksmen: police ready to shoot armed robbers caught in the act. In November 1990 Kenny 'Big Head' Baker was shot dead by a marksman from Scotland Yard's PT17 squad near Reigate in Surrey, during an attempted raid on a Securicor van, with members of the Arif family. He was the seventh robber in four years to be shot dead on the job.

On 23 November 1987 Tony Ash had been shot dead in the process of a wages snatch at the Bejam supermarket in Woolwich, south London. The police had been tipped off by informer Seamus Ray. Ash was a larger than life character who had never had the best of luck: he had once offered some stolen Scotch to a pleasant woman he met at a hotel dance in Ramsgate only to find out that she was an off-duty policewoman. Ronnie Easterbrook, another of the fifty-something robbers on the job, was also shot but survived. Ash's was a very public death: a Thames Television crew had been in the process of filming the Flying Squad at work. A wreath sent to his Camberwell funeral read: 'May your executioners and Seamus Ray live long and suffer every day.'

Eighteen months later Jimmy Farrell and Terry Dewsnap were shot dead when they tried to rob a post office in North Harrow on 13 April 1989. Police, who included the Yard's PT17 marksmen, had been tailing the team. Farrell had only been back on the street for eight months after serving a sentence for robbing the National Westminster Bank in Isleworth in 1977, a crime he claimed he had not committed. Dewsnap was one of the men whose name had been mentioned as the real murderer of Micky Cornwall.

The Great Train Robbers slip in and out of the national consciousness still. Bill Boal and Brian Field are dead. The latter died in a car crash in 1977, his new in-laws unaware of his previous history. Cordrey disappeared into England's West Country as a florist, Goody moved to Spain and James tried unsuccessfully to revive his racing career. Buster Edwards was back in the Old Bailey in 1992 but only as a witness in the murder trial in which two sisters, Michelle and Lisa Taylor, were accused – and eventually cleared on appeal – of murdering Alison Shaughnessy; he had sold flowers to the murder victim's husband. Charlie Wilson was to suffer a violent end, Bruce Reynolds decided to become a writer. Ronnie Biggs popped up at the Earth Summit in Rio de Janeiro in 1992, advising delegates, on the local radio, on how to avoid being mugged on the city's Copacabana beach. Ex-Superintendent Jack Slipper, the man who tried unsuccessfully to remove him from Brazil, even went out in the summer of 1993 for an old boys' reunion, courtesy of the *Sunday Express*, and shared memories of the past. Monty and Rommel meet again. Slipper told Biggs that he should come back and would probably face only four or five years because of the passing of the years. Biggs, pony-tailed, elegant and laconic to the last, said that he missed his jellied eels and pie and mash but not the dank, dark cells of Wandsworth.

At a time when robbers pour petrol over their victims or threaten to rape their wives, a rosy hue now suffuses the men of the Great Train Robbery. Even Sir Robert Mark wrote of Biggs in his autobiography that his escape had 'added a rare and welcome touch of humour to the history of crime'. Sir Robert observed drily that Biggs' retreat to Brazil made him the most memorable figure to undergo the punishment of banishment since Henry IV in 1398.

But the arrival on the scene of a beefed-up version of the old snitch, nark, canary or squealer was already changing the face of robbery. The supergrass had arrived.

8

THE SUPERGRASSES

Bertie,'King Squealer' and the Rest

Supergrass Bertie Smalls with detectives in 1973.

*T*he supergrass is a modern phenomenon, distinguished from the old-fashioned nark, who has been known as long as there has been a notion of crime and punishment. Jack Wild in *The Beggar's Opera* was an informer and Dick Turpin himself was tracked down by officers who used the promise of favours to his fellow criminals. Scotland Yard has long operated its Information Fund and by the end of the Second World War the informer in a case of stolen goods was entitled to 10 per cent of the value of the property, a system that continues, sometimes controversially, to this day.

But although they have always been a feature of criminal life, the men who broke the eleventh commandment of the underworld, 'Thou shalt not grass', have always had to suffer the penalties. The 'snitchers' in the fifties were sometimes punished with the 'mark of the nark', a razor slash from cheekbone to the corner of the mouth. A man with an obvious scar and without a Clydeside accent was often thought to be an informer.

The title of the first 'supergrass' – someone who gives evidence against many of his former colleagues in exchange for a lenient sentence and protection – is usually bestowed on Bertie Smalls, the London bank robber who helped the police in 1973, but there is debate on this. Leonard 'Nipper' Read, who investigated the Krays, claims that Leslie Payne, adviser to the twins, who gave evidence against them at their Old Bailey trial in 1969, was the first genuine supergrass.

The use of supergrasses in Britain was to mirror what was happening in the United States, where the first major cracks in the underworld's code of loyalty were appearing: Joseph Valachi, a veteran Mafia man, became in 1963 the first member of the organization to become an informer. His move led to the setting up of the Witness Security Programme, a less formalized version of which now operates in the United Kingdom.

By 1974 the policy was starting to work in Britain. Sir Robert Mark noted of a number of criminals that, 'Faced with honest and trustworthy detectives for the first time in their experience, they began to sing'. But a sentencing policy which had more than doubled the standard term for robbery is as likely a reason for the ending of the concept of 'honour among thieves'. While a robber might accept with equanimity, the six- or seven-year sentence that was normal in the fifties knowing that his family, hair and libido would probably still be intact by the time he came out, the notion of a dozen or more years behind bars concentrates the minds of even the 'staunchest'.

Smalls was a short, squat man who looked like the film actor Bob Hoskins and held ferociously right-wing views. Bobby King, one of the bank robbers on whom he informed, says, 'He loved violence. He couldn't handle straight company, he liked to be with "one of his own", an expression he used all of the time.' Before being a robber, Smalls had worked as a ponce, which some of his victims hinted was an indication of the decadence of character that would lead him to inform.

In 1973, faced with the possibility of a daunting sentence for his part in the Wembley bank job, and tracked down at a hide-out in Northampton through his au pair girl, he co-operated with the police and started on a process which would help to gaol many of his colleagues. Detective Jack Slipper believes that a key factor in the final turning of Smalls came when he first had to face the men who were then his colleagues at the committal hearings. Smalls was heavily hungover, having downed his regular bottle of vodka the previous day, and Danny Allpress, one of his seven co-defendants, taunted him by asking him who would be having his wife while he was away.

An agreement was drawn up with the Director of Public Prosecutions, Sir Norman Skelhorn, granting him immunity in return for complete co-operation. He, his wife and two children were hidden at a guarded address. By September 1974 he had helped to gaol twenty-one former associates for a total of 308 years. As he concluded his evidence in the committal proceedings, King and Danny Allpress sang 'We'll meet again, Don't know where, Don't know when ...' This scene was later used by screenwriter Peter Prince in *The Hit*, which starred Terence Stamp as a supergrass hiding out in Spain. Allpress even taught his prison budgie – pet birds are allowed to long-term prisoners and 'Do not enter, budgie loose' is a not-uncommon cell-door sign – to say 'Bert is a fucking grass'. Diane Smalls was sympathetic to her husband's victims: 'I wept all night because I considered the sentences (between sixteen and nineteen years) were inhuman,' she said of the gaolings of Allpress, King and five others. 'People may find it difficult to understand but my heart goes out to their wives, families and friends.'

The deal which gave Smalls immunity did not meet with universal judicial approval. In the words of former judge, Sir Frederick Lawton: 'He was undoubtedly a villain. He would only turn Queen's evidence if he was given a complete immunity from prosecution and wanted that in writing, which seemed the quintessence of impertinence. There was this criminal saying "I've committed a large number of offences and I don't believe a word you say about not prosecuting me, unless you put it in writing." It was outrageous.'

Some unexpected embarrassments for the authorities resulted from Smalls' co-operation. One man, Jimmy Saunders, who had been convicted of a robbery on the evidence of a supposed verbal admission to the police, was cleared on appeal when Smalls explained that Saunders could not have taken part in it.

Other grasses sprouted. The old habit of honour amongst thieves became dishonour amongst robbers: George du Burriatte, Billy Williams, Jimmy Trusty, Freddie Sinfield, Roger Denhardt, Billy Amies, John 'The Target' Moriarty, Tony Wild, Colin Francis, Charlie Lowe, Maurice O'Mahoney, Chrissie Wren, Dave Smith, George Piggott, Billy Young, Roy Garner and Micky 'Skinny' Gervaise all sang for their supper.

The tariff for telling tales became five years. Reducing Lowe's sentence from eleven and a half to five years, Mr Justice Roskill said: 'It is in the public interest that a person such as this should be encouraged to give information to police in order that others may be brought to justice.'

O'Mahoney, or 'King Squealer' as he called himself in his autobiography (complete with foreword by musician Rick Wakeman), was born in 1947 into a large Irish-Catholic family and was involved in a wide range of crime – robbery, burglary, extortion, blackmail, hijacking – from an early age. He was a violent man who had once bitten a diamond off the ring on a victim's hand and swallowed it. On his own admission, he took real pleasure from battering and cutting up his enemies or victims, beating them in the face with a hammer or smashing their kneecaps. He took contracts to wound people – £1000 for shooting a man in the legs, for instance – and acted as a debt-collecting heavy who would beat a debtor about the head with a hammer until he came up with the money. He boasted of having plotted to kidnap both Elton John and Elizabeth Taylor and of having robbed the actress Dinah Sheridan.

On 11 June 1974 O'Mahoney was arrested at gunpoint in London. His girlfriend, Susan Norville, had already made a statement to the police about a Securicor robbery with which he was charged. Some of his associates had also started to talk, he said later, and that was what persuaded him to go QE – Queen's Evidence. He claimed that they had threatened his lover and had suggested that they would gouge his eyes out with a toothbrush. 'I've had enough,' he said. 'Give me a high ranking officer from Scotland Yard. I want to confess.'

Confess he did. He admitted 102 offences, including thirteen armed robberies and sixty-five burglaries and involving £197 000 in cash. He dealt with Deputy Assistant Commissioner Ernest Bond, Commander John Lock and Jack Slipper.

O'Mahoney enjoyed the good life of the grass in Chiswick police station. The 'grass-house' as it became known was itself to provoke controversy: his girlfriend was allowed in to see him, he was granted a television and an eight-track stereo system and smuggled in whisky, brandy and beer. He celebrated major events with champagne and whiled away the time between making statements with games of Ludo with his girlfriend, Scrabble with fellow informers, fishing and snooker with the officers and trips to the golf course. Slipper defended the use of some facilities: 'Prisoners in a normal prison watch TV in the television room and supergrasses have to have the same facility in their cell or they would go bonkers.'

On 19 September 1974 O'Mahoney appeared at the Old Bailey and pleaded guilty to his 102 crimes. Prosecutor Michael Hill described him as the most guarded man in Britain. His assistance to the police had been 'incalculable'. His own barrister, Kenneth Machin, told the court that 'by his action he may have already signed his own death warrant.' O'Mahoney was then allowed to address the court himself: 'I know that what I have done in the past is wrong and I believe that what I am doing now is right ... I want to hit right at the heart of the criminal underworld.'

The judge, Sir Carl Aarvold, gave him the lenient sentence of five years and O'Mahoney wept with relief before being taken to a solitary cell in Oxford gaol. Word soon spread as to who the new guest was and cheery cries of 'You're going to be poisoned, you grass,' greeted him and notes threatening damage to himself and his family were shoved under the door.

He returned to court for the 111-day trial on 4 June 1975. Thirteen people faced charges of armed robbery, conspiracy to rob, receiving stolen property and conspiracy to pervert the course of justice. It was heard in front of Mr Justice Bernard Gillis, a genial and mild-mannered 'cove from Hove', whose slightly more lenient than average sentences had earned him the affectionate nickname 'Gillis-is-good-for-you'. O'Mahoney's evidence was convincing and a further seven people were convicted and given gaol sentences of up to fifteen years.

O'Mahoney finally refused to give any further evidence. He claims that this was because there was an increasing likelihood that juries would be nobbled and he did not want to risk himself without reason: 'That was it. King Squealer would sing no more.' His armed protection abruptly ceased, to his dismay, and he called the *Guardian* to complain: 'They've dropped me flat, the canary that fell from its cage. They've told me to go out and get a decent job. The only trade I know is how to break into banks. I'm in a terrible state. I could go round the corner and cry.'

But he dried his eyes and re-emerged as a security man on Rick Wakeman and David Bowie tours, selling dodgy jewellery and carrying out electrical work at the homes of his police minders. Amazingly, he was back at the Old Bailey in July 1993, charged with robbery and possession of firearms over the snatch of a money-bag outside a post office in Shepherd's Bush, during which police had fired four shots.

Appearing under his new name of Peter Davies, he offered a fantastical defence: that the police had themselves asked him to carry out the robbery so that they could frame another man with the stolen bag. Now grey-haired and pony-tailed, he told the court that he believed the police had been planning to kill him because he had hinted that he would do a second volume of memoirs in which he would expose police corruption. He said that he had often lied on the instructions of his handlers in order to convict men and named a former detective constable who ran a south London wine bar as one of his middleman. He was acquitted and immediately attempted to sell his story to the *Sun*.

Many other criminals followed O'Mahoney's example, although whether this was from the high motive of 'striking at the heart of the criminal underworld' or for the sake of a hefty sentence reduction is less certain.

Billy Williams also made the jump in 1974. He claimed that he turned when PC David Clements was shot at the wheel of a panda car by robbers escaping from a bank raid in July that year. He saw Clements flinch as the bullet struck him yet still manage to carry on the chase. This was his conversion on the road to Chiswick police station. He pleaded guilty to three armed raids and asked for thirty-six other offences, mainly robbery and conspiracy, to be taken into consideration. Williams became so nervous about giving evidence that he would vomit before appearing in the witness-box. He was sentenced to five years. Like O'Mahoney, he had to contend with threats – cyanide in his orange juice was one – and scalding water was thrown at him, a hazard for informers and sex offenders in gaol.

Williams was allowed out of his cell to marry his fiancée, Barbara Stanikowski, and the *News of the World* featured a photograph of him celebrating, wearing a policeman's helmet and apparently living the life of Riley inside. Philip Trusty, who shot the constable, was gaoled for twenty years for a series of robberies, while Trusty's brother Jimmy, by now an informer too, received a two-year and nine-month sentence.

One of the most enigmatic of the informers was Roy Garner, a former meat porter and property-developer turned cocaine dealer, whose prominence came from his relationship with Detective Superintendent Tony Lundy. Lundy described him as the most useful informer in the history of Scotland Yard and there is no doubt that Garner provided much vital information to the police without ever serving much gaol himself, at least initially. Lundy and Garner's association ran for fourteen years, during which Garner picked up around £200 000 in payments for information leading to the recovery of goods or money.

Garner prospered because, although his friends had suspicions, he was not yet known as an informer and was able to tap information through his clubland associations; he owned a north London villain's hang-out called Elton's and his financial success helped him to run stables for trotting-horses in Britain and Florida. Garner's charmed life ended when Customs and Excise nailed him for VAT fraud. Like many criminals, he had moved into a simple and lucrative fiddle: gold krugerrands were flown in from Holland and sold on without the VAT on gold being paid but with the VAT price added to them, representing a 15 per cent profit. Since shipments worth £1 million each were being brought in, the sums to be made were significant. Garner was gaoled for four years for his part in the game.

The relationship between Lundy and Garner was to attract greater attention than Garner's informing activities. The pair were shown together in a photograph at a 1974 charity function given by the Lady Ratlings (the women's branch of the Grand Order of Water Rats) at the Dorchester Hotel. Lundy's detractors suggested that there was something less than healthy about the relationship and queried how Garner had been able to collect so many lucrative rewards for robberies solved.

Lundy was then the subject of a series of disciplinary investigations which split the Yard and could be summed up in a *Sun* headline of the time: 'Brilliant or Bent?' Most damaging for Lundy was the remark of his superior, Deputy Assistant Commissioner Ron

Left: Roy Garner described by Detective Superintendent Tony Lundy (above) as the most useful informer in Scotland Yard's history.

Steventon, that: 'It is my belief that Mr Lundy is a corrupt officer who has long exploited his relationship with Garner.'

The robbery that was to spark the greatest controversy about the Lundy–Garner axis was the hijacking of £3.5 million worth of silver bullion on 24 March 1980 after Micky Gervaise, dressed as a policeman, had waved the lorry-driver into a lay-by for a bogus road test. Most of the ingots were recovered but twelve were missing, fuelling speculation about dirty dealings. Lenny Gibson and Dolph and Ron Aguda were gaoled for ten years for the robbery. Micky Gervaise received a shorter sentence because of his co-operation and the inside man, Bill Parker, got seven years.

Garner now wanted his reward and felt entitled to the 10 per cent that he might have anticipated. According to Martin Short's book on Lundy, £180 000 was eventually paid out. But Garner appeared to believe he was untouchable and was caught smuggling nearly 400 kilograms (880 pounds) of cocaine into Cornwall by Customs in what was called Operation Redskin. In March 1989 he was gaoled for twenty-two years, which was reduced to sixteen on appeal, and retired, furious, to prison threatening to spill beans. Nikolaus Chrastny, the German crook believed to be behind this enormous cocaine deal, was also arrested in the sweep. But on 4 October 1987 he escaped from the cell where he was being held for security reasons in Dewsbury, West Yorkshire. Because he was being so co-operative, he had been allowed model-making equipment, which he used to effect his escape.

Lundy's successes were undeniable and Martin Short in his biography of the detective describes him as the Yard's equivalent of Andrew Lloyd Webber: six trials involving him were on at the Old Bailey simultaneously. During a five-year period up to 1982 around fifty 'resident informants' (RIs) gave information that led to 451 people being charged, of whom 262 were convicted.

But the character of some of the supergrasses was starting to make the whole exercise less palatable. It emerged that one, Dave Smith, who admitted to around seventy robberies, had also been responsible for the death of Kurt Hess, a handbag manufacturer, who had died a month after Smith had coshed him and robbed him of £782. The charge was dropped to manslaughter because Hess had a thin skull, but there was unease that a man such as Smith could escape the normal penalties of his crimes. In September 1986, arrested and locked up after an attack on a Securicor vehicle, Smith did to himself what countless of his former colleagues would happily have done: slit his throat.

The Liverpudlian Billy 'The Queer' Amies was another super-grass whose conduct was less than saintly: he had been involved in one robbery where a man had been tied up and his teenage daughter stripped and threatened with rape unless the victim revealed the whereabouts of his money.

For his part, Lundy took early retirement on health grounds, blaming a combination of Masonic officers at the Yard, embittered criminals and gullible journalists for his demise. He went to Spain, where he ended up in the same neck of the woods as some of the men, like the Agudas who watched him on his morning runs, whom he had helped to gaol.

By the mid-eighties the tide was beginning to turn against the supergrasses. Some, like Tony Wild, who had given evidence in robbery and murder trials, had been reconvicted and had admitted to inventing evidence. Others decided against co-operation once they reached the witness-box, most notably in the trial of John 'The Face' Goodwin and Brian Reader in April 1982 for £1 250 000 worth of burglaries, when supergrass Gervaise indicated his unhappiness in mid-trial and a re-trial was ordered. Goodwin was cleared but was then charged with jury nobbling and gaoled for seven years. His conviction was overturned on appeal in 1984.

Goodwin was as wily as the rare birds of prey he used to keep in his country home: he tape-recorded drunken detectives discussing his case with him, using a bug hidden in a Christmas tree at a mutual friend's house. The detectives were eventually charged with corruption offences and ran a 'cut-throat' defence, in which they told mutually contradictory stories. One claimed he had never been in the house at all and that the voice on the tape was not his; the other claimed they had both indeed been there but that the £1000 Goodwin had offered them was merely so they would tell the truth in his trial and hence no corruption had taken place. The jury accepted this explanation. Goodwin's problems were not over; his wife, Shirley, was kidnapped while he was in prison and held for a ransom of £50 000. Charlie Pitts, the brother of 'Queen of the Shoplifters' Shirley and bank-robber Adgie was convicted of the kidnapping in June 1984 and jailed for eighteen years.

There was now a growing feeling that there was something inherently cynical about violent men who had profited from crime parlaying their way out of a long sentence by informing on their colleagues. Juries started to find them unpersuasive and they ceased to form a major part of the police's armoury. There were a few exceptions, such as the major Triad trial at the Old Bailey in 1992 where the chief witness was the first Chinese supergrass in Britain, but his evidence failed to convince.

A dark joke that floated around prisons in the eighties went thus: a Jewish criminal who hated Arabs had decided to join the French Foreign Legion, so that he could shoot as many of them as he wanted. On his first night on duty he was on guard on the battlements of a desert fort when the sentry tiptoed towards him and whispered – 'See, out there behind that dune, four Arabs hiding.' The sentry tiptoed away and the criminal took his rifle out and fired – and shot the sentry in the back. 'Why did you do that?' another legionnaire asked him, 'I thought you hated Arabs.' 'Yeah,' replied the criminal, 'but I hate a grass even more.'

Although remarkably few informers have suffered retribution despite frequent reports of prices on their heads, some of them did suffer violent ends. Johnny Darke was stabbed to death with a machete at the Ranelagh Yacht Club in Fulham in November 1978 after rumours that had been helping the police. Johnny Bindon, an actor who played opposite Carol White in the film *Poor Cow*, and who was famous in the press for the anatomically remarkable way in which he could lift beer mugs, was charged with the murder but acquitted. Patrick 'Paddy Onions' O'Nione was murdered in November 1982. Jimmy Davey, another underworld figure, was arrested a few months later for questioning in connection with the killing but died after being forcibly restrained in police custody.

By the nineties it had become clear that the old *laissez-faire* attitude of letting bygones be bygones had passed and that unwary informers whose faces had not already been altered by plastic surgeons could expect to have a slightly cruder job done for them by their former associates.

In 1989 the body of Alan 'Chalky' White, a small-time criminal and drug dealer who had been giving information to the police about his associates, was found wrapped in tarpaulin in a lake at the Cotswold Water Park. He had been picked up from his home in the idyllic village of Minchinhampton in Gloucestershire 19 kilometres (12 miles) away, stabbed to death and dispatched to a watery grave. One of the men against whom he was due to give evidence, Danny Gardiner, was convicted of his murder.

Dave Norris, a police informer, was shot dead outside his front door in Belvedere, south-east London, by two men wearing crash helmets on 28 April 1991. The trial of two men accused of murdering him was abandoned half-way through. Three other men who were believed to have been informers have also been killed.

The police say they continue to protect informers and since 1978 new identities have been granted in 170 cases. With families included this involves a total of around 700 people, some of whom have been moved to Australia and the United States. It is a complex business: bogus documents for bank accounts, educational qualifications and medical records have to be obtained and the men are sometimes guarded for years afterwards.

Some supergrasses seem untroubled. Smalls was spotted in pubs in north London in the early nineties. Colin Francis, who was given a five-year sentence in 1980 after informing on twenty colleagues, popped up again more than ten years later advertising himself as a security consultant. Some, apparently undismayed by the prospect of encountering some of the old lags they helped to gaol, have taken off to the sun.

9

COSTA DEL CRIME

Spanish Knights and the 'Silent Man'

Ronnie Knight
and wife Sue.

Charlie Wilson, the Great Train Robber, now fifty-seven, was slicing tomatoes and cucumbers for a salad at his home in Llanos de Nagueles near Marbella in Spain at around 7 p.m. on 23 April 1990 when the bell rang. A tall young man in a grey track suit and a baseball cap was standing there. He had arrived on a yellow mountain bike. He told Pat Wilson, who answered the door, that he wanted to see her husband and mentioned the name Eamonn. Wilson beckoned him in and they went to the patio where Charlie had built a barbecue and where he had been entertaining guests earlier that day to celebrate his wedding anniversary.

A few moments later there was the sound of voices raised in argument, then two loud bangs. Charlie Wilson staggered dying towards the pool, blood streaming from a wound in the neck where his carotid artery had been severed. Nearby, the Wilson's husky-Alsatian cross-breed, Bobo, also lay dying. Charlie had been kicked in the testicles, punched so hard in the face that his nose was broken and then shot with a Smith and Wesson revolver. The young killer fled by vaulting the back wall. An accomplice had probably been waiting nearby in a getaway car. The 'Silent Man', as he had been called during the Great Train Robbery trial, was silent for ever.

Charlie Wilson had bought his Spanish retreat in 1987 for the reasonable price of £25 000 and had spent lavishly to refurbish it, with pink Portuguese marble for the bathrooms and a turret inlaid with coloured glass. He called it Chequers. Apart from that one gesture of braggadocio, he kept a low profile. In the evenings he painted still lifes rather than clubbing like many of his contemporaries. The local Spanish police had been unaware that he was even living on their patch when he was murdered.

His funeral was attended by many of his old colleagues: Bruce Reynolds, Buster Edwards, Roy James and Robert Welch paid their respects while Charlie's favourite song, Frank Sinatra's 'My Way', was played. Ron and Reg Kray sent floral tributes. Many of the mourners wanted to know why Charlie had been killed. The likeliest explanation involved drugs. Although Pat Wilson was adamant that her husband had never been involved in trafficking, it is inevitable that Wilson mixed with those who were and he may have invested some money in the purchase of a shipment of cannabis from North Africa. But the specific reason for his death would appear to be connected with a south London drugs dealer called James Rose.

Rose had found his niche in criminal history by being a member of the first gang to be arrested after a co-operation agreement had

The funeral in 1990 of Charlie Wilson, attended by Buster Edwards (left) and Robert Welch (right).

been signed in 1988 between the then Foreign Secretary, Sir Geoffrey Howe, and his Soviet counterpart, Eduard Shevardnadze. He had been smuggling highly prized Afghan black, which had increased in value in the eighties as the result of the Afghan war, into Britain via Moscow and St Petersburg, hidden in sacks of liquorice. He realized that he might receive a lighter sentence if he named the gang leader, one Roy Adkins, who at the time was out of harm's way in Amsterdam. Rose apparently wanted Wilson's approval to name Adkins.

Whether Wilson ever contemplated such approval is not known and Rose had been gaoled in January 1990 at Chelmsford Crown Court for his part in the ring. When Wilson was last in London before his death, a man called Eamonn, acting as a middleman, had delivered a message from Adkins in Amsterdam censuring him for supposedly okaying his name. Wilson denied any involvement and his friends believed him. They say that naming another man was not his style.

Adkins was not to be reassured. It would seem that he brooded and one theory was that he got two young hoodlums to kill Wilson. The pair had been serving gaol sentences of thirteen and nine years respectively for armed robbery and drug offences and had escaped while being transferred from Albany prison on the Isle of Wight to Blundeston gaol. Both were wanted men. Not everyone buys this theory. Gordon Goody, another Great Train Robber who retired to Spain, told the *Sunday Times*: 'Charlie would never have given no one no names ... the young villains of today – for a couple of grand, a few lines of coke, they'll get a gun and use it.'

The police were not the only people who were anxious to find out who had disposed of Charlie. Norman Radford, a holidaying cousin of Charlie who had seen the gunman sitting nonchalantly by the side of the road earlier in the day, told reporters, 'His murder has upset a lot of big names out here. They are not happy men.'

In September 1990 two men walked into the Nightwatch bar of the American Hotel in Amsterdam and fired six bullets into Roy Adkins. But whether his death was a result of a feud with Wilson is another matter. The police believed not, saying that on the night he died he had met two Colombians with whom he was involved in selling smuggled emeralds. One of Adkins' associates had been robbed of part of the emerald assignment and the Colombians had arranged the meeting with Adkins who, as the middleman, was being held responsible for the loss. (Adkins' death was followed by another fatal shooting in Amsterdam, that of Micky Blackmore, a south London gangland figure who was owed money by Adkins.)

The news of the Adkins shooting caused fresh ripples in the bars of the Costa del Sol. At Charlie Wilson's inquest in Horseferry Road coroner's court in London, coroner Paul Knapman remarked: 'It is ironic that Charles Wilson should end his days being gunned down in the barbecue area of his retirement home in Spain.'

The notion of the 'Costa del Crime', the part of Spain that 'fell off the back of a lorry', was already a cliché, but the shooting blew a hole in the idea of a villain's nirvana where the chaps could still enjoy all the pleasures of 'home' – satellite football, Carling Black Label, bacon and the *Daily Express* – with none of the pain – rain, taxes and the Regional Crime Squad.

It was the collapse in the summer of 1978 of the extradition agreement between Spain and Great Britain, originally drawn up by Benjamin Disraeli a hundred years earlier, that had made Spain so attractive to men who, if not on the run, were at least travelling at jogging pace. The extradition arrangements had broken down because Spain felt that Britain was not playing the game and was making it too difficult for the Spanish to retrieve their fugitives from the United Kingdom. The British authorities had not realized at the time what their lack of co-operation would cost them. Spain became a safe haven for criminals: close enough for the family to come out and visit yet far enough away to avoid the attentions of the police. By the mid-eighties, British detectives reckoned there were between seventy-five and a hundred men on the Costa whom they would like to interview in connection with serious crimes.

The early pioneering villains wondered to themselves why they had not thought of the move earlier. The area had been chic in the late fifties and early sixties – the Duke and Duchess of Windsor and Sophia Loren watered there – before the big hotels and apartment blocks were built, and even in the seventies it suited many of the new immigrants perfectly: across the Mediterranean was Morocco and a plentiful supply of cannabis resin for which many had acquired a taste while in prison. Up in Morocco's Rif mountains, locals waved packets of the stuff at tourists driving through villages. A kilogram of cannabis resin in the late eighties, at the height of the trade, cost as little as £200 and was fetching £700 in Marbella and around £2000 in England.

Gradually the Costa del Sol became a sort of European Miami – sunny, spoiled, decadent and dangerous. The chaps didn't mind. They were free and the only bars they were behind had names like Sinatra's, Roxy's and El Bandito. They were joined by other, less spectacular, criminals: the bent businessmen with bad debts, the spivs offering time-shares to gullible tourists, the sort of blokes who liked to be judges in Miss Wet T-shirt competitions and couldn't be bothered to learn Spanish. They merged with the 100 000 other Britons who had moved south.

Then in 1985, after negotiations between the British and Spanish governments and a thaw in the traditionally chilly relationship between the two countries, the extradition decision was reversed. Spain's Justice Minister, Fernando Ledesma, announced that 'no Briton can escape the justice of his country'. The door had been closed but the new agreement was not retroactive. Those who did not commit an offence in Spain could stay. Few have been returned to Britain.

One who did return was Freddie Foreman, the old Krays henchman. He was wanted for a Security Express robbery in Shoreditch in 1983 and was hoisted back to Heathrow on 28 July 1989, still in his beach mufti, to stand trial and be gaoled for nine years. Some villains were picked up by the Spanish police and held in gaol while their papers were examined, others watched and waited. One of these was Ronald Knight.

If the underworld had its own aristocracy and its court jesters, then the man who was its ambassador to Spain was undoubtedly Ronnie Knight, known more or less equally for his bad-boy status in London and his marriage to the actress Barbara Windsor, star of many *Carry On* films and rated very highly by director Joan Littlewood who had spotted her talents early on.

Ronnie, born in Hoxton, east London, in 1934, was known to villains – and inevitably the law – as the man who ran the Artistes and Repertoire Club in Charing Cross Road. This club was to the criminal fraternity what Groucho's was to television executives and the Travellers Club to spies: a place for gossiping, drinking too much and being recognized. Despite its name, for many of its patrons the art was blagging and the repertoire was a recital of derring-do or more often derring-didn't. Knight, after a youth spent committing a few minor offences and lying in hospital with a leg-bone disease, became mine host to London's gangsters and the many actors and singers who liked rubbing padded shoulders with them. Like many criminals of the sixties, he was fascinated by celebrity. In his auto-biography, *Black Knight*, his memories of a party at Danny La Rue's were made of this: 'Noel Coward, tinkling away on the ivories for all he was worth ... That Russian ballet bloke, Nureyev, ponced around ... Roger Moore drew the girls like horse-flies to a cowpat.'

Over the years the A & R attracted them all, from the young Rolling Stones through to Freddie Mercury and Queen. But the more regular visitors were villains. One of the functions of the A & R and Knight's later club, the Tin Pan Alley, was that of alibi: many villains would claim they had been there at the time of a robbery or piece of mayhem.

Knight's other business, with his partner Micky Regan, was pool tables, which were just starting to take over from bar billiards as a major money-maker in pubs. Freddie Foreman, later to acquire the title 'the Mean Machine', acted as collector.

What was to become part of the spiral that eventually took Knight off to Spain was the killing in 1970 of his brother David. David had been beaten up in a pub in the Angel by a group that included a man called Johnny Isaacs. Ronnie and his older brother, Johnny, became obsessed with extracting vengeance or an apology for the episode and in May 1970 set off with David to the Latin Quarter

Club in Soho to find Isaacs. Isaacs was not there but a fight broke out none the less, during which young David was stabbed through the heart with a carving knife by Alfredo 'Italian Tony' Zomparelli. Zomparelli pleaded self-defence at the subsequent Old Bailey trial, was convicted of manslaughter and gaoled for four years.

On his release he started running a Soho bucket-shop travel agency while Knight, by his own admission, went hunting for him 'like a lion after a wart hog'. On 4 September 1974, while playing pinball on the Wild Life table in the Golden Goose amusement arcade in Old Compton Street in Soho, Zomparelli was shot four times with a .38. Knight celebrated the news of the death with a bottle of champagne. He had no idea who had done it, he said, but was delighted they had.

Nearly six years later Knight was arrested for the murder. George 'Maxie' Bradshaw, also known as Maxwell Piggott, a long-haired gangland hitman with a droopy moustache and a beard, had told the police that Knight had paid him £1000 to carry out the killing. To prove his own involvement, Bradshaw described in detail the spot by a golf course near Winchester where he had hidden the murder weapon. He said that he had knocked back several large brandies, put on a false beard, which he had later discarded because it looked so ridiculous, and had then, with an accomplice, shot Zomparelli, fleeing on the underground. He was remanded in custody in Brixton. Bradshaw, who had taken part in between thirty and forty robberies, was gaoled for life for murder and duly gave evidence against Knight.

Knight's trial, with Barbara Windsor making an appearance despite the fact that the marriage was nearly over, was a high-profile one. Knight and Nicky Gerrard, who was accused of being Piggott's accomplice, were cleared and Knight ran from the Old Bailey, his exit impeded only by a *Sun* reporter who foresightedly jammed the revolving door to stop him making a quick getaway with the newspaper that had actually bought his story. (Gerrard was shot dead in south London in 1982 after being seized by masked men who beat him around the head. His cousin, Tommy Hole, was charged with the murder but cleared.)

Freddie Foreman, brought back from Spain to stand trial for the 1983 £6 million Shoreditch robbery.

Knight sold his clubs and received an £80 000 pay-off for money that he had invested in Soho peep-show clubs. He had already made around £3000 a week from these establishments, where young women took off their clothes and did improbable things with rubber snakes for the entertainment of lonely men who shovelled coins into the slot machine that kept the peep-hole open. His more puritanical colleague, Micky Regan, was disgusted.

A silk-shirt-with-embossed-initials man, Knight had spotted the potential of Spain in the early seventies and, with brother Johnny, had bought 1600 square metres of land in the hills beyond Fuengirola. An American architect designed his four-bedroomed house, with pool and gym, and in 1975, after spending £40 000, Knight moved in. He took a share in the local Wyn's Bar and a supermarket and went into property and a car-hire company. 'It was Paradise found,' he said. Knight told his mates about the glories of the Costa del Sol and soon they were all buying plots of land. He extolled its advantages: 'Restaurants where there's only roast beef and Yorkshire pudding on the menu – and English mustard.' (He started the Mumtaz in Fuengirola because he missed a decent curry.) It was all like a little village, he reckoned. Los Boliches, one of the *barrios* of Fuengirola, popular with what the Spanish police called 'The Mafia Inglesa', was nicknamed Bethnal Green in the Sun.

Knight married Sue Haylock in June 1987 at Fuengirola town hall, with a blessing and reception at El Oceano, a restaurant-cum-club and sports centre on the beach. Sue wore a £3000 dress of ivory silk and satin and carried a bouquet of orchids and salmon roses. The press loved it and some fanciful stories about the cake being in the shape of Wandsworth prison and £10 000 being spent on a fireworks display were telephoned back to news-desks. Years later, the vicar who had officiated at the wedding appeared as himself in *Eldorado*, the ill-fated BBC soap opera.

The one nagging problem was the British police. They had hinted that they wanted to see him in connection with the 1983 Shoreditch Security Express job for which his brothers Johnny and Jimmy were gaoled for twenty-two and eight years respectively.

During the trial *The Times* had recorded that among those sought for questioning were five men: Ronnie Knight; Freddie Foreman, who by then had a penthouse apartment in Marbella's Alcazaba complex; Ronald 'Big Ronnie' Everett, a mate of Foreman's; John James Mason, a former company director who had been cleared of the £8 million Bank of America robbery in Mayfair in 1976; and

Clifford Saxe, former landlord of the Fox in Kingsland Road, Hackney, where it was alleged that the Security Express robberies were planned. The quintet soon became known to tabloid readers as the Famous Five. Ronnie has always said that robbery was not his game and has blamed the attention he has attracted on the fact that he was 'a West End face ... the police had me marked down as a gangster, a thief'. However, reports suggested that Knight ran a criminal outfit in Spain called The Office, which planned big robberies, and he and the other members of the quintet became irritated with the tales and innuendo. He blamed the press, for whom a trip to see what Ronnie was up to was a popular mid-winter jolly, and his own outgoing personality '... if there's one thing the press love it's a colourful charismatic character to play around with ... I worried they might extradite me from Spain for stealing the limelight from the monarch.' The worry gave him a burst ulcer with the Fleet Street 'reptiles descending like a plague of blood-sucking locusts.'

By 1989 the Famous Five had become the Nasty Nine as far as the *Daily Mirror* was concerned. The four other unfortunates supposedly being hunted by the British police were Keith Cottingham, wanted in connection with a murder inquiry; Jimmy Jeffrey, an amiable north Londoner who was later to be sentenced to four years in Madrid for drugs offences; Micky Green, an outgoing former north London night-club-owner, who had been wanted in connection with an alleged VAT fraud; and John Corscadden, a liquidator (of the financial sort) from Manchester, wanted in connection with major fraud.

The sun did not shine so brightly any more. Eight drunken Welsh rugby players planned to kidnap Knight for a mythical £60 000 reward – they were supposedly going to abseil into his house and smuggle him across to Gibraltar. Others tried different approaches: a policeman who had pursued him even invited him to his own wedding in Loughton in 1989 on the grounds that detectives had attended Ronnie's in Spain. The Knights regretfully declined. They had a prior engagement. For Ronnie, at least, Spain still provided the safety that had eluded Freddie Foreman and Charlie Wilson. He told people he would go back to England if the police gave him a guarantee of bail.

Another arrival was Derek Maughan, an ex-con and former boy soldier from north-east England who went out to Spain in the eighties with the idea of opening a pub. But through the ex-prisoners' grapevine, he met up with hash smugglers who offered him a chance to join the lucrative market. 'When I first came down to Alicante, I didn't know anybody there. I rang a friend in England and he said he had a friend in Marbella and that he might be able to put me on to something. I didn't like the Marbella atmosphere too much, it was too flashy. It was dangerous, there were too many villains milling around, gold chains, cock of the walk kind of thing, so I moved out of town.'

London fraudsters with large amounts of capital were bank-rolling drug-smuggling trips but they wanted people with 'pedigree' at a middle-management level, to be in charge of operations. This would involve going out in Zodiac dinghies, meeting the mother-ships loaded with hash from Morocco and bringing the cargo back to a safe beach in Spain. The Moroccan authorities were paid off so the main problem was ensuring a safe arrival in Spain. 'They'd pick a beach which was isolated or near a town and have a car with a radio three or four kilometres along the road,' says Maughan. 'There would be another car on the other stretch of road in constant contact – "the road is clear, the road is clear" – and they'd do the same with the dinghy: "Come in now." We were rarely caught on the beach. I thoroughly enjoyed it, it was very exciting and it gets the adrenalin pumping.'

The hash would be stored in a safe house until it could be loaded into a container lorry bound for Holland or Germany or England. But the problem was the quality of the personnel. 'If you do a big job in England, you check people's pedigree and you certainly wouldn't rob a bank with people you hardly knew. But in Spain you'd meet people one day and they'd be on the boat with you next day. When trouble arose, they weren't reliable. They didn't have any loyalty.' Maughan speaks from experience: he was gaoled in Spain for three years for his part in a major operation.

As a drug smuggler he was chased by a helicopter on one occasion and shot at on another. But the money was good: 500 kilograms of cannabis, an average load, was worth £1 million, and Maughan would make on average £25 000 a trip in the late eighties. The big sums involved made dishonesty tempting. On one occasion, a bogus 300 kilogram (660 pound) load was sold from Morocco: 'There were serious repercussions. People went to Morocco to look for the people who did that. I understand a couple of people got killed down there.' There were other casualties.

'One man whose firm kept losing load after load was pinpointed as the source of the leak and they told him to go to Morocco to operate from that end. From there he was asked to go on the boat and was put in a sleeping-bag and dropped over the side,' says

Maughan. 'There's been some terrible hidings for stealing small parts of loads.'

Unusually, Maughan himself is not a drug user although he sees no harm in it. He has married a Spanish woman and started a family. He has also learnt Spanish, which few of the other ex-pat ex-cons did: 'It's unpleasant to sit in a bar and listen to them, and the Spanish look at them with disgust ... getting drunk all day and driving big cars, open-top BMWs, Range Rovers, on the pavement. Most of them don't even let their kids go to Spanish schools.'

The villains meanwhile have started eyeing other parts where the hassles would be less: Turkish Cyprus, to where Polly Peck owner Asil Nadir fled while awaiting trial for fraud, has no extradition treaty with the United Kingdom. Greece, Israel and Tunisia were also inspected as the joys of listening to 'Viva Paloma Blanca' on soft Spanish nights started to pall.

A final exodus will perhaps be caused by the growth of another group of exiles: retired police officers who, by the spring of 1993, were so numerous that they decided to set up their own 'Viejo Guillermo' ('Old Bill') association. The Spanish watch developments with puzzlement. For the British criminal in Spain, there is a touch of irony: for many years it was the wily Mediterranean in Britain who was seen as the root of vice and wickedness.

10
VICE

The Messinas,
Tommy Smithson,
Silver and Mifsud
and Soho

Carmelo Messina
celebrating his
release from gaol.

'*He* dresses in a semi-flashy style and oozes a lubricious self-satisfaction,' wrote Rhoda Lee Finmore in the introduction to her book on the trial in 1951 of Alfredo Messina for living off immoral earnings. 'A gross exterior was married to practical illiteracy but with a shrewd organizing brain.'

The Messina brothers were perfectly cast in the role of purveyors of vice to post-war Britain. They had lived in Italy and Malta and Egypt. They had avoided fighting in the war because of their 'reserved occupation'. They even looked, with their little moustaches and their fancy suits, suitably foreign and spiv-like.

But the Messinas did not quite invent the vice trade in Britain. The various Acts of Parliament still in force in the second half of the twentieth century give testament to the fact that if prostitution was not the oldest profession, it had not exactly escaped the notice of the English legislators: the 1751 and 1818 Disorderly Houses Act and the 1824 Vagrancy Act and 1847 Town Police Clauses Act had all been in operation for more than a century before the Messinas had their camelhair collars felt.

In the twenties, vice prosecutions were frequent and more than 5000 arrests for street offences were recorded in 1922, with 2231 in London alone. But the police faced criticism for their zealous interpretation of the law and the number of arrests in the capital in 1923 dropped to 595 as a result of successful appeals which showed that, in many cases, it had not been proved that the person accosted had been 'annoyed'.

By 1953 there was even a boom in the demand for prostitutes' services which peaked at the time of the coronation of Elizabeth II as thousands of men, many visitors from overseas, expressed their monarchist enthusiasms in a less obvious way than waving Union Jacks or buying mugs imprinted with the faces of the new queen and her consort. Police estimated that around 150 prostitutes began work in the West End in the period leading up to the crowning.

Nor was organized prostitution a twentieth-century innovation. In 1885, in a series of famous articles, the *Pall Mall Gazette* under the editorship of W. T. Stead had exposed a trade in child prostitutes from England to the Continent, in particular Belgium. Stead was gaoled for his pains; to prove his point, he had nominally purchased a young girl whose father was then persuaded to make an official complaint.

Lurid tales of a burgeoning 'white slave' traffic circulated in the twenties, but were much exaggerated. In Britain, according to

'Nutty' Sharpe, former head of the Flying Squad, it was 'a sordid, small-time affair – there is more rot written about white slavery than any other subject in crime.' The biggest racket, he claimed, was importing Frenchwomen and marrying them off to down-and-outs under the protection of a ponce: 'A new girl appearing in London without a "protector" would be torn to bits like a tame canary amongst a bunch of hawks. When the word goes round that "she's Johnny the Basher's new girl" the other women leave her alone.'

Europeans and North Africans were the most high-profile members of the vice business in the years between the two world wars, and of these the Algerian Casimir Micheletti and the French Juan Antonio Castanar were the most active. The former had a reputation for ruthlessness when crossed and the latter was a tango-teacher who used his job to recruit prostitutes. Both controlled dozens of girls and both were deported to France in 1929. Their feud continued and in 1930 Castanar shot and killed Micheletti. Violent trouble had been connected with their enterprises and a French pimp, 'Charles the Acrobat', had been murdered at the Cochon Club in Frith Street. French involvement in prostitution continued to claim victims. Emile Allard, whose cover was diamond dealing, and Michel Vernon were rivals in the field, a rivalry that ended in January 1936 when Allard, who was also known as 'Red Max' Kassel, was found shot dead in St Albans in Hertfordshire, although he had actually been killed in Vernon's Soho flat. Vernon was convicted of the murder in France, whither he had fled, and sent to a penal colony.

'The extent of the evil is often exaggerated,' said the first post-Second-World-War Metropolitan Police Commissioner, Sir Harold Scott, of the gaming dens that often co-existed with the brothels. 'It is mostly confined to lower-class establishments in the West End and East End and the promoters and players are largely Cypriots, Maltese or coloured people.' Not that Sir Harold subscribed to the view that immigrants were largely responsible for vice: 'Most of our criminals are home grown.' But in the period's climate of moral hypocrisy, it was perhaps not surprising that outsiders seemed best equipped to cater to the tastes of a nation more repressed in sexual matters than its European neighbours.

Prostitution was dangerous work. In the forties prostitutes working Shepherd Market in Mayfair paid as much as £20 a week for protection. Detective Robert Fabian was impressed with their toughness: 'Strong as a young bullock with legs like marble – she does so much standing about. She would ask £5 and take £3.' He had his own psychological interpretation of the women: 'The greater majority of London's prostitutes are very much under-sexed, almost at zero, by contrast with an ordinary respectable housewife and that is a professional asset to them.'

John Gosling, head of the Vice Squad for two years in the fifties, offered similar bromides: 'Their faces go before their time, their skin coarsens, their speech turns foul until at last it is true to say that they are almost completely de-womanized in every gentle aspect of that word. This, like the mark of Cain on the brow of the murderer, is the stigmata of prostitution which none can escape.' Another Yard detective, Superintendent Arthur Thorp, said that the British women, rather than the French and Germans, caused the police most trouble: 'Unlike the foreigners, they seem to let go of themselves, to lose every shred of self-respect and decency when they go on the streets. Perhaps that is because they are more conscious of the depths to which they have sunk.'

By 1952 clubs were raided on a regular basis, about every fortnight, by plainclothes men and 'zombies', the police slang of the time for policewomen, posing as revellers. Gosling felt that the London of the fifties had become as shamefully amoral as 'Marseilles and Port Said'. The prostitutes 'lie in ambush like brigands, along the defiles through which money passes.' He noted the arrival of the 'car prostitutes', young women who cruised the West End to pick up clients. By the late forties, the area of operation had extended from the West End to take in the main-line stations like King's Cross, Euston and Victoria, the previously respectable area of Maida Vale, and Stepney, which the police believed was coping with 'the demand from the City'.

The police reckoned that by 1950 there were around 3000 prostitutes. When the evangelist Billy Graham visited London at the time he found so much sex in Hyde Park that he said: 'It looked as though your parks had been turned into bedrooms, with people lying all over the place.' His remarks provoked questions in the House of Commons and the Home Secretary, 'Rab' Butler, defensively reported that the police were actively making arrests in the park with half a dozen prosecutions a day.

Eddie Chapman, the safe-cracker, noted that one of the remarkable aspects of the boom in prostitution was that so many of the women were living in Church of England property – 'they [the Church] were the greatest ponces of God's earth.'

The Messinas had entered this world in the mid-thirties. The paterfamilias, Guiseppe, a furniture repairer, had been born at the foot of Mount Etna in Sicily in the 1860s. He moved to Malta where he married a Maltese woman and where the two oldest boys, Salvatore and Alfredo, were born in 1898 and 1901. In 1905 the family moved to Alexandria in Egypt where Guiseppe opened a brothel and where Eugenio, Attilio and Carmelo were born. The brothels expanded to the extent that the Egyptian authorities became concerned. Salvatore was gaoled and the family was expelled in 1932. Two years later Eugenio, by now married to Colette, a French prostitute, came to England to assess the market.

His brothers followed him and over the next decade the family vice business expanded in the centre of London, using women from the Continent who were often married off for a small fee to local ne'er-do-wells. Each prostitute was given her own maid whose role was to ensure that clients did not stay any longer than was physically necessary, under what became known as the 'ten-minute rule'. The brothers also provided legal services and paid the frequent fines incurred by the women at the local magistrates' courts.

Other criminals had meanwhile noted the profits being made and another gang of 'Epsom Salts' (Malts), led by Carmelo Vassalo, demanded protection money from the women, who went to the police. As a result four of the Vassalo mob were sentenced to penal servitude for up to four years. Violence had already broken out between the Messina and Vassalo gangs and in 1947 Eugenio was gaoled for three years for cutting the tips off two of Vassalo's fingers. His brother Carmelo was gaoled for bribery. The burgeoning gang warfare became public and the Norwich Member of Parliament, John Foster, asked the Home Secretary, Chuter Ede, to set up a commission to look into organized vice in London. Ede declined to do so.

The Messina brothers were classic vice kings from the tips of their manicured fingers to the toes of their two-tone shoes but all had sensibly adopted solid-sounding English names: Attilio became Raymond Maynard, Salvatore chose Arthur Evans, Eugenio was Edward Marshall, Carmelo was Charles Maitland and Alfredo selected Alfred Martin. All of them played the part of the respectable, if somewhat flashy, businessman. Eugenio drove a yellow Rolls-Royce.

Their operation was finally exposed in the *People* by Duncan Webb, a classic crime reporter who was a confidant of gangster Billy Hill. Webb, who had come to the *People* via the *South London Press*, the *Daily Express* and the *Evening Standard*, and was known to his friends as Tommy, was an intriguing enough character in his own right. He had become the lover of Cynthia Hume, a night-club hostess and the wife of Donald Hume who had been gaoled in connection with the killing of a car dealer. Webb was one of a breed of larger-than-life crime reporters who were in their heyday in the fifties when papers had crime bureaux rather than a single correspondent. Their number included Percy Hoskyns, Tom Tullett, Ted Sandrock and Stanley Firmin. Jimmy 'the Prince of Darkness' Nicholson, who worked for the *Daily Sketch*, the *Daily Express* and the *News of the World*, was the only one of the genre still reporting in the nineties. The fifties was also the time when it could be fairly said that the *News of the World* was 'the judge's trade paper' because it published long and detailed reports of criminal trials.

Webb did not sell himself short. 'The reason the underworld chaps talk to me ... is because they trust me. They know I cannot be bought or sold, nor is there a lot of which I am afraid.' And he reported in *Dead Line for Crime* that, 'There was a distinct dearth in the vice trade in London after I exposed the notorious Messina brothers.'

Not that the Messinas were his only target. Antonio Rossi, or Tony Ross, who had been born in Corsica but claimed Scottish ancestry, was another. Webb invented the rather awkward nickname of 'the Hyena of Soho' for him, although it seems unlikely that anyone ever referred to him as such. Webb bearded him in the estate agent's shop he had in Soho with the immortal lines: 'I am Duncan Webb. The last I heard of you was that you were going to cut my throat. Here is my throat. Cut it.' Rossi resisted the temptation.

Webb had started his investigations into the Messinas with a prostitute called Ellen. It says something of the times that he was able to write, straight-faced, in his memoirs: 'When she knew I was a newspaper reporter, she offered me one night's hospitality if I would persuade a certain well-known male film star to use his influence to get her an actress's job.' He recorded that, as he continued his inquiries, someone attempted to run him down in Old Compton Street in Soho: 'A streetwalker came up to me. With a sneer on her lips, she said "That was meant for you, dearie".'

Reckoning day for the Messinas came on 3 September 1950 when Webb named the 'four debased men with an empire of vice which is a disgrace to London'. At that stage the brothers owned properties that operated as brothels in Shepherd Market, Stafford Street, Bruton Place and New Bond Street, all in the West End. Webb catalogued their connections with prostitutes and exposed their cover addresses before passing his dossier on to a very grateful Scotland Yard, who later said they had already been aware of much of what was happening. The following week, Webb reported that he had been attacked in the street and that his assailant had informed him: 'The Messinas are pals of mine. It's about time you journalists were done proper.'

Scotland Yard set up a task force to deal with the ring and all the brothers, with the exception of Alfredo who had not featured in the *People* exposé, decamped to France.

Alfredo did not have long to wait for his come-uppance. Detective Superintendent Guy Mahon and his officers paid a visit to the sober suburban address of 45 Harrowdene Road in Wembley, north London, interviewed him and arrested him for living on the immoral earnings of Hermione Hindin, with whom he shared the house. Remarking 'Let's be friends, we are men of the world,' Messina hospitably offered the officers champagne, whisky, tea and turkey and, if they would drop the charges, a £200 bribe. While some tea and Haig whisky – leading Superintendent Mahon to venture the information that he had led the hunt for the acid-bath murderer, Haigh – was consumed, the rest was resisted.

Mrs Hindin had 104 convictions for soliciting around the West End. She was one of the most loyal and hard-working of the Messina prostitutes, along with Cissy Cohen, Georgette Borg, Blanche Costarki, Marthe Watts and Jean Gilson. Watts wrote about the brothers in her memoirs, *The Men in My Life*, and had '*Gino le Maltais, homme de ma vie*' tattooed on her left breast. Watts hated Webb and once attacked him ferociously in a pub.

The charge against Alfredo Messina was, effectively, that he dropped Hindin off in the West End of an evening and financed his comfortable life style on her earnings. He denied even knowing that she was a prostitute, although they had lived together for eight years, saying that he imagined she went to see her mother or to the cinema on the nights she was not in Wembley.

Alfredo was tried at the Old Bailey in May 1951, prosecuted by Christmas Humphreys and Mervyn Griffiths-Jones, both later to become judges, in front of Mr Justice Cassels. Enough emerged about his financial arrangements to give an idea of the scope of the Messina operation. He had bank accounts with the Bank Italo Egyptiano, the Banque de Commerce in Brussels, Barclays Bank in Gibraltar and Barclays Bank in Paris as well as money held in a safe-deposit box in Selfridges department store. He also had accounts in Casablanca and

Messina
brothers
Alfredo (left)
and Carmelo.

Tangier. Much was made of the fact that he had paid £987 10s for a mink coat for Mrs Hindin in 1945.

Messina's version of events was that Mahon saw the 'money' in his safe – with three diamond rings, a champagne swizzle stick and a gold fountain pen – and called his assistant Bert Foster into the room and announced that he was going to charge Messina with bribery. The jury did not believe him. Mr Justice Cassels was equally disapproving. He summed up, allowing himself the indulgence of some judicial wordplay but making it plain what he thought of the defendant: 'It is perfectly right and proper that you should be invited to let pass through your minds the reflection that it would be unlikely that a police officer, who could have no other interest in this case other than discharging his duty would stoop so low – as well as stooping low to get money out of the safe – as to pull out of the safe £200 and then round and say to this man "I am now going to charge you with bribery".' Before sentence, the judge delivered a stern rebuke: 'You thought that so far as the police of this country were concerned, you could do anything. You are an evil man.' Alfredo was gaoled for two years on each charge, to run concurrently, and fined £500.

Attilio meanwhile slipped back into the country and set up home in Chalfont St Giles in Buckinghamshire with one of the leading members of their team, Robena Torrance who was a prostitute. He was gaoled briefly in 1959 under the Sexual Offences Act but escaped deportation to Italy when the Italian government refused to accept him. John du Rose, one of the detectives on the case who later became a Deputy Assistant Commissioner at the Yard, recalled searching Attilio's flat and finding a book called *The Road to Buenos Aires*, which gave details of how procurement and prostitution functioned. Sentencing him, the recorder, Gerald Dibson, said: 'You made a sumptuous but revolting living from the suffering bodies of the women you trapped, seduced and reduced to a form of slavery. You caused great suffering and it is only right that you should suffer.'

Eugenio and Carmelo shifted their operation to Brussels, where they recruited Belgian women, but were arrested there in 1955 in possession of loaded revolvers and stood trial in Tournai in 1956. Eugenio was gaoled for seven years but Carmelo, now in poor health, was sentenced to nine months for passport and firearms offences. He was deported and moved to Ireland before finding his way back to England under a false name, Carlos Marino, and with a Cuban passport. He was arrested, gaoled and deported to Rome where he died six months later at the age of forty-three. Attilio managed to lie low in Bourne End, Buckinghamshire, where he had a house called, appropriately enough, Hideaway and affected the manner of an English country gent in tweeds and cap, but he was eventually deported to Italy. Salvatore moved to Switzerland and only Alfredo remained in England. He died in Brentford in 1963.

Remarkably, the Messinas' operation survived some of these upheavals. The brothers controlled it from France and the prostitutes travelled to Paris to make their payments. Initially Marthe Watts assisted but, as she wrote, 'I could not help feeling a sense of pity and remorse as I thought of my own young days and saw these foolish young creatures deceived into a new way of life that could only bring them unhappiness.'

Messina relatives took on some of the business. Anthony Micalleff, who operated from a boarding-house in Earls Court, was targeted by both the police and the press. In 1958 he was found guilty of allowing the Norfolk Hotel to be used as a brothel and also of permitting his children to be there while it was so used. He was fined £100. That year there were no fewer than 16 900 arrests for prostitution in London.

The Maltese connection survived well. Joe 'Mantini' Spiteri, who came to London as a young man in 1952 and was gaoled with the Messinas, was so innocent that when he first saw prostitutes in the West End he thought they were well-dressed beggars for why else would they be approaching people in the street? The women stayed willingly with the Maltese men, he says, preferring them to the less hot-blooded Englishmen.

The vice world also became more overtly violent as people like Tommy Smithson arrived on the scene. Smithson, a rangy Liverpudlian, ex-boxer and ex-stoker in the merchant navy, first emerged as a force to be reckoned with in 1953. He had protected one of the main Maltese vice operators, George Caruana, a handsome man said to look like Tony Curtis, from an attack by a heavy called Slip Sullivan, organized, so one version has it, by Gypsy Hill, Billy Hill's paramour. Sullivan was badly slashed about the arm and throat and Smithson was summoned to the Black Cat factory at Camden Town, according to his old ally Jim Barnett, who tells this dramatic version of the attack: 'There was Moshe Blueboy, Billy Hill, Jackie Spot and they said look, Tommy, you know you're carrying a gun, give us the gun. He gave them the gun and Billy Hill hit him over the head with it.'

At that stage, says Barnett, a furniture van arrived and eight to ten men poured out including Sonny Sullivan, Slip's brother.

Smithson nearly lost, literally, an arm and a leg as the attackers slashed and cut him: 'You could put fingers in the scars in his arms and legs, where they tried to cut it off. Then they threw him over a railway embankment.' One account suggests he was dumped outside the National Temperance Hospital, another that a small child spotted him and summoned help. Spot, for whom Smithson ran a Soho club, made financial amends for the attack and for Smithson's refusal to help the police.

Known for his fearlessness, his scarred face and his padded shoulders, for a while Smithson ran the deceptively-named Publishers' Club and a bookie in Soho. His main money, however, came from protection rackets and his practice was to cream a shilling in the pound off all bets in the spielers under his control. The protection was double-sided: no other villains attacked the premises and the police would only raid by appointment. As Jim Barnett, his partner, recalls: 'The police would tell us when they were going to come so we would arrange to have a few friends round, a little money on the table, next to nothing. Somebody would be carrying the rent book and he would be the one who went in front of the magistrate. After he'd been pinched a couple of times, someone else would carry the book.'

Some of the magistrates were clearly well aware of the charade played out in front of them. One, Roland Thomas at Marlborough Street court, responded to one rent book carrier who wished him a happy Christmas in court: 'Merry Christmas to you, too, but it's still £90 and nine guineas costs – but don't worry, there's a man at the back of the court who'll be only too pleased to pay the fine for you.'

Smithson's punishment for offenders was less gentle and many of the Maltese lived in fear of him. Although guns were rarely used, Jim Barnett explains that there was no shortage of alternatives: 'A wall is a marvellous weapon. You ram someone's head into a wall, that's a pretty heavy thing to hit them with. Tables, heavy ashtrays, chairs, your hands, your feet. And another good weapon is to drive yourself raving mad.'

The 'mad' act was invariably successful and the owners of clubs and brothels paid up regularly. The enforcers lived a crazy life of little sleep, purple hearts and black coffee, breakfast at the corner shop, visits to the Turkish baths where they would throw away their dirty underwear and shirts and then a plunge back into the day. Money changed hands swiftly in Soho in those days: clients paid prostitutes who paid pimps who gambled the money and paid protection and would be out hunting for more money all within a few hours. Smithson's cut, often as much as £500 a night from the clubs, was also squandered on fast living and, according to Barnett, through his generosity to those down on their luck. Smithson was not above taking money from people to beat others up and then splitting the money with his intended victim and organizing a bogus fight to satisfy all sides. On one occasion he 'beat up' Barnett for £200 on the instructions of a bent Flying Squad officer.

According to Barnett, Smithson grew jealous of Hill's power, started pressuring people too heavily and demanding too much money, upsetting many people. In June 1956, ten days after Fraser, Warren and Co. had been jailed for the attack on Spot, Smithson was shot dead in a lodging-house in Carlton Vale in Maida Vale, West London. As the *Daily Mirror* had it, he was 'murdered Chicago-style, in broad daylight ... the crêpe-soled killers walked in Indian file. In the upstairs room at Number 88, there were two dull "plops".' An indication of the importance with which such events were treated at the time is the fact that it was reported by no less the nine members of the *Daily Express* Crime Bureau.

Smithson's widow, Jessie, who had left him when he joined the gangs, said: 'His wasted life should be a warning to others ... the time for tears was many years ago.' In Leytonstone, in east London Smithson was given what was then becoming the ritual criminal's funeral, complete with limousines, wreaths inscribed 'to a gentleman' and dark glasses for the mourners.

Zoe Progl, a fraudster, thief and general good-time girl, who called herself the 'Queen of the Underworld', recalled Smithson's demise: 'Tommy's death seemed to have a peculiarly stultifying effect upon all the prominent members of the underworld and so many of his friends, including me, for some time lost the urge to graft and tended to live on the proceeds of past jobs while we drank in various groups and mourned the passing of a friend.'

There were almost as many theories as to why Smithson died as there were scars on his body. Barnett believes that the Maltese had become tired of paying Smithson off and organized his murder, which Barnett did not approve but accepted: 'If you were having rows with Tommy Smithson, you had to kill him. He was somebody that had had so much damage to him, nothing stopped him any more.' He believes that the message for the British gangsters was: 'Watch out for the Malts, they will retaliate.' Joe 'Mantini' Spiteri agrees: 'Everyone was pleased about it, they felt more relaxed.'

Certainly Smithson had had an argument with Caruana, from whom he wanted money, possibly for his friend Fay Sadler, of Pen Club fame, who had been arrested because of his bouncing cheques. There had been a row and Caruana had been slashed with a pair of scissors. The police theory was that Smithson was becoming an irritation to two new vice organizers, Frank Mifsud and Bernie Silver, possibly blackmailing them, and that they wanted him off the scene, with the added advantage of having Caruana implicated; Caruana was believed to be branching out on his own, against the wishes of Silver and Mifsud. The murder was, according to detective Bert Wickstead, 'A landmark inasmuch as it let every other contender for the vice position in the West End know that the Syndicate [Silver and Mifsud] were in poll position and would brook no interference to thwart their powers.'

But the real reason for the murder was much more mundane, according to the man who actually pulled the trigger, Phillip Ellul. Smithson had previously tried to recruit Ellul to his protection team but had been rebuffed. Ellul, who now lives on welfare in an apartment just off Broadway in San Francisco, remembers Smithson having a fight with Caruana after which Ellul and he had squared up to each other with knives. The moment passed but Ellul then heard that Smithson had been looking for him with a gun.

'So I thought to myself – mmm – and went and got me a gun,' says Ellul. He lay in wait for Smithson to appear at his normal gambling haunts but saw no sign of him for ten days. With his colleagues he set off for Maida Vale, looking for Caruana and not expecting to find Smithson: 'I knocked on the door. It was nothing like they said in court. I didn't go there to kill him, I didn't know he was there.' A woman opened the door and told them that Smithson was upstairs.

'He was sitting on a chair with a little pair of scissors,' recalls Ellul. 'I said he had a pair of scissors that big but that wasn't true. I was going to let it go at that because sometimes I'm looking for somebody and I'm mad, ready to explode inside and then the next minute I might be buying them coffee.

'I said – "Listen, Tom, you carry a gun, you use it. I'm carrying one and I'm going to use it." And I just – BANG – shot him in the shoulder. He said "Phillip!" So I cocked it and it jammed. So I hit him and he went right over the bed.' Ellul left the room to try and fix the gun and Smithson locked the door and shouted 'That man's crazy!'

Victor Spampinato, Ellul's confederate, and another Maltese heavy, tried to calm things but Ellul kicked the door in – 'One kick, you get the strength. I just walked in, put the gun to his neck and BANG. I said let's go.

'Smithson's behind me, he's bleeding. I said "Now you're satisfied. It had to come to this." I never had any qualms about what happened there.' He believed his dignity required him to use his gun once he had produced it. He borrowed £2000 from Caruana who, according to Ellul, knew nothing about it and fled with Spampinato to Manchester. They read the newspaper reports of the killing over breakfast the following day in a Maltese café on Trafford Road.

'We were busy looking at all those papers. It said that Scotland Yard knows who did it. They said "he died in his shoes" and all that carry on. So I thought to myself, well, Smithson's dead now.'

A hunt was launched for Ellul and Spampinato. Both were lured back to London apparently on the understanding that a deal had been done and that they would face only a manslaughter charge and a probable five-year maximum sentence. But, after they had given themselves up, murder charges were placed against them. At their trial prosecuting counsel Reginald Seaton QC warned the jury that many of the characters they would encounter were 'by no means admirable persons or useful citizens'.

Ellul, who had told Smithson to 'say your last prayers' before he executed him, was convicted and sentenced to death, being reprieved forty-eight hours before the hangman was due to arrive and eventually serving eleven years. Spampinato was cleared. Spiteri, who was meant to be part of the hit team, had a lucky escape: he had been chatting up an old girlfriend called Sharon when the other two set off from a Cable Street café on their errand and was too late for the kill. But more attention was focused on the two men eventually to be charged with plotting the murder and paying for it: Silver and Mifsud, who were credited with filling the vacuum left by the Messinas.

Silver, who had been born in Stoke Newington in north-east London, had been in the parachute regiment during the war until he was discharged on medical grounds in 1943 and had worked as a market trader and jobbing builder before moving into vice, where he was one of the Messinas' apprentices. Initially in the fifties he had a brothel in Brick Lane in east London and a strip club in Soho's Brewer Street but he was expanding speedily. He had expensive tastes and was in the process of buying a £27 000 yacht at the time of his arrest on vice charges in 1973. He claimed to be an 'estate agent and art dealer'. Mifsud was an aggressive and erratic former traffic policeman from Malta. Spitteri says he was a generous soul, forever buying drinks, although he 'used to dress like a bum, loaded with money but always dressed like a bum. Torn shirt, maybe even torn trousers.'

In the sixties the two men virtually controlled Soho's vice rackets. They owned around twenty strip clubs between them and made a fortune on the backs of the young women who rented their properties. They used strong-arm tactics to move people out of their properties if it interfered with their 'flat farming' and were said to have set fire to the staircase of one flat they wanted vacated.

There were hiccoughs. Mifsud and Caruana were prosecuted under the Metropolitan Police Act for running an unlicensed theatre, namely the Stripperama in Greek Street, but were rescued by the Lord Chamberlain, whose decision that stripping could not be classified as a 'stage play or dramatic entertainment' may well have been true in the rather joyless establishments run by the men. For more than fifteen years the Syndicate flourished, making what the police claimed was as much as £100 000 a week and becoming the 'Rolls-Royces of the criminal fraternity'.

The vice world had its ear to the ground and in October 1973, before Bert Wickstead's first planned raid in response to new intelligence, Mifsud and Silver and their associates fled, tipped off by a policeman. 'I then enlisted the aid of the press,' wrote Wickstead later. He persuaded them to print stories with headlines like 'The Raid That Never Was' and to give the impression that the operation had been abandoned. This ruse appeared to work because the crew drifted back from abroad and were mostly in their old haunts when the real raid took place in December 1973 and 170 people were held.

Five of them were found in the Scheherazade Club, which was in full swing and where, as Wickstead recalls, a 'buxom blonde' was singing. Guests, staff and band were rounded up and taken in buses for questioning at Limehouse police station: 'I put them all in the charge room and they were thoroughly enjoying themselves, the band was playing and everybody was singing.' Mifsud was not among them. He was later arrested in a tent on the Swiss-Austrian border and booked into a private Swiss psychiatric hospital where he claimed to be suffering from a mental condition that would make travel back to England unwise.

However, the vice charges did stick and in September 1974 Silver and Mifsud found themselves at the Old Bailey, accused of

Above: Frank Mifsud (centre) with Bert Wickstead (left) after extradition from Switzerland in 1975. Right: Bernie Silver, accused of running 'the Syndicate' with Mifsud.

running what was described as the 'Soho Vice Syndicate' and of making £100 000 from their 'slaughterhouses of love', as Henry Miller called brothels.

In what was the biggest vice trial since the Messina days, it was claimed by Michael Corkery for the prosecution that this was a 'vicious empire ... an unsavoury world of prostitutes, ponces and pimps' that rented out flats to prostitutes at what were then seen as exorbitant rates – £100 a week for a little room above a strip club. Witnesses reeled off the exotic names of the clubs alleged to have housed prostitution: the Perfumed Garden and the Taboo, the Casbah and the Gigi. One of the prosecution witnesses, Frank Dyer, Maltese despite his name, claimed that when police raids became a problem, 'a man at the Home Office was fixed to have it stopped'. Dyer said that he himself had been threatened, beaten up and offered £20 000 to disappear and not give evidence. Joe 'Mantini', who also gave colourful evidence, accusing defence counsel Michael Havers of being a 'ponce', claims that he was offered £10 000 not to go into the witness box and threatened with death if he did. Years later he was still carrying a knife, spike and hammer for self-protection.

On 19 December 1974, after a sixty-three-day trial, Silver and six other Maltese men were gaoled, Silver for six years with a fine of £30 000. The judge, Lord Justice Geoffrey Lane, told them: 'The profits you reaped were enormous ... the only mitigating fact I can see is that there is no suggestion that you drove any girl into prostitution. You employed every device and artifice which your considerable intelligence enabled you to use in order to try and escape detection and to avoid conviction.' The court appeared not to have been moved by Silver's claim that he had once organized prostitutes to cheer up the British troops in Northern Ireland, and that he had been allowed to run a brothel there in the hope that it would lead to information about the IRA.

Smaller fry, Anthony Mangion and Emmanuel Bartolo, were each gaoled for five years with Mangion's loyal sister shouting from the public gallery 'Don't push him, he's a good man,' before being hustled out, screaming abuse. Frank Melito, Frank's younger brother Joseph and Romeo Saliba were also gaoled for acting as front men. Reports of the time claimed that £50 million had passed through the Syndicate's hands to be stashed in Swiss banks, but little evidence was advanced for such vast sums.

Bert Wickstead had meanwhile been reinvestigating the ancient Smithson case and decided that Mifsud and Silver must have ordered it. Both men were to face murder charges. Silver was convicted on 8 July 1975, a conviction quashed on appeal on 18 October 1976. It is fair to Silver to say that he was also exonerated both by Ellul, the killer, and by contemporaries who have no hatchet to grind on his behalf and who believe he was wrongly charged.

Spampinato was traced to Malta and gave powerful evidence against Silver and Mifsud at the Old Street committal hearing. He arrived straight from the airport and cut a dramatic figure, dressed all in black and with a Fu Manchu moustache. He said that he had been given the message that 'this punk [Smithson] has got to be exterminated' and described in detail how Ellul had shot Smithson. He recalled the sight of 'thick blood like liver from his mouth'.

Wickstead had been to the United States in pursuit of Ellul, who had served his sentence for Smithson's murder, and found him, remarkably enough, after making a television appeal. A 'true crime' magazine had printed Ellul's photograph and he was spotted by a diligent reader, in a hostel in San Francisco. Eventually he was brought back to England and asked to give evidence.

But the time awaiting the big drop had made him a nervous customer and, although the police let him go to a betting-shop every day to calm his nerves, he said that he wished to return to the States for medical reasons because of his ulcers. He never came back to give evidence and Silver in the end walked free, as did Mifsud.

Silver's troubles were not over. In 1978 he was deported from Malta, then a popular watering-hole for criminals. Back in England the *People* were still on his case – they had described him as a 'human vulture' as early as 1953 – and announced in August 1979 that 'Godfather Bernie Is Back in Business', citing half a dozen clubs with Silver connections and suitably exotic names. He suffered personal unhappiness when his wife, Albertine Falzon, a French former prostitute, committed suicide by jumping from her room in Soho.

Mifsud faced other charges but was cleared of conspiracy to murder Smithson, convicted (but on appeal cleared) of attempting to rig an Old Bailey trial by suborning a Soho hot-dog seller to give false evidence and had his five-year sentence and £50 000 fine set aside. In the original trial Mifsud was alleged to have approached a man to implicate Anthony Cauchi, a club rival in Soho, in an explosion at one of Mifsud's Greek Street clubs.

Mifsud and Spampinato retired to Malta where the former berates those curious about his past with threats of legal action and the latter looks after his elderly mother.

The years when the Syndicate was all-powerful had seen the vice world changing for reasons other than arrests and gaoling. Public attitudes had shifted. 'In the late forties and fifties, the ordinary member of the public regarded vice as something which ought to be put down,' says former judge Sir Frederick Lawton. 'But later many people took the view that the kind of activities which I used to have to prosecute ought not to be prosecuted at all.' He cited the 1967 legislation concerning homosexuality as an example of this change in attitude.

The arrival of the Street Offences Act on 16 August 1959 had driven many prostitutes off the streets, the police remarking that it was like a 'vacuum cleaner'. Instead of the £2 fine for soliciting there was £25 for a first offence, and double that for a second one. The sentence for a third offence was gaol. Prosecutions for soliciting in the first quarter after the Act came into effect were down by a remarkable 90 per cent, from more than 4000 to just 464. But the trade – and there were estimated to be 5000 prostitutes working in London at the time – moved speedily elsewhere. A euphemistically named *Ladies Directory* appeared with photographs and telephone numbers of prostitutes. Its publisher was convicted of conspiring to corrupt public morals.

'Near-beer' joints, which were not licensed, acted as pick-up places for prostitutes. Advertisements rich in *double entendre* started appearing in newsagents and in telephone booths. Many strip clubs were able to offer prostitution services, and establishments that charged enormous sums for bottles of bogus bubbly, on the often false understanding that a woman would be provided, also flourished.

New figures emerged on the scene and disappeared: 'Big Jeff' Phillips became a millionaire through the porn trade and survived by paying substantial backhanders to the police. But in 1975, after serving a brief prison sentence and naming corrupt officers, he killed himself because of an unrequited love affair.

Others made their profits from renting out parts of property empires for prostitution. One of these was John Gaul, gaoled and fined £25 000 in 1962 for living off the earnings of prostitutes. He was later to become better known when his wife was killed by hitmen. After Gaul's imprisonment Alec 'The Count' Kostanda took over some of his properties until he himself was convicted and gaoled for six months. In west London, one of the people who profited from the climate was racketeer landlord Peter Rachman. There was male prostitution, too, but on a tiny scale, although the police believed

194

that Hungarian refugees in the late fifties found it an easy way to make money.

Soho remained an area of vice up to the eighties, when the police, in co-operation with the local Westminster Council, clamped down on the many peep-shows and porn clubs. By this time, prostitution had moved off the streets of the West End. The top end of the market worked as 'escorts' for hundreds of pounds a night, catering to high-rolling and often foreign businessmen, while the bottom end moved to Finsbury Park, Streatham and Kings Cross, the place where, in 1991, the Director of Public Prosecutions, Sir Alan Green, was stopped for kerb-crawling.

But a development had already taken place which was to change the face of vice in London. Working hand in sweaty glove with corrupt police officers, one of the main pornographers of the seventies, one Jimmy Humphreys, was emerging.

Humphreys, a crook but not a major one, was among the first to profit from the sixties boom in pornography. He moved into Soho clubland with his wife Rusty, an attractive and self-willed stripper, who had the distinction of having modelled industrial safety boots on factory training films. He had his early brushes with the police, paying over money, he complained later, to a detective called Harry Challenor. The policeman, for his part, denied taking the bribes but was to reappear in the annals of the underworld soon enough. Humphreys' neighbour in his Soho club was Silver and it was Silver who was to be helpful when he ran into problems with expanding his empire, helping out with advice on the necessary bribes that had to be paid.

Prostitution and the clubs provided a combination of illegality and cash that was to prove too tempting to the very people whose task it was to control them, who soon found themselves swimming with the tide rather than against it. A vice that was to be as corrosive as any being offered by strip clubs or pimps turned out to be a corruption at the very heart of the police themselves.

11

GOOD EGGS AND BAD APPLES

Police Corruption and the Underworld

Disgraced former head
of the Flying Squad, ex-
Commander Ken Drury.

*D*etective Sergeant Harold 'Tanky' Challenor, was a resourceful man. He had served in the Special Air Services with distinction during the Second World War and played an active role in the Flying Squad before being moved to West End Central, at the heart of London's crime in the early sixties. Always imaginative, on one occasion he persuaded a small-time crook to take him to a criminals' pub so that working villains could be pointed out to him. Since the man was not prepared to be seen with a policeman, Challenor 'got hold of a woman's wig, borrowed one of Doris' [his wife's] longest skirts, a roll-neck sweater, high-heeled shoes, nylon stockings and a cloak-like coat and handbag.' Heavily made up, he sat nursing his gin and tonic while the villain nodded at the professional heisters and hoisters present. Challenor's cover was nearly blown when he entered the gents by mistake and told a startled drinker that, 'I've recently had a miscarriage and must still be a bit light-headed'. He was even propositioned, and rescued by his 'boyfriend' for the night, who kept up the deception and called him a 'silly old cow'.

By the time he had established himself in the West End, Challenor was being called worse things than a silly old cow. He already had a reputation in the Soho patch in which he worked for what could be euphemistically described as eccentric behaviour. He had for some years been suffering from a mental disorder which had been noted by his colleagues but never confronted. On 11 July 1963 there was a demonstration against Queen Frederika who was staying at Claridges Hotel and who was seen as symbolic of the repressive right-wing regime then in power in Greece. Challenor, furious at what he saw as impertinent anti-royal activities, arrested a number of the participants, gave them some whacks and planted half-bricks on them with the words: 'There you are, me old darling. Carrying an offensive weapon can get you two years.'

One man he arrested, Donald Rooum, who was a member of the National Council of Civil Liberties (now Liberty), was able to prove that since there was no brick dust in his pockets he could not have concealed a brick there and he was cleared. Challenor was suspended and eventually stood trial in June 1964 with three young detectives. He observed later that, 'The whores danced outside the Old Bailey when Oscar Wilde was gaoled, glad to see a menace to their profession out of the way. I'm pretty certain that though there may not have been quite such an exuberant display of relief when I was publicly disgraced, a few glasses were raised in the clip-joints and strip clubs by the men who controlled organized crime and prostitution in the West End.' His three colleagues were convicted of conspiring to pervert the course of justice and gaoled for a total of eleven years. Challenor was found unfit to plead.

He was clearly not the full sovereign. He had convinced himself and his wife that he was being prepared for a secret mission by being hypnotized and brainwashed and as he travelled to Brixton in the prison van during his trial he would chant to himself, mantra-like, 'Who Dares Wins', the SAS motto.

In his memoirs, Challenor says that he has no recollection of planting the bricks and fabricating evidence and is adamant that corruption was not his practice when dealing with vice in Soho. Plenty of the area's denizens claimed otherwise. Challenor said that these were the sort of men who, when on trial, would suffer from what was called in the Met a 'fit of dock asthma' during which they would fix their gaze on the jury and roll their eyes while a police officer was giving evidence, to convey the impression that the officer was lying. All too often they may have been right. Challenor admits that he was not averse to delivering a right-hander when he felt one was merited and, when he felt someone was due for a prison sentence, he would brush their lapel and say genially 'I thought I saw some porridge on your suit'.

Although psychiatrist William Sargent agreed that Challenor was 'mad as a hatter', others took a more cynical view and for a while pretending to be mad in court was known as 'doing a Challenor'.

But Challenor's manic dishonesties were as nothing compared to a much greater cancer that had grown inside the detective force of the Metropolitan Police by the early sixties. Bribery had long been endemic. Safe-breaker Eddie Chapman reckoned that bail and adjusted evidence could always be bought at a price and said he once paid a policeman £30 000 to say in a pre-trial statement that he would be available to give evidence on his behalf. The case was duly dropped. Criminals of Chapman's era who wanted the same favours used a middleman, often a taxi-driver called Jack the Liar, who would arrange the hand-overs.

The judge who was to gaol Charlie Richardson, Sir Frederick Lawton, also has his theories about corrupt officers. He believes that the rot set in because of wartime regulations which exposed the police to bribery when businessmen and industrialists were able to buy their way out of trouble if they had committed offences.

Eric Mason, a major gangland figure from the fifties through to the seventies, recalls: 'I've paid the police plenty of money over the years to get bail or lessen the charge or even knock a few of my previous off before sentencing. There's hundreds of ways they elicit money from you and that was part and parcel of your business and you accepted that.' He remembers a local superintendent in Cardiff, where he was held for a bank robbery, remarking on the London detectives and how they could afford 500-guinea suits and double Scotches. 'The Cardiff top coppers knew that every copper in London was bent.' Sir Frederick also recalls a man who had made a 'confession' full of Cockney slang and Yiddish expressions, but who was a well-educated Pole. The case fell and led to a successful action for malicious prosecution.

'The practice of police putting words into the mouth of a suspect who they're arresting started in the fifties,' says Sir Frederick. He recalls one sergeant whose suspects would, on arrest, always say: 'Blimey, who's grassed me this time?' This was regarded as a classic verbal in that the statement immediately suggested that the man was both a member of the criminal classes, because he knew the word 'grass', and that he had been in trouble before.

The Yard hierarchy took the Nelsonian view. When, in 1955, Superintendent Bert Hannam produced a report on corruption, particularly in West End Central police station, the Metropolitan Commissioner, Sir John Nott-Bower, not only ignored its findings but went personally to the station to stand on a chair and reassure the troops that he did not believe a word of it.

While the payment of bribes to detectives may have been routine in the sixties and seventies for career criminals, it was in the specialized areas of drugs and pornography that the most systematic forms of police corruption emerged. Both fields offered enormous profits to their protagonists, who were happy to pay a percentage if it ensured that they were not bothered by the law. Public ambivalence as to whether drugs, in particular cannabis, and pornography should have been illegal anyway further confused the issue because the police could reassure themselves that they were essentially condoning what many saw as 'victimless' crimes.

It was in this climate that *The Times* on 29 November 1969 published a remarkable story, by reporters Julian Mounter and Garry Lloyd, about police corruption. It stated baldly: 'We have, we believe, proved that at least three detectives are taking large sums of money in exchange for dropping charges, for being lenient with evidence offered in court, for allowing a criminal to work unhindered.'

The article named three officers: Sergeant John Symonds,

Detective Inspector Bernard Robson and Detective Sergeant Gordon Harris. *The Times* reporters had tape-recorded and photographed the officers' meetings with a small-time criminal called Michael Perry. One of the telling remarks in the taped conversations was Symonds saying: 'We've got more villains in our game than you've got in yours, you know.' But the most memorable snippet was when Symonds said reassuringly: 'Always let me know straight away if you need anything because I know people everywhere. Because I'm in a little firm in a firm. Don't matter where, anywhere in London I can get on the phone to someone I know I can trust, that talks the same as me. And if he's not the right person that can do it, he'll know the person that can.'

It was this theme of a 'firm within a firm' that was to send tremors through the Yard over the next three years as a tale of cynical and pervasive corruption was slowly and painfully revealed. By the end of this time, a number of policemen were behind bars, the work of three major squads had been mightily damaged and the reputation of the police had been severely dented.

The initial inquiry into *The Times*'s allegations was entrusted at an operational level to Detective Chief Superintendent Bill Moody. With hindsight, it was a breathtaking appointment: Moody was himself one of the Yard's most corrupt officers and would follow the men he was investigating to the dock of the Old Bailey within five years. The flashy Moody, who drove a Lancia purchased from a porn-dealer friend, must have enjoyed the irony of investigating officers whose dishonesty was almost amateurish in comparison with his own.

The task of overall head of the inquiry was given to Frank Williamson, one of the inspectors of constabulary, Home-Office-appointed officials whose duty it is to oversee the police. A former chief constable from Cumbria, Williamson had made no secret of his distrust of some of the Met's habits. The Home Secretary, James Callaghan, indicated that he should report either directly to him or to the Commissioner of Scotland Yard, Sir John Waldron. Williamson later said that he found his inquiries frustrated through 'a misguided loyalty to the Criminal Investigation Department, arising from a deep-rooted desire to avoid publicity from prosecution of police officers.' He said that he believed there were three types of officers at the Yard: those who were corrupt, those who were honest but did nothing and those who were too stupid to realize that there was any corruption in the first place.

The cornered Symonds tried his best shots: first he threatened libel actions against *The Times*, then he concocted a story that the whole tale had been fabricated by the Richardson gang as a way of settling scores over his (minimal) role in their demise. But despite attempts to impugn the honesty of the reporters and a battery of sound experts who sought to cast doubt on the taped evidence, Robson and Harris were gaoled on 3 March 1972 for seven and six years. Symonds went, in the argot of the underworld, 'on his toes' and fled the country, reputedly to southern Africa, but gave himself up seven years later and was gaoled for eighteen months.

The seven-week trial cost around £500 000 and the bribes the men were convicted of taking totalled a mere £275. But the story of what prosecuting counsel John Mathew called 'complete and utter corruption' was a pebble thrown into a pool of dishonesty and the ripples were about to wash through the Yard. Indeed, they were already lapping at the edges of the Drugs Squad.

A London heroin addict called Kevin Healy, facing a cannabis charge in Oxford, had been recruited as an informer and encouraged to set up a large LSD deal. However, he felt uneasy about the police's methods; he had been part-paid with some of the drugs seized. He reported his misgivings to the Oxford police, who relayed the story to the Home Office. The first official concerns about the work of the squad were now being privately aired.

Healy had come into contact with the man who was in effective charge of the growing squad, Detective Chief Inspector Vic Kelaher, who after time in the Flying Squad had become the youngest DCI in the Yard's history. He and his loyal deputy Detective Sergeant 'Nobby' Pilcher relied heavily on informants and were making a mark for themselves as a new can-do team who provided high-profile convictions. Pilcher was known as someone who loved carrying out raids on the famous, most notably John Lennon and Yoko Ono who were raided in 1968 in an over-the-top operation in which officers burst in SAS-style through the windows. The team's methods were well known to the hippie dealers of Notting Hill but complaints from that direction could be safely ignored.

At the time, relations between Customs and Excise and the police were at a low ebb; the former regarded the latter as being, at best, flash and superficial in their approach and at worst, dishonest and corrupt. It was no accident that the game started to unravel for Kelaher when Customs targeted Basil Sands, a cannabis dealer, who was gaoled for seven years but who claimed loudly that he had been acting with Kelaher's knowledge and agreement in order to snare the main dealers in the operation. Kelaher was not prosecuted at this stage but was moved to desk duties, which he carried out until he left the force three years later.

But he had not escaped. On 5 November 1972 the *Sunday Times* published a detailed exposé of the Drugs Squad and two days later Kelaher was charged with conspiring to pervert the course of justice, along with officers Prichard, Lilley, Acworth and McGibbon. Prichard and Lilley were gaoled for eighteen months, Pilcher, who had initially fled to Australia, for four years and Kelaher was allowed to resign from the police on medical grounds. Mr Justice Melford Stevenson made what was to become a famous sentencing speech in which he told the shamed officers: 'You poisoned the wells of criminal justice and set about it deliberately. What is equally bad is that you have betrayed your comrades in the Metropolitan Police Force which enjoys the respect of the civilized world – what remains of it – and not the least grave aspect of what you have done is provide material for the crooks, cranks and do-gooders who unite to attack the police whenever opportunity occurs.'

But if the revelations about the Drugs Squad were messy, what was to happen to the Obscene Publications Squad – the Dirty Squad as it was presciently known – was muckier still.

The scandal arose from the corrupt associations between the leading Soho pornographers, who in the sixties were starting to reap the harvest of blue films and dirty magazines, and senior officers who were paid to cast a blind eye to the activities, tip off the dealers when raids were imminent or eliminate competitors in a cynical abuse of power.

At the heart of the relationship which was eventually to fell the Dirty Squad was Jimmy Humphreys, who had seen the opportunities on offer from the vice world of Soho and was now, with the help of his wife Rusty, firmly establishing himself in that world. The couple's timing was impeccable and they were soon profiting heavily from three clubs which they ran with as much flair as was possible in the seedy backwaters of Soho. One of the dancers Rusty hired was Norma Levy, who later gained notoriety as the prostitute involved in the downfall of the cabinet minister Lord Lambton.

Humphreys had arrived on a scene in which vice racketeers Bernie Silver and Frank Mifsud were already operating successfully with the knowledge of the police. Humphreys and Silver used to vie with each other as to who could provide detectives with the best tables at charity boxing events at the Grosvenor House hotel in Park Lane.

Senior CID officer Commander Wally Virgo and the resourceful

Moody, head of the Obscene Publications Squad, were alleged to have received regular payments for their help. Virgo's rate was said to be £2000 a month with a 'Christmas bonus' of £2000. Humphreys' scrupulous diary-keeping indicated that £53 000 had been paid to Virgo and Moody in sixteen months. In addition, as sweeteners, they and their subordinates had been treated to holidays, cars and clothes. The pornographers were happy to pay since it safeguarded their interests and their profits were high enough for the bribes to be seen as no more than the normal expenses of running a business. They provided the occasional necessary bodies – usually harmless small fry – so that the squad would be perceived as carrying out its job. But the police got greedy. One pornographer, John Mason, noted that his monthly payments rose swiftly from £60 to £1000. What the police had done was to create, in the words of Mr Justice Mars-Jones when they finally came to trial, 'a vast protection racket'.

In February 1972, the remarkable hospitality arrangements for the police were subjected to intense scrutiny: the *Sunday People* showed the head of the Metropolitan Police's Flying Squad, Commander Ken Drury, on holiday in Cyprus with none other than Mr Jimmy Humphreys. Drury tried to wriggle out of the embarrassment by claiming to the *News of the World* that he had been on the hunt for Ronnie Biggs, the escaped Great Train Robber.

Alas for Drury, Humphreys' diary showed that he had met the commander no less than fifty-eight times, feeding his investment so generously with the profiteroles and pastries of the Soho gâteau trolleys that he felt obliged to buy him an exercise machine to slim off some of the excess bulk.

It transpired that Drury's come-uppance was the work of a gangland figure, Joey Pyle. He had been raided by police searching for Freddie Sewell, who had murdered a Blackpool policeman, and charged with a firearms offence. He was acquitted but apparently 'got the hump' with the Met sufficiently to tip the press off about the Drury-Humphreys relationship.

In the meantime, the new Serious Crimes Squad, established in 1971, was looking into the West End porn world. As they did so, events were unravelling. Peter Garfath, the former lover of Rusty Humphreys, was given a severe slashing in the Dauphin Club in Marylebone in October 1972. It was believed that this was a warning to him to end his relationship with Rusty, who was about to emerge from Holloway gaol where she was serving a brief sentence for a firearms offence.

The attack was to act as a catalyst for the police who were seeking a reason to pounce. Silver and Mifsud had discreetly left the country as they realized, with people being arrested, that the rules were changing. Humphreys fled with a false passport to Amsterdam where the pursuing British police arrested him in December 1973 with the words 'It's all over, Jimmy'. He was gaoled for eight years over the Garfath attack but always pleaded his innocence.

Humphreys then made a series of statements to the police implicating thirty-eight detectives and quoting extensively from his damning diaries. On 28 February 1976 twelve officers were arrested, including Drury, Virgo and Moody. Drury was taken from his home with a blanket over his head.

It was the greatest internal police scandal since the 1877 'trial of the detectives', in which a third of the detective branch at Scotland Yard had been charged with taking bribes. Gilbert Kelland, the officer who had played a major part in cleansing the twentieth century Augean stables, wrote later that, 'We strongly believed that, for the eventual benefit of the force the crow of corruption had to be nailed to the barn door to convince and remind everyone of the need for positive action and eternal vigilance to combat this particular evil.' Of the seventy-four officers investigated, twelve resigned, twenty-eight retired, eight were dismissed and a total of thirteen were gaoled.

Virgo and Moody were convicted and gaoled for twelve years and had to find costs of £15 000 and £10 000. Virgo was cleared on appeal on the grounds that the judge had misdirected the jury on corroboration evidence. He died a few years later. Drury was gaoled in 1977 for eight years and died in 1984. A group of junior officers received lesser sentences. At the end of the Drury trial Commissioner Sir Robert Mark commented: 'Many police officers, very senior ones, knew what was going on, may have been part of what was going on, could certainly not have been blind to what was going on and are still serving today.' He also remarked sardonically that, 'A good police force is one which catches more criminals than it employs.' The authors (Barry Cox, John Shirley and Martin Short) of the book on the whole saga, *The Fall of Scotland Yard*, summarized the way in which the corruption had become institutionalized: 'Catching small fry specially set up for you by the big fry who were your "friends" was much easier than catching all sizes of fry on your own. Many an honest but overworked detective was seduced by this possibility.'

Not all villains looked down on Virgo. Cat burglar Peter Scott reckoned he was a decent man who had been used by other officers.

Ex-Commander Wally Virgo, accused of turning a blind eye to pornography dealing.

'Wally was really out of his depth. He was manipulated by other officers. I don't think they really thought of it in terms of corruption. They just thought it was a perk.'

Sir Robert Mark had been appointed commissioner in 1972. It was a bold move because essentially he was an outsider. He had started as a policeman in his native Manchester and had been Chief Constable of Leicester for ten years before being brought to the Met in March 1967 as an assistant commissioner, the 'Lone Ranger from Leicester'. To say he was made unwelcome would be an understatement: 'I felt rather like the representative of a leper colony attending the annual garden party of a colonial governor.' When he was elevated to the top job with an aim of 'making virtue fashionable', there were still plenty of officers, mainly detectives, who greeted his appointment with dismay. 'I had served in two provincial forces for thirty years and though I had known wrongdoing, I had never experienced institutionalized wrongdoing, blindness, arrogance and prejudice on anything like the scale accepted as routine at the Met,' was his assessment of his task. In his autobiography *In the Office of Constable* he was moved to quote Hamlet:

The time is out of joint: O cursed spite
That ever I was born to set it right.

Partly because of Sir Robert's strategy of going public with his reforms, the era just prior to his clean-out has been seen as one of the most corrupt in the history of the British police. Certainly, it was a time when policemen appear to have been at their most cynical; but their underworld reputation for routine dishonesty was longstanding, as was public cynicism about police honesty: 'If you want to know the time, ask a policeman' comes from an old music-hall song based on the widely held view that officers stole the watches of drunken toffs they found in the streets.

Sir Robert had already made some changes in his role as assistant commissioner, immediately sacking officers who were convicted of criminal offences. (Incredibly, they had previously been allowed to remain on the payroll until their appeal, invariably unsuccessful, was heard months or even years later.) He also returned to uniform any detective whose disciplinary record suggested that he was unfit to work unsupervized, a source of mild enjoyment to the uniformed officers who, for a number of years, had mistrusted their plainclothes colleagues. During Mark's five years as commissioner, 478 men left the force following, or in anticipation of, disciplinary

**Metropolitan Police Commissioner Sir Robert Mark (right),
'Making virtue fashionable'.**

procedures. Of these, fifty were prosecuted. The vast majority retired in advance of events. The annual rate of departure was around six times higher under Mark than in the immediately preceding years.

Mark identified three main forms of corruption on a sliding scale: the first was charging for bail, suppressing previous convictions and dropping more serious charges; the second affected the more senior officers who were involved in crimes like bank robbery, drugs and obscene publications; and the third applied to officers who believed the system of justice was weighed against them and felt justified in bending the rules. The ranks themselves had a snappier classification: 'Bent for yourself' (taking bribes) or 'bent for the job' (fitting up people who were believed to be guilty but could not be proved so). Paul Condon, who took over as Commissioner of the Metropolitan Police in 1993, was later to describe, without condoning, 'noble cause' corruption, whereby a police officer massaged evidence to ensure the conviction of someone he was sure was guilty.

A newly created body to investigate allegations of police corruption was set up in 1971. It was called first A10 then CIB2 and nicknamed the 'rubber heels', because of its members' supposed habit of creeping up silently on their prey. It was initially headed by a uniformed commander, the hand-picked Ray Anning, thus breaking some of the power of the detective side of the force. Service was limited to two years and all allegations of corruption had to go directly to A10 to prevent the old problem of CID men at the Yard tipping off colleagues in the field.

Mark meanwhile had summoned the representatives of the CID to what they thought would be a placatory discussion. 'I told them that they represented what had long been the most routinely corrupt organization in London, that nothing and no one would prevent me from putting an end to it and that, if necessary, I would put the whole of the CID back into uniform and make a fresh start.' One of the detectives clandestinely taped the chat and leaked it to the press but this strengthened rather than weakened Mark's hand. As far as he was concerned 'the century-old autonomy of the CID had ended'. Home Secretary James Callaghan wrote him a note: 'Dear Commissioner, Quick, decisive, right. All I hoped you would do. Congratulations!'

The next time the notion of police corruption received a wide public airing was in 1978 with Operation Countryman in which officers from the Dorset police force were brought in to investigate allegations of corruption within the detective branch of the Met. Officers from thirteen provincial forces took part in the biggest ever external corruption inquiry into the Metropolitan Police.

It was sparked by allegations made by a supergrass, Geoff Simms, who had been gaoled for ten years for a wages snatch and was facing further trials. He told Regional Crime Squad police in Hertfordshire that police officers had helped to plan robberies in the City of London and that criminals were routinely paying officers for bail and assistance in their trials. Simms, a strange young man who kept his cricket gear and his guns in the boot of his car, suggested that bribed police deliberately stayed away from areas when they knew a robbery was about to take place.

The allegations coincided with rumours circulating in police and underworld circles that officers in London had been indirectly involved in the 1978 robbery of the *Daily Mirror*, in which a guard was killed and £200 000 stolen, in the 1976 payroll snatch at the *Daily Express* in which £175 000 was stolen and in the 1977 robbery at Williams and Glyn Bank in the City in which £225 000 was taken.

More than a hundred officers worked on the inquiry, interviewing criminals, police officers and journalists in a bid to establish the truth of the rumours. Led by Arthur Hambleton, Chief Constable of Dorset, under the operational control of Leonard Burt, his assistant chief constable, Operation Countryman started in a prefabricated building at the back of a Met police station in Camberwell in south London before moving to more secure headquarters in Godalming in Surrey.

After six months, the team had a list of seventy-eight officers from the Met and eighteen from the City of London against whom there were allegations of corruption, perjury and conspiracy. One officer was said to have profited by £40 000 from a bank raid, others had arranged for early parole, it was claimed. Others had been paid thousands for information that would lead to robberies. Even given that some of the allegations might have been malicious or score-settling, they were deeply disturbing.

Alf Sheppard, who acted as a go-between for police and villains, provided the startling information that £80 000 had passed through the hands of Detective Chief Inspector Philip Cuthbert, much of it handed over in a restaurant opposite Bishopsgate police station. He described Cuthbert as 'a criminal who chose to be a policeman' and said that the officer had told him of potential places to rob, including the post office headquarters where Cuthbert claimed to 'know the form'. Said Sheppard: 'He told me he wanted to be rich and very quickly so he could retire and live off the proceeds.' A secret tape-recording showed Cuthbert talking about the extent of corruption and discussing which senior officers he used to 'bung' (bribe).

Cuthbert was the chief catch of the inquiry along with the man described in court as his 'cheerful assistant', John Goldbourn, a former detective sergeant. Cuthbert, an arrogant man and a master of a Freemason's lodge from Brentwood in Essex, was told at his trial on 20 July 1982 by the recorder of London, James Miskin QC: 'Each of you has tried unsuccessfully to pull the wool over these sensible jurors' eyes. You failed.'

But the investigating team, dismissively nicknamed 'the Swedey' by the Met because of its rural origins, had started to encounter problems early in the inquiry. Files would mysteriously disappear and the investigators took to requesting whole batches of documents so that it was unclear which ones they sought. They were not taken over-seriously by many of the Metropolitan wide boys who did not believe – correctly, as it transpired – that they would be able to penetrate the tightly knit lodge mentality of the Met. By 1980 the inquiry was in difficulties. Two senior Scotland Yard men were appointed to the team and the provincial officers, seething at what they saw as a further sidelining of their work, departed. The souvenir tie designed for the Countryman officers tells its own story: it shows a fluttering eagle (the symbol of the Flying Squad) and, beneath it, a little country mouse making a V-sign. (Such ties are often struck to commemorate a major investigation, but usually of a more traditional crime.)

By the end of the inquiry in 1982, £4 million and four years after it had been established in 1978, there was a feeling that the nettle remained ungrasped. Operation Countryman had investigated a total of 200 corruption allegations and submitted forty-one reports to the Director of Public Prosecutions but only four prosecutions were sanctioned. A total of 2000 statements was taken.

After it was all over Hambleton publicly attacked the obstruction he encountered. He claimed that an earlier statement he had made in 1979, suggesting all was well, had been signed to save the inquiry. 'Basically, you may say that we were stopped from cleaning up the Yard,' he said.

In October 1982, the Attorney-General, Sir Michael Havers, suggested that the officers had got 'carried away on a wave of optimism' in their investigation. In his memoirs Sir David McNee, who had been commissioner during the inquiry, is scathing about it. Of Hambleton's complaints he says: 'If they thought their inquiry was being obstructed, all they had to do was tell me. Neither of them ever did.' He also had little respect for the inquiry: 'All sorts of tittle-tattle by criminals, by associates of criminals or by disgruntled complainants was listened to and acted upon ... I was not impressed. Wholly innocent officers were going into the pool of suspects often only on the word of rogues.'

The most significant inquiries into police malpractice since Operation Countryman have concerned the West Midlands serious crime squad based in Birmingham and the Stoke Newington police. The former, carried out between 1989 and 1992, ended with more than a dozen cases brought by the West Midlands police being thrown out on appeal, but no officers convicted of any offences.

The focal allegation of Operation Jackpot, the Stoke Newington inquiry, between 1991 and 1993, was that officers had been involved in recycling crack cocaine and other drugs seized from dealers on Sandringham Road, north London's 'front line'. Police were also accused of fabricating and planting evidence on locals, mainly those of Jamaican origin. At the centre of the corruption was Detective Constable Roy Lewandowski, a long-haired Liverpudlian wide boy. He was arrested for stealing goods worth more than £2000 from the victim of a brutal killing. A recluse, David Berman, had been tied up and left to die by burglars. Lewandowski, as the exhibits officer in the case, had access to the rare books in the house and had helped himself. He was gaoled for eighteen months. His activities had diverted attention away from the fact that drugs had now become the most lucrative of all the underworld's trades.

12

DRUGS

From the Brilliant Chang and Fabian to Howard Marks and 'Operation Wrecker'

Three of the passport photos used by cannabis smuggler Howard Marks.

During the First World War the Mayfair chemists Savory & Moore advertised cases containing sheets impregnated with morphine and cocaine in *The Times* as 'a useful present for friends at the front'. Barely a decade later the same drugs, 'fear-banishers' as some of the troops called them, were to provoke one of the biggest scares of the twenties. The ensuing panic led to a fear that would never be banished again.

What has been suggested as 'London's first drug bust' involved a young man called Willy Johnson, who had convictions for theft, lived with a prostitute and was arrested in 1916 for selling boxes of cocaine for 2s 6d in the West End. There was at the time no specific drugs legislation and he was charged under the Poisons and Pharmacy Act, which only made it an offence to sell. Since he had been unsuccessful in the actual sale, he was acquitted. The law was soon to change. From 28 July 1916, under the Defence of the Realm Act, possession of cocaine and opium without prescription became a criminal offence.

The Dangerous Drugs Act was passed in 1920, but the scares began before then. As was to happen so often in future, the involvement of a celebrity focused attention on the issue. A chorus girl called Billie Carleton, who had graduated to the lead role in *Watch Your Step* at the Empire in Leicester Square, had supposedly been introduced to opium by the club-owner Jack May, who ran Murray's in Beak Street in Soho. She soon also acquired a taste for cocaine and was supplied by a costume designer called Reggie de Veulle who got his drugs from Lau Ping You, a Chinese in Limehouse, and his Scottish wife Ada.

On the night of 27 November 1918, after she had performed in *The Freedom of The Seas* and attended the Victory Ball at the Albert Hall – an event of patriotic kitsch with Lady Diana Manners playing Britannia and other celebrities playing the parts of other loyal nations from the colonies – Billie Carleton retired to bed. Her maid went in to wake her the next day and found her dead, a little gold box half-full of cocaine on the dressing-table. Arrests followed: Ada Lau Ping, described as 'the high priestess of unholy rites' by the Marlborough Street magistrate Frederick Mead, was sentenced to five months hard labour. Lau Ping himself was only fined £10 in the belief that opium was a national vice of the Chinese and therefore understandable.

Reggie de Veulle stood trial at the Old Bailey in front of Mr Justice Salter on charges of manslaughter and conspiracy to supply cocaine. The jury cleared him of the former charge and he pleaded guilty to the latter. He was sentenced to eight months hard labour and despatched to Wormwood Scrubs. Marek Kohn, in *Dope Girls*, questions whether Carleton really did die of a cocaine overdose, which is extremely rare, and suggests that a more likely scenario is that she took a depressant and choked.

No matter. Following her death there were a series of newspaper articles of the sort that have now become familiar whenever the offspring of a famous person dies of drug abuse. The *Daily Express* series was a classic: 'You will find the woman dope fiend in Chelsea, in Mayfair and Maida Vale. An obscure traffic is pursued in certain doubtful teashops . . .' The *Daily Mail* told its readers: 'Men do not as a rule take to drugs, unless there is a hereditary influence, but women are more temperamentally attracted.' Voices in Parliament called for the flogging of dealers and the deportation of all Chinese.

The member of the Chinese community on whom the greatest attention focused was the man who had given evidence at the Carleton inquest: the Brilliant Chang – his real name was the less exotic Chan Nan. Born in Canton in 1887, to a merchant family, he originally worked in England as a marine contractor before opening a Chinese restaurant in Regent Street where, according to the *World Pictorial News*, he 'dispensed Chinese delicacies and the drugs and vices of the Orient'. The same paper, in a series of articles about Chang, noted that his 'obsession' with white women led him to demand to be paid for his drugs in kind. When he discovered that the women would oblige, 'the flame of evil passion burned more brightly within and he hugged himself with unholy glee'. The story, told by a 'Special Commissioner' of the paper, commended women who retained 'sufficient decency and pride of race' to turn down this fellow with 'lips thin and cruel tightly drawn across even yellow teeth'.

Chang, a short, elegant, self-confident figure who dressed in fur-collared coats and grey suede shoes, became a marked man. He was linked with the drug-related death of Freda Kempton, a young dancing-teacher, and abandoned his Regent Street restaurant for the Palm Court Club in Gerrard Street, before opening the Shanghai Restaurant in Limehouse. But his Limehouse warehouse was raided, cocaine was found and he was gaoled for eighteen months in 1924. At his trial the Recorder of London told him sternly: 'It is you and men like you who are corrupting the womanhood of this country.' After he had served his time, he was deported. He was escorted by taxi from Wormwood Scrubs to Fenchurch Street station and then by train to the Royal Albert docks, where he was seen off, according to one report, by 'unhappy girls … with dope-sunken eyes and pallid cheeks'.

Legend followed him abroad and there was a choice of stories to believe: he jumped ship in Port Said, set up a drug business in Zurich, moved to Antwerp or died blind and disgraced in Shanghai. According to the *Daily Telegraph*'s crime reporter, Stanley Firmin: 'A strange Nemesis overtook him. He went blind and ended his days not in luxury and rich silks but as a sightless worker in a little kitchen garden.'

Politicians and journalists were happy to add to the general xenophobia surrounding Chang, although not all police were convinced. 'Nutty' Sharpe described him as the most libelled of men. 'The Chinaman,' he concluded, 'is a pretty honourable fellow.' Marek Kohn suggests: 'If the ultimate menace of drugs had to be summarized in a single proposition, it would be that they facilitated the seduction of young white women by men of other races.'

The trade was essentially associated with foreigners. In 1922 Sitaram Sampatrao Gaikwar, the nephew of the Maharaja of Barod, was arrested after he had collected a package of cocaine at Lyons Tea Shop in Waterloo, and his case was seen to symbolize both the weakness of foreigners and their involvement in the trade. Germans had been arrested importing cocaine via Newport in Wales but it was the Chinese who were suspected of bringing opium up the Thames. In 1922 the *Empire News* was warning that, 'Mothers would be well advised to keep their daughters as far away as they can from Chinese laundries and other places where the yellow men congregate.'

There was, however, a general uncertainty about the drugs and their effects. *The Times*, for instance, felt the need to put its readers straight on cocaine: 'Most cocainomaniacs carry revolvers to protect themselves from imaginary enemies.'

Besides the Brilliant Chang, the other main demonic figure was Edgar 'Eddie' Manning, known as 'the Villain' by police and press. Born in about 1888 in Jamaica, one story suggests that he was christened Alfred Mullin and was the son of two former slaves. The version he himself told was that his real name was Freddie Simpson. He had worked in Britain during the war in a munitions factory and played in the band at Ciro's night club. In 1920 he shot three men in the legs with a Colt revolver in Shaftesbury Avenue in London's West End after one of them had punched and insulted an actress friend, Molly O'Brien. For this he was gaoled for sixteen months. He was also damaged by association: a man called Eric Goodwin, an ex-serviceman with a drug habit, overdosed on heroin at Manning's house in 1922, which drew more attention to the Jamaican. He was eventually arrested in Primrose Hill in north London in possession of cocaine and opium, and a silver-topped cane that had a secret compartment for hiding drugs. He received a six-month sentence, the maximum under the 1920 Dangerous Drugs Act, and one month for possession of a firearm. The spiral had begun: in 1923 he was arrested again and gaoled this time for three years after being caught with opium and cocaine. The *News of the World* recorded the event with the headline 'Evil Negro Caught'.

In 1926 he wrote a highly fanciful account of his life in *World Pictorial News*. In this, his humble background was transformed and he claimed that he had actually come to England to study for the bar rather than work in a factory and had been seduced and corrupted by a woman he had met in a night club.

Gaoled for three years in 1929 for possession of goods stolen from Lady Diana Cooper's car, he was described by Detective Sergeant Powell as possibly 'the worst man in London'. He became ill in Parkhurst prison and was taken to the prison hospital where he died from acute myelitis, toxaemia and heart failure on 8 February 1931.

If the Brilliant Chang and Eddie Manning were the *éminence jaune et noir* of twenties immorality, the home-grown queen was Kate Meyrick, who had come under scrutiny when Freda Kempton, who was one of her dancers, had died of a supposed overdose. Born in County Clare and famed as the first woman in Ireland to ride a bicycle, she entered the entertainments industry in 1919 after her husband abandoned her, leaving her to support two sons at Harrow and four daughters at Roedean. She co-managed Daltons in Leicester Square, which was known as a pick-up place for cheerful prostitutes and was frequently raided by the police who went in wearing night-club mufti of top hat and white tie.

One of the officers in charge of the West End raids was Sergeant George Goddard, who topped up his meagre police salary so heavily with bribes that he was charged with corruptly receiving money and gaoled for eighteen months in 1929. Goddard, whose imagination had clearly been enriched by so much exposure to the heady life, claimed in court that the £18 000 savings he had acquired were the result of successful betting at the races, the sale of rock at the Wembley exhibition and astute foreign exchange dealing.

Kate Meyrick also ran the 43 in Gerrard Street, the Folies Bergere, the Manhattan, the Little Club and, most famously, the Silver Slipper in Regent Street. The 43 saw the mix of gangsterism –

Ruby Sparks was a regular – and show business that was to become the pattern of such clubs until the seventies. 'Nutty' Sharpe described the raids: 'I went to the Manhattan Club in evening dress and opera hat with a friend who was a man about town. We gained admittance without difficulty and at the same moment a colleague similarly attired found his way into the "43", where the licensing laws were being flouted. The main body of the raiding party, thirty or forty members of the squad, waited in cars on the Embankment, near the Tate Gallery ... The music stopped as the cry went up "It's a raid" ... I think the majority of them regarded it more as a lark, for it gave them a thrill, but they changed their views when they appeared before the beak.'

Although Mrs Meyrick was gaoled for six months in 1924 she continued to run the clubs through her daughters. But the law pursued her. She was sentenced to a further eighteen months hard labour and additional small sentences eventually drove her from the game. Having made and lost a small fortune from her clubs, she died in 1933. Sharpe, who had helped to gaol her, reminisced affectionately about her clubland days: 'Personally, I can't see that much harm was done.'

Kate Meyrick (third from right) on her release from gaol in 1924.

By the thirties attention had begun to shift to marijuana, 'the vicious drug which causes men to lose all sense of responsibility and perform the most reckless acts,' as the *News of the World* described it in 1938. The case which promoted this assessment was that of a soldier, Andrew Vanderberg, who was gaoled for ten years for a series of crimes, culminating in a gun battle with the police, which he said were carried out under the influence of marijuana.

In 1928 Britain had ratified an international agreement controlling cannabis which the Egyptian government had proposed three years earlier. However, marijuana was not considered a major issue and it was 1950 before the annual number of cannabis arrests passed the hundred mark and 1951 before the Dangerous Drugs Act, which regularized the various statutes on narcotics in a major piece of legislation, became law.

In their report on drugs to the League of Nations in 1928 the government noted that there were 620 drug addicts in Britain, 320 of them women. More than a hundred of the total were doctors. Imported drugs were carefully monitored, said the report, which recorded that 211 969 pounds (96 150 kilograms) of raw opium had been imported legally, with more than 90 000 pounds (40 800 kilograms) of raw coca leaves, 8000 pounds (3600 kilograms) of Indian hemp and 16 000 pounds (7200 kilograms) of crude morphine.

1928 also saw the remarkable, if exaggerated, posthumous intervention of Major Cyril McNeile, 'Sapper', the creator of Bulldog Drummond, into the world of drugs. As the *News of the World* reported it, Sapper 'disgusted by the degenerate parasites of the West End against whom the police were powerless' had suggested in an army mess shortly before his death that 'any young man of energy' should take a tip from Bulldog and form a 'black gang' to deal with the low-lifes. These energetic young men were reported to have pounced on miscreant 'dope peddlers and other crooks' in the West End and to have taken them to a garage off the Great West Road where they flogged them with dog whips until they promised to mend their ways. The paper reported the extent of the menace with the story of a young officer whose engagement had been broken off because his fiancée had become addicted to marijuana: 'She has been going to these cigarette orgies. It will be years before she is well.'

A drugs squad was set up but disbanded not long after, and by 1950 the police were satisfied that drugs had practically ceased to exist except amongst foreign seamen and the new Caribbean immigrants.

It was clear how these 'coloured fellows' were regarded in some quarters: Superintendent Robert Fabian describes them in *London After Dark*, published in 1954, as 'like schoolboys ... simple folk, believe me, but they so often get bad names through the young trollopes who become their "camp followers" ... they have the brains of children, can only dimly know the cruel harm they do these teenage girls who dance with them and try thrilled puffs at those harmless-looking marijuana cigarettes.'

Fabian noted the shift from cocaine and opium to marijuana and found its market amongst the 'jazz crazy youngsters – there is I believe some scientific foundation for the claim that marijuana addiction can help a musician for this drug has some effect upon that part of the brain which responds to rhythmical vibrations.' He warned the innocent of the dangers of under-estimating the drug. 'Chelsea drug addicts! You wouldn't think them glamorous if you could see them as I have,' wrote Fabian. 'That pale dull young man in the frayed grey suit and duffle coat who is not enjoying his beer. The middle-aged woman with dyed hair streaky with grey. She wears black corduroy trousers and a purple utility box jacket.'

Chapman Pincher of the *Daily Express* took up the theme: 'Coloured men who peddle reefers can meet susceptible teenagers at the jazz clubs.' And in 1957 *The Times* agreed that, 'White girls who become friendly with West Indians are from time to time enticed to hemp smoking ... this is an aspect of the hemp problem – the possibility of its spreading among irresponsible white people – that causes greatest concern to the authorities. The potential moral danger is significant, since a principal motive of the coloured man in smoking hemp is to stimulate his sexual desire.'

The authorities did not see drugs as a major problem at this stage. Former Flying Squad Commander Frank Cater recalls that in 1959 the Drugs Squad had one car at its disposal – provided it was booked well in advance. In 1961 Sir Ronald Howe, the post-war head of the CID at Scotland Yard, wrote without irony that, 'In this country drug trafficking presents a very small problem. Englishmen don't take drugs, they prefer Scotch whisky.'

Although it is easy with hindsight to smile now at the notion of drugs being virtually obsolete in Britain by the fifties, it was certainly a minor business as far as the underworld was concerned. It was left to others to supply the chaps in frayed grey suits and the gels in their black corduroy trousers. The organized criminal was still far removed from the trade.

But all that was soon to change. A new breed, who had a more romantic vision of drug smuggling than Messrs Fabian and Pincher, had arrived.

'It was a summery sort of night, very warm and balmy. There was incredible phosphorescence in the water. It was actually magical, coupled with the nervous tension of waiting and wondering whether the opposition was going to emerge from the hedgerows and bushes, whether the boat was actually going to get there. Romantic is the right word for it. It seemed to have a timeless quality. The classic scene – a deserted estuary, a sailing boat, moonlight, secrecy and I felt that I was part of a long, long tradition that stretched back for years and years, the brandy smugglers of the eighteenth century and so on. It was like something out of a Robert Louis Stevenson novel.'

Thus Charlie Radcliffe, drug smuggler. With the sixties had come the sea change for trafficking. A generation that did not get its travelling experience from National Service in Cyprus or Aden had, for the first time, the money and the time to take advantage of cheap foreign travel in Morocco or India or Peru or Thailand. Many young people tried their first joint in Tangier or their first chillum in Benares and some found it easy enough to bring small supplies back into Britain, where sniffer dogs and a drugs-alert Customs force were not yet in place.

From these young men – and a few women – came the first of the new generation of drug dealers. Many were university educated, bright, trusting and without links, at that stage, in the criminal world. For a while they could operate with apparent impunity, in the same ways as new immigrant teams of criminals; the police had no entrée into their world and did not speak their language. Their methods at first were fairly crude. The simplest hiding place was the space below the side window of a van; drugs could be packed there without distorting the shape of the vehicle. But Customs officers soon grew wise to drivers who had difficulty in winding down their window. Dealers in Asia and North Africa used mechanics and technicians to construct an array of ingenious devices for smuggling – model elephants that were hollowed out and filled with hash, entire buses stripped down and packed with it, false-bottomed boots, tubes of toothpaste, packs of tea, delicately carved chess sets.

The growth of travel on the hippie trail, through Greece and Turkey and Afghanistan to Pakistan, India and Nepal or through Spain to Morocco, meant a constant flow of buses which could be packed and loaded during a stopover and driven profitably home.

Cocaine was lighter and easier to carry than marijuana. Some could be coloured pink and brought in as mouthwash – although the British market proved to be as conservative about its white coke as about its white sliced bread. Mixed with distilled water, it could come in as white wine. It could be smuggled in hairbrushes and eventually, and sometimes fatally, wrapped in condoms or plastic bags and swallowed by the 'mules' who were fired at Europe from bases in Colombia, Venezuela, Nigeria, Jamaica and Peru.

There were highly publicized arrests, of Keith Richards and Mick Jagger of the Rolling Stones who were sentenced initially to a year and three months respectively on benzedrine and cannabis charges, provoking *The Times*, only a decade after they had warned of the dangerous race-mixing effects of the drugs, to ask in an editorial by William Rees-Mogg: 'Who breaks a butterfly upon a wheel?' There was talk, too, of legalizing or at least decriminalizing cannabis, and in 1969 a committee under the chairmanship of Baroness Wootton recommended reducing the penalties for cannabis possession. But the establishment was not to be persuaded. The drug remained illegal and the subject of a massively expanding trade.

Radcliffe was a typical smuggler. The son of an army officer and product of a military public school, where he had smoked his first joint, he had planned a career in publishing or journalism when the opportunity to become a cannabis smuggler gradually presented itself. At that time, dealers chose different ways of operating: 'Some people took so many precautions that their lives weren't really worth living. They'd move address every few days and emerge wearing dark glasses and behaving as if they were part of some spy movie. Others were recklessly upfront. I suppose we saw ourselves in the vein of Robin Hood.'

In the late sixties the ounce price of drugs was based on a tenth of the pound price: a £100 pound of cannabis would split into sixteen £10 ounces. Lebanese drugs used to come in 200 gram sacks, muslin- or cotton-wrapped, with stamps of the Syrian army, the Palestine Liberation Organization or the Christian Militia, depending on who controlled the passes. Army involvement was standard; the Moroccan army and police often assisted dealers to their boats with their loads.

'There was a phenomenal level of trust and comradeship across rival companies,' says Radcliffe. 'It's like antique dealers. They work together, they co-operate over certain things and other times they are fiercely competitive. When Bob Dylan sang "If you live outside the law you must be honest", it struck a very resonant chord.'

There was some heaviness, however. In the seventies a Glasgow gang descended with shotguns on a deal in Ladbroke Grove and took all the hash and money. The possibly apocryphal tale was that retribution followed and the Lebanese importers involved cut off the robbers' hands in symbolic punishment. Smuggling by sea gradually came to seem a more sensible option than running drugs through points where there were always Customs officers. The drugs were off-loaded on the shore and driven up to London in hired camper-vans that were filled to the gunwales. The drugs would be hidden in the garage of a house in which a homeless and unsuspecting friend had been installed.

The money was good although nothing like the 'street value' given by Customs and police in court. 'The street valuation has always been a bone of contention between the forces of law and order and the forces of unlaw and disorder,' says Radcliffe. 'When you appear in court the assumption is that you bring in a ton of dope and you then cut it up into one-pound deals and sell it at your local pub and you amass this huge fortune. In reality, it is all about margins. For every one you invest, you get three back.'

As Radcliffe describes it, there was a chairman of the board and shareholders who put up the money. He acted as managing director and personnel officer. The team required was around eleven people: four on the main boat doing the fortnight-long trip from Morocco using British Admiralty charts from World War Two, two on the landing craft, one in Spain, one in Morocco, two to drive the shipment to London and one to guard it. On one occasion there was a panic when the boat went missing. 'It had never occurred to me that I'd ever have the kind of embarrassing situation of ringing wives and girlfriends and saying, "I hate to tell you this, but I've a feeling your old man isn't coming home."' But although the boat had sunk, the crew survived and even managed to save some of the cargo, which was remarkable in the circumstances: 'Two were non-swimmers, they were all Londoners and I think their combined nautical experience was half an hour on the Serpentine.' Eventually Radcliffe decided to get out but was persuaded to back that one final run. It ended like many a 'one last big job'.

'At about two o'clock in the morning there was a noise like a sledge-hammer and I said, "Who the fuck is that at this time of the morning?" A big deep voice came back: "This is the fucking Customs and Excise and if you don't come down and open this fucking door we'll fucking knock it down with a fucking sledge-hammer." My hair was standing on end. It was Nemesis. Customs officers produced, with some pride, a scroll, a "writ of assistance", their equivalent of a search warrant. It was a scroll which began rather alarmingly "In the name of Her Majesty the Queen, greetings," which I thought was somewhat inappropriate at the time, but I was delighted to have her greetings anyway.' The Customs officers, in bulletproof vests, asked for his gun and did not believe him when he told them he was a pacifist who would not allow his children to play with guns.

The evidence compiled by what had been called Operation Yashmak was enough: notes with figures, drugs hidden in the garden in screw-up drainage tubes, £10 000 in small boxes and £40 000 stashed in a safe under the stove along with safe-deposit-box keys. It was a thorough search: 'Customs showed me a photograph of one of their officers holding a goat, which belonged to a neighbour and which used to graze in our garden, by the tail with its backside slightly raised and shining a torch at it. Written on the back was "We've looked everywhere".'

Customs told Radcliffe that their arrest-conviction rate was 90 per cent and that his wife had been arrested: 'Initially they were making, it would be unfair to call them threats, but they were saying, "The council looks after children pretty well these days, it's not so bad being in care as it used to be in Victorian times."' He agreed to make a statement if charges against his wife were dropped. On 22 October 1980, barely six months after his arrest, Radcliffe found himself confronting a different type of Victorian institution. 'I got a five-year prison sentence from a civilized sort of judge from an academic background who clearly didn't have a big thing about cannabis being the source of all evil. I think he referred to us as gentlemen smugglers, and at the time it was like something out of *Boys Own Paper*, the sort of thing Biggles did. It had a kind of schoolboy feel about it.'

Prison followed and he met old villains who would say ' "Come here, son, I want to pick your brains ..." I didn't see it as a progressive step, having a lot of people prepared to use firearms.' These were the new drug dealers, heavy-duty men who were more Jimmy Hoffa than Jimi Hendrix. 'While we were on remand they'd found a handless corpse in a quarry and I thought – God, this isn't like the Round House '66. And there were Customs officers getting shot. It seemed a different world.'

So he quit. Took, as he put it, voluntary redundancy from Customs and Excise and concludes: 'I have a lot of regrets but then, on the other hand, I had a more interesting life than I would have had if I had stayed on the straight and narrow. It's been an adventure.'

Another smuggler was Surya 'Chris' Krishnarma, an Indian who owned a casino and restaurant that were in financial difficulties on the Isle of Wight. He entered the business in the early seventies because he saw cannabis smuggling as a swift way out of his problems. A married man with four children, he did not believe the drug should be illegal anyway. 'Cannabis had been used throughout history. Only the other day I was reading about an archaeological find in Israel which suggested that it was being used for pre-menstrual tension in the fourth century. I was breaking a law I believed to be bad. There were 100 000 tobacco-related illnesses and 100 000 alcohol-related illnesses but there had not been one single cannabis-related death.'

Krishnarma started modestly enough in Morocco buying cannabis at £40 a kilo. 'I thought of it as a great adventure. We had code words and signs, we didn't consider the dangers.' He and his associates would load a car and take the ferry from Tangiers to Southampton: 'It became a well which wouldn't run dry, you just went and dipped in, your life style expanded.' By now they were buying for £35–£40 a kilo in Morocco and selling for £200 a kilo in England. But they realized that there were greater profits to be made. They set up a trekking company offering cheap holidays to young people in North Africa, drove the coaches down, deposited the holiday-makers in thatched huts on the beach and then loaded the cannabis into the coach at a villa. The drugs were hidden in side-panels that could only be reached by removing all the seats, an operation that took around an hour and a half.

Krishnarma learned a lesson which might have been useful to him when, on his return from a non-drug-smuggling trip, he asked a Customs man why he was always stopped. 'He told me it was because I looked as though I had just very recently come into money. I didn't have money built into me. They could see that I wasn't quite happy with money, that I was still flashing it about.'

But cannabis smuggling was still a relatively gentle trade: 'The violence and the business, the professionality, all that came later.' An indication of this was the occasion when Krishnarma's driver telephoned to say that a London gang had broken into their hotel and had stolen the diesel van. Later he heard that his driver was selling the supposedly stolen haul in Brighton.

'This guy said "Do you want me to get it back?" and I said, "Well, of course we do." He said it would cost 20 kilos of cannabis, no money. He said, "We'll just go and threaten the man." I got a call much later that same night to say, "We've got the load back, we've got the driver, do you want us to break his legs?" And I said "No, no, no, let him go." ' The gang had held the driver's girlfriend hostage and when he returned he had agreed to take them to the stolen drugs. 'I thought – now I am well and truly in the criminal underworld.'

Arrest was not long in coming. 'Customs and Excise wanted to bring the case and they would say, "Chris, answer these questions and we will handle this, we are much better than the police." And the police would say, "Have nothing to do with Customs and Excise, we'll look after you." There was this rivalry between them.' Nineteen of the team were arrested and two turned Queen's Evidence. Arrested on 5 June 1973 Krishnarma was gaoled on 11 July the following year for ten years, one of the biggest sentences of the early seventies and one of the first major police-Customs joint operations. He was to face two further sentences. 'In prison in Winchester, we were stars. We were pointed out in the exercise yard.'

Krishnarma met many armed robbers who were realizing that bank robberies were increasingly hazardous and were becoming interested in the prospects of bringing 'puff' in from Morocco. The old, slightly puritanical, underworld attitude to drugs was changing – with results that could scarcely have been foreseen – and in Spain some of the ex-robbers, who knew little about the quality of drugs, tried to enlist him as an adviser. He had met Great Train Robber Charlie Wilson in Long Lartin gaol and visited him for breakfast at his villa. 'If you belong to the same club somewhere, it's likely that when you move on to some other place and you hear an old club member is there, you go and see him.' A month later, Wilson was shot dead.

But the man who epitomized this era of drug smuggling in the seventies was Howard Marks, an effortlessly charming, Welsh-born Oxford physics graduate who won over everyone he met, with the eventual exception of some of the officers of the United States Drug Enforcement Administration and a judge in a Florida court-house. In Oxford he had lived in a house that was later to be rented by an American student who had also smoked cannabis but famously 'did not inhale': Bill Clinton, who was later to become the President of the United States.

Born in 1945 to a merchant sailor father and a schoolteacher mother in Kenfig Hill, near Port Talbot steelworks in Wales, Marks had done well enough at Garw Grammar School to be accepted for Balliol College, Oxford. After graduating he drifted into drug dealing and set up an Oxford boutique called Annabelinda's as a front for laundering his funds. Around thirty or forty friends were employed in the network. He started by bringing a ton of cannabis in a car from Frankfurt to Switzerland on behalf of an American group, for which he was paid £3000. There was a clear attraction and, for someone who would not have objected to being a rock star, there was the compensation of being able to live like one. Marks also enjoyed the ingenuity required in working out routes from, say, Karachi to Switzerland so that cases could be shifted from plane to plane.

With an eccentric and devious Irishman called Jim McCann, who had told key people at Shannon airport that he was smuggling guns for the IRA, Marks managed to set up a new bridgehead in Ireland, placing the drugs in an industrial estate that was used for export goods and avoiding Irish Customs. The drugs were driven out piece by piece and taken to a lonely farmhouse where they were redistributed into cars to be driven via ferry to London. The driver would be paid £2000–£3000 to take more than 200 pounds (90 kilograms) of cannabis. There was no shortage of volunteers.

Marks' entrée into the world of drugs had coincided with a strange twist in his life. At the end of his university career, he was briefly recruited by MI6 through a Balliol contemporary, Hamilton 'Mac' McMillan, who thought that his friend could find out what was happening in the twilight worlds that his Bohemian charm opened to him. He was originally hired, according to David Leigh in *High Times*, to attempt to win the friendship of women in the Czechoslovakian Embassy. However, the intelligence service link was to have a remarkable side-effect.

All went smoothly until, in 1973, Marks was arrested. 'I'd got too big for my boots, I was very arrogant.' The team had been smuggling into the United States, using sound systems for major British bands and the special Customs licences which meant that they were not subject to the usual search. A smart sniffer dog nipped at the ankles of this burgeoning enterprise: 380 kilograms (838 pounds) of hash came into New York *en route* for Las Vegas, one of the speaker cabinets got left behind and was spotted by the dog on a routine patrol. The Drugs Enforcement Administration moved into action. At the end of an international operation, Marks was arrested in Holland, accused of involvement in dealing in England, Holland, Italy and the United States.

For the first time he was able to play his MI6 card, telling the Customs men who came to interview him in detention that he had been asked to infiltrate IRA drugs-smuggling operations. None the less, he was extradited to England and held in Brixton prison for three weeks before being granted £20 000 bail.

The already confused saga was further complicated by the role of McCann, a man who has scruples like a hen has teeth, who lived in a netherworld between reality and fantasy, and whose claims to be an IRA man were drawing attention to the operation. Marks had meanwhile rented a house in north Oxford as he prepared for his trial. One morning in April 1974 a large man in a raincoat came to the door and asked for him. Marks emerged carrying his baby daughter and the man introduced himself in front of the landlady as being from 'Customs and Excise'. 'You'd better come with us,' he said. Marks gave the baby to the landlady and, looking shaken, departed. The forces of law and order were not to see him again for six years. Speculation about what had happened was rife: he had been abducted by the Mafia and assassinated by their hitmen, he had staged his own disappearance, he had been spirited away by MI6.

Detective Superintendent Phil Fairweather of Thames Valley police was aware of the security aspect and contacted MI6 in London. The cannabis, as a saying of the time had it, was about to hit the air-conditioner. The press, naturally enough, were intrigued. Eddie Laxton of the *Daily Mirror* was to pursue the Marks tale across the years and his first effort appeared on the front page of his paper in May 1974: 'Where Is Mr Marks? A man who vanished before an Old Bailey drug-running trial has been named to detectives as a link between an American drugs ring, the IRA Provisionals and MI6 – the British secret service.'

Marks read the various newspaper reports in a hide-out on the Isle of Dogs in east London, where he was trying to grow a moustache. He was about to embark on a marathon stretch on the run. Travelling with a false passport, as a geography teacher called McKenna, he went via Harwich to Denmark then flew to Italy and holed up in the resort of Pineta di Arenzano, a few miles north of Genoa. Streams of friends and hangers-on drifted out to visit the always hospitable Marks. But Eddie Laxton, that old sniffer dog of a reporter, was still curious. In October 1974 the *Mirror* splashed again: 'HE'S ALIVE! WHY THE MAFIA HID MARKS.'

Over the next seven years, Marks slipped in and out of Britain, disguised and running under the *nom de guerre* of Albi, sometimes Albion, Jennings. The surname was in honour of the American country singer Waylon Jennings, who was one of the 'outlaw' breed of singers taking on the conservative Nashville establishment, and also of an old scallywag called Albert in Kenfig Hill. Marks lay low, spending a summer in camping-sites where he always pitched his tent near the toilets so as to be close to the telephone.

The drug-smuggling machine soon started moving again. He set up a 700 pound (315 kilogram) deal for Pakistani hash to be brought by sea from Karachi to Dubai and thence to Rome. The money flowed in. Marks travelled the world with three different identities, setting up nine deals over the next eighteen months – the largest a 5 ton shipment – and keeping one or two moves ahead of the authorities. He returned to Britain, under the name Albert Lane, for the birth of his second daughter in Wimbledon in October 1977. He seemed untouchable. He would pop up at parties and even sing Elvis Presley songs in the Nashville pub in Hammersmith. He was the bubbles in the champagne of many a media party and enjoyed playing the part of the velvet pimpernel. He went to Thailand to invest in the newly profitable Thai sticks, which were stronger than hashish and had been a favourite with American servicemen enjoying rest and recreation from the Vietnam war in Bangkok hotels.

'I was a fugitive for six and a half years and I smuggled as much cannabis as I could. I felt that this was my destiny, this was my karma. I suppose I felt like a prizefighter. One day one's going to get knocked out on the canvas. You have to carry on until you're beaten.' The quantities smuggled were enormous, Marks taking the view that a car was as likely to be stopped by police as a container lorry.

Meanwhile the dealing and smuggling world was changing. People from the supplier countries like the Lebanon, Pakistan and Morocco wanted a greater involvement in Europe by taking part in the whole operation. Diplomats were able to use their immunity to act as smugglers, almost untouched. Marks was ready for the big one, a job that was to make him £1 million and involved shipping drugs from Aruba Island off Colombia over to Scotland's Western Isles on New Year's Eve of 1979.

The front on this occasion was to be a film company called Worldwide Entertainments which provided a good excuse for large vehicles and odd movements. It was going to make a 'semi-documentary film located in the Western Isles and set in the latter half of the last century.' It was about Freud and had all the necessary props in terms of cameras, lights, even a genuine film director.

In truth, Marks and his associates were enacting a far more remarkable tale than any nineteenth-century yarn they could have

Howard Marks.

dreamed up. New York heavies, ex-CIA men, were waiting to off-load what would make the team's fortunes from two 40-foot (12-metre) yachts, *Bagheera* and *Salambo*. The engines of the 3 ton lorry were cut so that it would not attract attention before it hit the main road. There was a police car on the road and an officer emerged. Marks approached him and said he was a film-maker checking the light for a dawn shoot. The policeman amiably inquired if he had any petrol he could borrow and Marks obliged.

The operation was immaculately planned. Black rubber Zodiac dinghies shipped the drugs from the mother-vessels to the Scottish shore on Loch Linnhe. Fifteen tons came ashore and the team of fifteen or sixteen, all furiously smoking dope, unloaded in 45 minutes. The cannabis was stored at four different warehouses – two in Scotland, one in Essex and one in Northamptonshire.

One of the hauls had to be jettisoned in Scotland after a panic over a message heard on the radio. Bales of marijuana surfaced off Kerrera in Scotland and were washed up on the shore, provoking apocryphal tales along the lines of Sir Compton Mackenzie's *Whisky Galore*, in which a consignment of whisky is shipwrecked off the island of Barra. There were stories of cannabis galore, including one of farmers feeding their hens the strange substance and of the resultant laid-back hens.

But the Colombian and American ends of the operation were becoming anxious that their shipment was not moving fast enough, certainly not at the rate of American shipments. They started to make their own inquiries: 'This was simply mad,' according to Marks. 'In the end they approached a man who turned out to be a Customs informant and that is how it all got discovered. Just impatience really.'

In 1980, customs searched the room in the Dorchester hotel in London where the syndicate pair – the American end of the operation – were staying and found a Knightsbridge number for 'Albi'. Arrest and the seizure of around 10 tons of cannabis followed. When Marks booked himself and his girlfriend, Judy Lane, into the Swan in Lavenham in East Anglia, he noticed that there were two young men at the bar. As Marks ordered a sherry, one of the young men, Higher Executive Officer of Customs and Excise, Nicholas Baker, leaned over. 'He said "Can I have a look at your watch?" and he was putting handcuffs on me at the same time.'

The following day the newspapers reported the arrests of those alleged to have been involved in Britain's largest-ever cannabis haul. But Howard Marks was not dead yet. He still had his MI6 card to play. It might be tattered, it might be rough round the edges but it might still be an ace.

The trial started in 1981 with Marks and his colleagues in the dock in Court Six of the Old Bailey. It was reported in the *Sun* under the headline: 'Eggheads Ran £20 million Drug Ring.' The *Daily Mail* recorded that, 'An Oxford graduate was the mastermind in a brainy gang.' The case seemed so overwhelming that Marks had been prepared to plead guilty for a seven- or eight-year sentence, something the judiciary would not contemplate, stating that the matter was so serious it would have to go to full trial.

Howard's charm spilled over the dock and into the jury benches. One of the jurors even drew a heart as she doodled her way through the evidence. When he was asked by the stern judge, Mr Justice Peter 'Penal Pete' Mason, why he was smiling, Marks replied: 'I still try to smile although I have spent the last eighteen months in prison. It is the only way of dealing with adversity and is in no way smugness or contempt.'

When it looked as though the case was slipping away from Marks, there arrived to give evidence a mysterious Latin American. He claimed to be a member of the Mexican security police involved in anti-terrorism and his mission and his work were so secret that the court had to be cleared of press and public. He told the jury that he had paid Marks $150 000 for his help in setting up a contraband and drugs deal that would assist Mexico's anti-terrorist work. He could not give his name nor further details of his work 'for security reasons'. It worked. Marks was acquitted despite Crown Counsel John Rogers' entreaties to the jury to dismiss the tale as rubbish. The joker had proved to be the ace.

'It was obviously such a nonsensical story,' says Marks. 'I'm sure the jury didn't believe it really, they were just looking for an excuse not to consign me to years and years in prison. I had to somehow link up MI6 with the Mexican secret service if such a thing exists, a really bizarre story. Someone came over from Mexico who was a genuine government employee, to do with law enforcement, and confirmed that I had indeed worked for the Mexican secret service but that he wasn't allowed to give any details. As far as I know, they don't exist.'

He pleaded guilty to the earlier charge for which he had fled and was given a three-year sentence which meant that he was free again in a matter of months because of the amount of time he had spent on remand.

Eventually, however, he was tracked down on 25 July 1988 in Palma, Majorca, by a team led by Drug Enforcement Administration man Craig Lovato, who had become obsessed with the case, possibly after reading Howard's indiscreet account of events in David Leigh's book. The British, American, Spanish and Canadian police and Customs forces combined to snare him.

One of his Judases was the unlikely figure of a *louche* remittance man, Lord Moynihan, the half-brother of the former Conservative Party minister Colin Moynihan. Marks and the peer had discussed setting up a cannabis plantation on an island off the Philippines where Lord Moynihan worked as a sort of corporate pimp, running massage parlours staffed by young Filipinas. Faced with the possibility of imprisonment, Lord Moynihan made a deal with the authorities to tape-record conversations with Marks which would establish the latter's drug-dealing intentions. He died not long afterwards.

Marks was faced with the choice of fighting the case and running the risk of a sixty-year to life gaol sentence or pleading guilty and being gaoled for twenty-five years. He took the latter course at Palm Beach Federal Court in Florida before being moved to the federal penitentiary in Terre Haute, Indiana. There, surrounded by men serving an average of seventeen years, he has been given the job of teaching English grammar to the inmates and runs a voluntary philosophy class in the evenings attended by Mafia men, members of Colombian cartels and one of the surviving members of the real-life French Connection team. He is teaching philosophy to the Dons. By the end of his drug-smuggling career, he had 'made and lost a couple of million – no more than the average yuppie'.

While Marks' cannabis enterprise was taking off, an equally complex and ambitious effort was being put into the production of LSD – acid. It came to an end when one of the conspirators, Henry Todd, walked to his front door which was quivering under a barrage of blows. He unlocked it and stepped back to dodge a swinging sledge-hammer wielded by a plainclothes police officer: 'I suppose you've come about the television licence,' he said.

Alas for Mr Todd, no. On 26 March 1977, Inspector Dick Lee and his team discovered six million tablets of acid and carried out a series of arrests of the team that was manufacturing and distributing them. It was the largest such police operation ever mounted in Europe. Codenamed 'Operation Julie' after Sergeant Julie Taylor, one of the officers on the case, it had involved hundreds of police, many acting undercover.

The conspirators were a diverse crew. Dick Kemp, who was producing some of the purest acid ever manufactured, had been educated at Bedford Grammar School, St Andrews University and Liverpool University, where he gained his Bachelor of Science degree in 1966. He had moved in with Christine Bott, who had graduated in medicine at Liverpool University. Brian Cuthbertson was the son of a civil servant. A Reading University mathematics drop-out, his travels throughout the world had given him a wide range of contacts if no visible means of support. Henry Todd brought his entrepreneurial and organizational skills to the operation. The son of an RAF squadron leader, Todd had two A levels and a theft and false pretences conviction; he was a keen mountain climber; played rugby for a London Scottish side and had worked as an accountant. The American in the group, David Solomon, had come to Britain in 1967 and had met Kemp two years later.

The main point was that these people and their associates were not from what was normally seen as the criminal underworld. They had only one previous conviction between them, they were brains not muscle and there was no fire power. When arrested many made full, detailed confessions, far removed from the world of 'no comment until I've seen my brief'. They shared a common interest in the properties of drugs and the operation was never set up solely as a commercial enterprise. Kemp started producing LSD in about 1971 in flats rented in London. Todd brought in a group of friends centred around Reading University, including Brian Cuthbertson, Russell Spenceley and Nigel Fielding. Internal problems caused a split in the team and Kemp and Bott moved to Plas Llysin in Wales in 1974.

Nigel 'Leaf' Fielding, who produced and distributed the tablets, recalled their original motivation: 'We began as idealists who had seen much wrong in human affairs. We thought we had found a non-violent means of effecting great changes in the world – changes that would, we believed, be of lasting benefit to the human race. As psychic guerillas, we willingly risked our liberty in the pursuit of a global expansion in consciousness.' This was not exactly how Mr Justice Park was eventually to see it when he sat in judgement on them.

The operation had some strange side-effects. In the course of searching the London laboratory where spillage had saturated a carpet, three of the officers had ingested LSD. Their depositions indicated their puzzlement, amusement and fear at what happened: in the pub after the search one of them thought his pint was too heavy to lift, another became fascinated with the foam on his glass and a third hid

233

Christine Bott of Operation Julie, and the farmhouse near Tregaron in Wales that was at its centre.

behind a pillar. Unable to reverse their car out of the pub parking lot, they walked back to the laboratory pointing out to each other, as Fielding says, 'the thousand mysteries of the south-western suburbs'. They were found collapsed with hysterical laughter watching *Jesus of Nazareth* on television and taken to Kingston hospital.

Kemp and Todd were gaoled for thirteen years, Cuthbertson for eleven, David Solomon and Russell Spenceley for ten, Christine Bott for nine, Nigel Fielding for eight and others for sentences that in all totalled 124 years. They were released during the eighties and disappeared into more normal occupations – in the City, computing, publishing. One became a police surgeon.

Both Dick Lee, who led the Operation Julie inquiry, and Craig Lovato, who hunted Howard Marks, expressed a grudging admiration for their quarry. Lee described the gaoling of Kemp as, 'A waste of genius ... where might he have gone but for his warped ideals.'

But by the late seventies the business of drug dealing was already changing. There was too much money around for it to be left to people who liked playing Grateful Dead music and reading Herman Hesse. The headbands were giving way to the head-cases. Drugs were to become the major criminal currency of the next decade, a period that was to see violent deaths and shootings.

One dealer who made his money in the seventies and early eighties recalls the moment when he and his team realized that the game was changing: 'A Customs guy stopped a lorry, opened the door and got shot. It was a great shock. We thought: "Who are these guys? What's happening? We'd better all look for another way of earning a living."'

It was 19 October 1979 and the man shot dead was Customs investigator Peter Bennett who was attempting to arrest Leonard 'Teddy Bear' Watkins on the Commercial Road in Stepney, east London. He was the first Customs officer to be killed on duty in 182 years. It was the culmination of 'Operation Wrecker' which, with a force of 120 officers, was targeted at a major cannabis-smuggling scheme that brought 'Paki black' in from Karachi.

Bennett was shot with a Beretta and his colleague Detective Sergeant John Harvey of the Hampshire drug squad was wounded as Watkins attempted to escape before being felled with the aid of a pensioner who hit him about the head with a walking-stick.

The architect of the scheme was said to have been Colin 'The Duke' Osbourne, a flash dresser who had met Watkins, along with two other drug smugglers, in Maidstone prison. In fact, Osbourne's role was probably no larger than that of his colleagues. Watkins, who had been serving a three-year sentence for a supermarket robbery, ran a straight transport operation after his release under the name of Edward Bear Motors – which gave him his 'Teddy Bear' nickname – in Fareham, Hampshire. Container lorries were fitted with false floors and dispatched to the Indian subcontinent ostensibly with sanitary goods for sale in Pakistan, returning with cheap sports shoes for sale in Britain. After each operation, the lorries were cut up and disposed of. By the time they were caught the team had, police estimated, made around £10 million, although this seems almost certainly an exaggeration. The quality of their cannabis was high, however, and they embossed it with the Rolls-Royce emblem and a gilded treble-seven motif, the international gambling symbol for the jackpot.

On what Customs believed was the fifth such trip – although it seems many more had been made – Watkins was driving a lorry from Felixstowe docks and was being shadowed by Bennett. He was unable to throw him off and was in London's Docklands, attempting to hide the load, when he stopped to make a check call to his colleagues and was told that an orange van would arrive to guide him to a hide-out. At this moment, Bennett approached him and was fatally shot. Inside the lorry were two sawn-off shotguns and some ammunition, which Watkins unsuccessfully claimed was there merely as a means for him to commit suicide if caught. His defence was that he thought Bennett and Harvey were part of a rival gang.

Gaoled for life at Winchester Crown Court in November 1980 with a recommendation that he serve a minimum of twenty-five years, 'Teddy Bear' cheerily told the judge and police: 'You win the battle but you won't win the war. I hope you die screaming of cancer.' Lesser members of the gang – Brian Bird who had been the 'overseas manager', Graeme Green and James Johnson – were gaoled for six, six and five years respectively for their part in the smuggling. Osbourne was never caught. Six weeks after the shooting he was found dead on Hackney Marshes. An inquest recorded an open verdict but former associates say he died of a heart-attack and was kept in a deep-freeze while his colleagues decided what to do with him.

The quantities seized by police and Customs grew ever larger and the smuggling methods more ingenious. In January 1991 a van supposedly carrying inert nuclear-waste samples from the Dounreay power station was stopped by a policeman in Newtonmore in the Highlands of Scotland. Inside, in cellophane and Gucci wrappers, was 500 kilograms (1100 pounds) of cocaine worth, it was said in court later, £101 million. So ended Operation Klondyke.

For more than a year Scottish Customs officers posing as fish farmers, tourists and film crews had been following the smugglers, who were mainly young Scots who had met while working on the oil rigs. The smugglers had taken their work seriously and had memorized the faces of all the officers who appeared in a documentary series on Customs work called *The Duty Men*. To no avail. The four men who were caught were gaoled for a total of fifty-seven years. Chris Howarth, a Yorkshireman who lived in Ullapool, received twenty-five years. The case demonstrated that the Scottish Highlands and Islands, with 4000 miles of coast and 700 separate islands, offered fabulous opportunities for sea-smugglers.

One Highland cannabis smuggler, Boyd Keen, gaoled for eight years in the mid-eighties, described the experience in almost lyrical terms: 'I took my old harmonica out and gave the distant Africa coast

Operation Wrecker: police examine the drugs-smuggling lorry and (inset) Leonard Watkins, gaoled for life.

a burst of "Leaving Port Askaig" and followed it with the jaunty air of "John D. Burgess of Coll". Both tunes written by men leaving old familiar places, men going out into the unknown to face their future.' Keen soon discovered that one of the disadvantages of taking the high road was the heavy sentencing policy of Scottish judges.

In England, barely a month seemed to pass without new record seizures or record gaol sentences passed, although neither seizure nor sentence seemed to dent the market whether for the old (cannabis) or the new (Ecstasy).

On 28 May 1993 the country's largest Ecstasy trial concluded with sentences of ten years for Thomas Slater, eight and a half for his son Zachary and six for Gary Eales. Slater senior was ordered to pay £600 000 of his profits under the Drugs Trafficking Offences Act in a trial that had lasted twenty weeks and had itself run into the millions of pounds. A new generation of drugs trials had started. As cannabis smuggler Derek Maughan says: 'A lot of younger guys come up today who didn't come up the way the older criminal did, by being a thief or a fence or whatever. Now all of a sudden, they're buying three or four thousand Ecstasy pills in Holland and getting £15 or £20 a time for them. They're making bundles of money. They're millionaires at twenty-three.'

But more significantly, perhaps, the old robbers had already moved emphatically into the game. In August 1989 the Great Train Robbers Tommy Wisbey and Jimmy Hussey were both gaoled for cocaine dealing. Mr Justice Robert Sanders, sentencing them at Snaresbrook Crown Court in east London, said: 'You are both old enough and experienced enough to know exactly what you were doing and your motive was greed.'

Wisbey explains: 'We were against drugs all our lives but as the years went on, towards the seventies, it became more and more the "in" thing. Being involved in the Train Robbery, our name was good. They knew we had never grassed anyone, we had done our time without putting anyone in the frame ... But it's another ten years out of my life.'

Frank Simms, a robber from Stratford in east London, who had been gaoled for fifteen years for the 1972 £400 000 silver bullion robbery at Mountnessing in Essex, was one 'face' who saw the attractions of drugs. He financed one of Britain's largest amphetamine operations from a Hertfordshire cottage and was gaoled for thirteen years after a police raid in November 1990 uncovered the laboratory.

'In the sixties if you were a drug-taker, you could never be a proper thief,' says Simms, now a gaol keep-fit fanatic. 'It wasn't accepted.' But that had all changed by the time Simms saw the chance of fast profits in the speed business. He was accused of supplying 40 per cent of the amphetamines in the country and running a £200 million operation, a proposition he dismisses as ridiculous, citing the tendency of the authorities to exaggerate the worth of drugs hauls. But he agrees he was fairly caught, attributing to the police 'more strokes than a cat o' nine tails' and ruing a cocaine habit which he thinks made him nastier and affected his judgment.

He says that some of the team he was financing were taking advantage of him, making money behind his back: 'It's all going to pot. There's no loyalty. The youngsters are probably looking at us saying "Look at that silly old sod." We're like the old Dad's Army.'

Other underworld names have been weighed off in the nineties.

In October 1990 Eddie Richardson was gaoled for twenty-five years for his part in a multi-million-pound cocaine- and cannabis-smuggling operation. The judge, Mr Justice Schiemann, at Winchester Crown Court, told him: 'It was a terrible crime. It would not be fanciful to liken it to spraying bullets into a crowd.' Under the Drugs Trafficking Offences Act a confiscation order for £356 979 was slapped on him. Richardson and his colleagues were alleged to have tried to bring in 153 kilograms (339 pounds) of cocaine and two tons of cannabis worth £6 million in a balsawood container shipped to Southampton. His sentence did not surpass the longest in a drug-smuggling case – that given to Paul Dye who was gaoled for twenty-eight years in 1986 for heroin smuggling.

In October 1992 Joey Pyle, the enigmatic figure who had popped up in the history of the underworld so many times, found himself in the Old Bailey on a drugs charge. The man who had been present during the Pen Club killing in 1960, who had shared drinks and jokes with Charlie Richardson, who had acted for the Krays, but who had walked free from many cases, was caught on a heroin and morphine sulphate charge. At the age of fifty-six, he was gaoled for fourteen years after being caught in a classic sting in which undercover officers infiltrated his own office staff.

One of his co-defendants was Pete Gillett, the adopted son of Reg Kray whom Gillett had met in Parkhurst prison. Gillett had been hoping for a career as a pop singer and had even recorded a song called 'Masquerade' that Reg had written for him. Pyle, who had show-business connections and an office at Pinewood Studios, was helping to relaunch his career.

In April 1993, Robert Tibbs of the Tibbs family, described in court as a company director now based in Suffolk, was gaoled for eight years for a one-and-a-quarter-ton cannabis shipment that had made its way from Morocco to Oban on the west coast of Scotland. He was ordered to pay £200 000 under the DTOA or alternatively face another three years inside.

The old criminal families and gangs were now linked to the new world of drugs. For many of them, the real money was no longer in safes or security vans with all the attendant risks of capture. Drugs could provide a far steadier, if less spectacular, income. But for some the old lure of that one massive job lingered on.

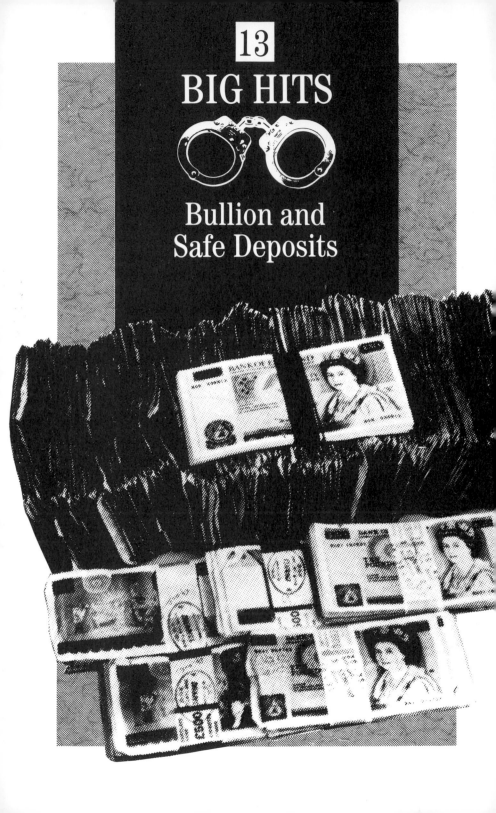

13

BIG HITS

Bullion and Safe Deposits

*T*he leader of the raid on the headquarters of Security Express in Shoreditch, east London, on 2 April 1983 was described as a 'Jack Hawkins figure'. This was a reference to the 1960 film *The League of Gentlemen* in which Hawkins played a mysterious ex-army officer who led a team of disillusioned ex-servicemen in a meticulously planned robbery which was to make their fortunes. In the original version of the film the robbers escaped but the rules of censorship of the day demanded that crime should not be seen to pay and the team were all caught in the final reel of the revised version. Although some of the men who robbed Security Express of £5 961 097 were also rounded up, many have never been found. More significantly, the raid was the first of a series of multi-million-pound heists that were to set new records and cross fresh boundaries of crime.

The robbers, around fifteen men all dressed in black, broke into the Curtain Road building known locally as Fort Knox, captured the supervisor, Greg Counsel, and forced him to admit the unsuspecting staff, who were tied up as they arrived. The robbers obtained the combinations of the vaults where the money was held by pouring petrol over one of the staff and threatening to set fire to him. They spoke in bogus Irish accents – as had the team in *The League of Gentlemen* – and were clearly well briefed, knowing that one member of staff smoked a pipe and another owned a dog. It was the largest robbery since the Great Train Robbery and the stolen goods weighed 5 tons. Security Express offered a £500 000 reward.

It was nine months before there was a breakthrough. In January 1984 Johnny Knight, brother of Spanish exile Ronnie, was arrested. He had deposited around £250 000 in bank and building society accounts around north London and had bought a villa on the Costa del Sol. Knight and another man called Terry Perkins were gaoled as ringleaders of the group. Both received twenty-two years at the Old Bailey in June 1985 after being told by Mr Justice Richard Lowry that they were ruthless and evil men. 'Your aim was to live in luxury,' he admonished them. 'Other guilty men have not been caught.' Knight's brother Jimmy, John Horsely and William Hickson were given smaller sentences but the police accepted that many of the gang, including the man with the vital inside knowledge, had not been found. Around £2 million from the robbery was traced, but searches in banks in Spain found 'the cupboard bare' the court was told.

Nearly five years later Freddie Foreman, famous for his old associations with the Krays, was gaoled for nine years after being brought back from Spain to stand trial. The claim was that Foreman had boasted to Spanish police that he had taken part in the robbery, a scenario that, given Foreman's criminal background, seems highly unlikely. However, he had previous convictions for cannabis importation and for being an accessory after the murder of Jack 'The Hat' McVitie and the Spanish authorities were clearly keen to pull the beach towel out from under him. He was finally whisked out of Spain, in shorts and a foul temper, in July 1989.

Foreman was cleared of taking part in the robbery but found guilty on the fourteen lesser offences of handling its proceeds. What probably convicted him was the fact that, prior to the raid, he and his wife had a mere £75 in their bank accounts but within the next seven months had deposited some £362 280. His barrister, John Mathew QC, said, 'There has been a suggestion that he was leading the life not only of Riley but of a very rich Riley. He was not. He was certainly not doing a nine-to-five job in Spain but it was not a life of luxury or ostentation.' No matter. The 'Mean Machine', as the press liked to call him, had been disconnected. But the capture and sentencing of the Shoreditch team did not have the desired deterrent effect as another group of security men were to discover.

'Get on the floor or you're fucking dead,' were the straightforward if unoriginal words that first alerted the guards at the Heathrow International Trading Estate that they were about to be the victims of the largest robbery in British history.

The instructions were delivered just before seven on the morning of Saturday, 26 November 1983, and were the start of a heist and an investigation that were to end in the death of an undercover officer, the recycling of tens of millions of pounds worth of stolen bullion and gaol sentences that totalled more than 200 years. This was the robbery that was to become known in both police and criminal circles simply as 'Brink's-Mat'.

As with so many major robberies, both the strength and the weakness of the operation was an inside man, in this case security guard Tony Black. He was the brother-in-law of career criminal Brian 'The Colonel' Robinson, who was then living in New Cross, south London. Black was already working for Brink's-Mat in 1980 and had supplied Polaroid snaps of the insides of the security vans for Robinson, who courted him on weekend fishing trips. Black was promised that something would be put away for him in a Swiss bank account if the job succeeded, but told that he would have to continue working there for at least a further five years to allay suspicion. He was given Plasticine and cuttlefish so that he could make impressions of the warehouse keys which he then passed back to the team which had been assembled by Robinson.

On the morning of the robbery Black overslept – he had been too nervous to enjoy a normal night's rest – and his criminal colleagues thought that, in the elegant vernacular, 'his arsehole had dropped out'. But he fulfilled his part of the bargain, at least initially. Excusing himself to go to the toilet, he managed to give a wave to the waiting robbers who crashed in fully armed to tie up the security guards.

As Black lay bound on the floor one of the robbers, the hot-headed Micky McAvoy, whispered encouragingly to him: 'It's all right, we've got the lot.' Indeed they had, a far greater haul than they had imagined. They had expected to get between £1 million and £2 million which was the normal amount of cash deposited on a Friday night. But a large consignment of gold for onward transit on the Saturday had arrived late the previous night and when one of the guards failed to remember his part of the combination-lock number of the safe containing the cash the team settled on the gold bullion. Its enormous value inevitably provoked a massive investigation.

But if Tony Black had facilitated the entry of the robbers, he was soon to facilitate their discovery. It was not long before the Flying Squad found the weak link – there was surprise in their ranks that Robinson would have used someone so identifiably close to him. Black had no criminal pedigree and was soon making statements and identifying the robbers. Robinson, McAvoy and a man called Tony White were arrested.

On 17 February 1984 Black pleaded guilty and was sentenced to six years, after the court had been told that he would assist in the prosecution of the main conspirators. The judge, Mr Justice David Tudor-Price, told him solemnly that, 'You and your family will for ever be fugitives from those you so stupidly and so wickedly helped.'

Robinson, McAvoy and White, the men Black had named, appeared at the Old Bailey on 25 October. They offered alibi evidence in their defence and challenged the evidence of Black. White was cleared but both the other two men were gaoled for twenty-five years after a trial during which the jurors were given police protection and had their telephone calls intercepted.

But if the robbers were now inside facing long sentences, what had happened to the bullion? The police had their suspicions but little hard evidence. It was some time before they targeted Kenneth Noye. A businessman in his mid-thirties, Noye lived in a mansion in the village of West Kingsdown in Kent with his wife Brenda and their two children. He was a bright and ambitious man, who had established lucrative haulage and property companies and had worked hard to capitalize on his successes which gave him an entrée into an affluent Kentish world of charity dinners, Freemasonry and squash clubs. He had, however, a number of minor offences to his name. These were for receiving stolen property and evasion of duty on importation of a firearm.

Noye was observed shifting large sums of money and purchasing gold bars in St Helier, Jersey. The police also took an interest in a visitor to his home, an unassuming man called Brian Reader who had gone on the run to the Continent while awaiting trial in a case in which supergrass Micky Gervaise was due to give evidence; he had convictions for store-breaking and burglary. By the beginning of 1985, following information from London gold dealers, the pair were under heavy surveillance. The police were also particularly interested in a bullion company in Bristol, Scadlynn Ltd, whose managing director was Garth Chappell. There was evidence that it had experienced an upsurge in its activities not long after the robbery.

It was decided that Noye's home should be staked out by two undercover officers. In January 1985 Detective Constables John Fordham and Neil Murphy hid in the grounds in camouflage gear. The Noye home was guarded by two Rottweilers and the suspicious animals scented the men's presence and started barking. Murphy tried to feed them the yeast tablets which had been recommended as a way of keeping them quiet, but to no effect. He beat a retreat, gesturing to Fordham who he imagined would follow suit.

The Noyes and Reader, who was visiting them, had been alerted by the barking and Kenneth, taking a torch and a knife from the garage, went to investigate. As he was later to tell it, he saw a figure in a Balaclava: 'I thought that was my lot. I thought I was going to be a dead man ... As far as I was concerned, I was fighting for my life.' He said that Fordham had struck him and that he had lashed out with his knife, stabbing the officer ten times. He demanded to know who the wounded figure was and Fordham gasped out 'SAS – on maneouvres', which was presumably his final attempt to maintain the secrecy of the operation. In the meantime, Reader had fled the house.

Brenda Noye, hearing the commotion, had come to her husband's aid with a shotgun and, on discovering what had happened, had returned to the house to call an ambulance and fetch a camera to record Fordham's appearance. 'You see a man in a Balaclava and a camouflage suit, you don't say "excuse me, before I hit you, are you a police officer?"',' said Mrs Noye later.

Murphy could tell that something had gone terribly wrong and was already radioing his concerns to the control point. Soon the Flying Squad was arriving in numbers. Fordham was pronounced dead later that night and Noye was arrested. Reader, who had tried to hitch a lift away from the area, was arrested. Both the Noyes and Reader were charged with murder.

The charges against Mrs Noye were later dropped but Reader and Noye stood trial at the Old Bailey in 1986. It was a highly-charged affair; Murphy, who had suffered a breakdown, had difficulty giving his evidence. Noye's defence was straightforwardly put by John Mathew QC, best known as a devastating prosecutor: that Noye had been alerted by the dogs, that he had seen a man dressed like a rapist, that the man had attacked him and he had defended himself. To the anger of the police, the jury acquitted both men. But Noye was now a marked man and official determination to convict him for connection with Brink's-Mat hardened.

Five months later Noye and Reader were back in court again, with five others including Garth Chappell, charged with disposing of the proceeds of the robbery and accused of handling stolen goods and evading VAT. Noye, Reader and Chappell were convicted of handling. Noye was given the maximum sentence of fourteen years, which he believed had more to do with what had happened to Detective Constable Fordham than the offence, Chappell received ten years and Reader nine. The case was described as 'the worst case of handling stolen goods that we have encountered' and the robbery itself as 'astounding in its audaciousness' by an unsympathetic Lord Justice Watkins when it eventually reached the Court of Appeal.

Solicitor Michael Relton, who had handled much of the laundering through foreign banks, was also convicted for his part and gaoled for twelve years, later reduced on appeal. Relton was the archetypal bent lawyer so hated by the police – or most of the police, since he did defend large numbers of officers charged with corruption offences. His success in laundering and investing the money had been such that he was virtually able to give up his law practice.

But the saga was not over. The police were still searching for people they believed had been involved. John Palmer, a Birmingham-born man who had picked up the nickname 'Goldfinger', was arrested in July 1986 on his return from Brazil where he had flown after being expelled from Spain. He stood trial on charges of handling the

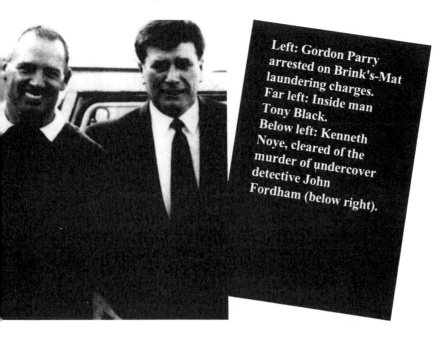

Left: Gordon Parry arrested on Brink's-Mat laundering charges.
Far left: Inside man Tony Black.
Below left: Kenneth Noye, cleared of the murder of undercover detective John Fordham (below right).

proceeds of the robbery and was acquitted. He blew a kiss to the jury and disappeared to Tenerife where he was reported to be running a time-share company a few years later.

The case trickled on. In September 1992, following an eight-month trial, four more members of the team – Gordon Parry, Brian Perry, Jean Savage and Patrick Clark – were gaoled for a total of thirty years for laundering £14.5 million of the money. Some of the loot had been invested in Docklands during its eighties boom and the rest moved through banks in the Channel Islands, the Isle of Man, Ireland, Switzerland and Liechtenstein. It was the ninth trial related to the robbery and raised the cost of the prosecution high into the millions.

But while Brink's-Mat was wending its way through the courts another, even more spectacular, robbery was being planned and executed. When it, too, finally came unstuck, even the trial judge seemed mildly impressed.

'The stakes were colossal,' Mr Justice Robert Lymbery told the immaculately dressed young man in the dock in front of him on 30 January 1989. 'Having lost, you have to pay the price accordingly. In this court I have seen a man of charm and courtesy, a man of substantial abilities. But these qualities, combined with others, serve to make you a very dangerous man.'

It was probably an assessment with which the man at whom it was directed, Valerio Viccei, would have broadly agreed. The Italian, who had just been convicted of the multi-million-pound robbery of the Knightsbridge Safe Deposit Centre in July 1987, was never one for false modesty or, indeed, any other kind of modesty. Had he decided to leave London speedily after the heist, instead of cruising its more expensive streets in a Ferrari Testarossa, he might have remained free instead of facing a twenty-two-year sentence.

The robbery itself was possibly the largest one that has ever taken place in the United Kingdom. The caveat is necessary because it is still unclear exactly how much was stolen. Many holders of the safety-deposit boxes have declined to say how much they lost and Viccei claims that cocaine and laundered money was contained in them. At the time of the trial the police estimate was £40 million. The cover of Viccei's autobiography, *Knightsbridge, the Robbery of the Century*, tells of 'How I escaped with £60 million', although nowhere in the book itself is the figure mentioned.

The robbery was significant in more ways than just the sum that was stolen. Viccei had assembled what was essentially an international team to carry out the job, breaking the fairly traditional English mode of such operations where only tried and tested 'staunch' allies were entrusted with so major a robbery. To carry out the spectacular crime the Italian recruited an Israeli, a Russian, a Pakistani and some home-grown English heavies.

Viccei himself came from Ascoli Piceno on Italy's Adriatic coast, the son of a lawyer father and a furrier mother. He had studied law briefly then joined up with a group of neo-fascists in 1972 and blew up the cables of a television station he considered too left-wing. Claiming Nietzsche as his inspiration, he burned out the offices of left-wing political parties but was eventually arrested and gaoled. In his autobiography, he records his transformation from teenage neo-fascist fire-bomber to mature career criminal: 'I have abandoned the rarefied pure air of my idealized forest and travelled all the way down to the polluted town. I switched targets and instead of destabilizing society, I long to make money just like its most respected citizens do.'

He arrived in Britain in the mid-eighties on the run from the police in Italy, linked up with members of the underworld and carried out a robbery of a branch of Coutts bank with one English colleague, despite being tackled by a game woman clerk who bit his fingers. The profits helped him move into a smart flat in St John's Wood in north London and he undertook a further bank robbery, netting £50 000 and escaping on a motor cycle. But in January 1987 the police tracked him down with an extradition warrant and he only escaped by kicking his way out of a car and hiding out briefly in Lord's cricket ground, dressed as a hard-hat workman. After a holiday in Colombia, where he was able to indulge his appetite for pure cocaine, he returned to England. He was still undeterred in his desire to carry out the mythical 'one big job' and to fund it he and another robber stole around £70 000 in travellers' cheques from the Mayfair branch of American Express in May.

Viccei had meanwhile met Parvez Latif, the Pakistani manager of the Knightsbridge Safe Deposit Centre, where Viccei was storing his ill-gotten gains. Latif had impressed him by his discretion over what were clearly illicit dealings, and when Viccei found that a friend in London's night-club circuit also knew him, he realized that the centre could be the big job he was waiting for. He approached Latif and over dinners and champagne at Tramp's night club gradually massaged him with flattery, promises of amazing wealth and some of the purest Colombian cocaine. Viccei also started an affair with Latif's glamorous girlfriend, Pamela Seamarks; he later repaid her friendship with a lubriciously soft-porn description of their liaison in his memoirs.

Viccei's strategy was simple and in some ways almost old-fashioned. Latif would arrange to have the Centre closed for a brief period; he would then allow Viccei and his team, posing as potential clients, to enter. Latif would continue his act as he and his colleagues – a supervisor and two guards – were tied up and the boxes robbed. With the inside knowledge from Latif, Viccei would be able to break into the most profitable boxes and make an escape with enough time to throw off the police.

On Sunday, 12 July 1987, armed with a Beretta and a sawn-off shotgun, Viccei led his team to the building. It had been closed and a note left on the door explained that, 'We apologize to all our customers for any inconvenience caused to them during the improvements to our security system. Business as usual from tomorrow. Thank you.' Dressed in Armani (suit), Hermes (tie) and Ferragamo (loafers), Viccei and a colleague rang the bell and were greeted by Latif. They pretended they were ordinary customers who had telephoned a few minutes earlier asking for an appointment. This exchange was watched by the guards who were not in on the plot and therefore had to be misled.

Viccei was then taken on a phoney tour of the premises during which he pulled a gun on Latif and 'forced' him to call the guards.

Viccei made an overt homosexual overture to one of the Centre's employees, which so upset the man that he was offguard when Viccei pulled a gun and subdued him. The robbers were then able to let in two colleagues to help with the attack on the boxes. With power drills, crowbars, sledge-hammers and screwdrivers, the team prised open the steel boxes and grabbed the banknotes, jewels and drugs inside them. But in his eagerness to whack open the doors, Viccei did not notice that he had torn his glove and cut his finger, leaving blood and fingerprints all over the vaults.

As the team left Viccei warned the Centre's employees, who were tied up, handcuffed and fearful, that he was leaving one member of the gang behind for a period and that if any of them attempted to escape the man had instructions to shoot. The team loaded the haul into a white Renault van and sped off. As Viccei remembered: 'The atmosphere was one of pure ecstasy: we had written a page of criminal history. We had just pulled off the boldest, largest and most spectacular robbery in recent times.' To celebrate, he fulfilled an old fantasy and filled the bathtub of the hide-out flat with money and jewels.

The reaction of the media was not dissimilar to the way they had reacted to the Great Train Robbery. Here was a daring robbery in which no one had been killed and in which the financial victims, either fairly or unfairly, elicited little sympathy. There was even an element of *schadenfreude* in watching the damp-eyed souls who gathered outside the Centre to find out if their boxes had been emptied.

But the bloody fingerprints, coupled with weak links in his team, were to prove Viccei's undoing. In addition, his self-confidence got the better of him and, instead of fleeing the country, he stayed and played. His arrogance – he was, in the Italian vernacular, a man who 'liked the smell of his own fart' – was his undoing.

Inspector Fred Leach soon realized that Viccei was a part of the operation and knew that he had been associated with an Israeli called Israel Pinkas when he had slipped away from the police earlier in the year. The police put Pinkas under observation and noted that he was using Whites Hotel just north of Hyde Park as a base. They decided to check on Whites' other guests and found that one was a man called 'Raiman' (Viccei's alias) and, the key factor for them, that he was Italian. The police now realized that the man who had just left the hotel in his Ferrari was the man they sought.

Viccei was finally cornered in a traffic jam at Marble Arch and dragged out through the windscreen of his beloved car with, according to the arresting police, the words, 'Right, chaps, the game is up now

Valerio Viccei (left), gaoled for the £40 million Knightsbridge safe deposit robbery, and his inside man Parvez Latif.

and you have no need to be nasty. You are the winners so calm down and everything is going to be fine.'

The trial was in many ways a formality for Viccei. One of his team, Steve Mann, decided to co-operate with the police and received five years. Peter O'Donohue was gaoled for eleven years, David Poole for sixteen and Eric Rubin for twelve. Israel 'Izzy' Pinkas got ten years, later reduced to nine. Parvez Latif, who had betrayed the trust of his employers, received the heavier sentence of eighteen years. Pamela Seamarks was given a suspended sentence. Viccei's twenty-two years was the heaviest sentence and he was soon in Parkhurst, knocking out his story with the help of James Nicholson, the Prince of Darkness. In 1993 he was, as he had predicted, transferred to an Italian gaol to await trial for offences in Italy.

In *The League of Gentlemen*, as the police close in one of the robbers tells another: 'Give them their money's worth at the trial and then flog your memoirs to the Sunday papers.' After the Knightsbridge trial *News of the World* readers were to discover that on one occasion 'sultry Pamela Seamarks lay naked on her lover's bed and felt her skin crawl as she looked down at the £4 million plum-sized diamond nestling in her navel. It was part of the treasure Italian Stallion Valerio Viccei had stolen ...'

The underworld crimes of the nineties had a less light-hearted air to them.

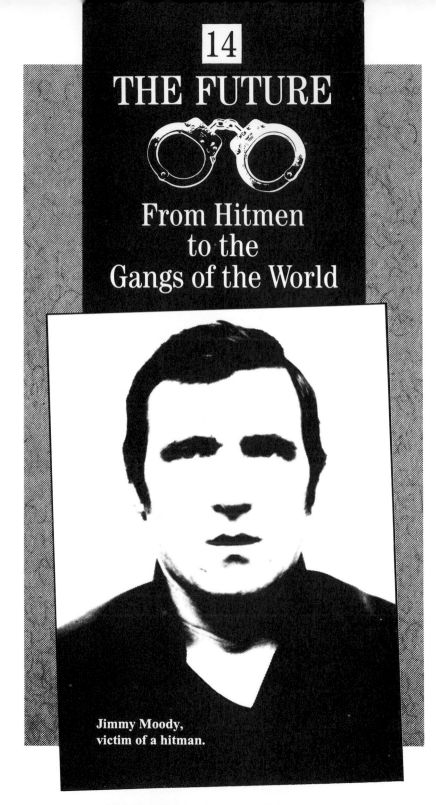

14

THE FUTURE

From Hitmen
to the
Gangs of the World

Jimmy Moody,
victim of a hitman.

The massively built character known to the regulars at the Royal Hotel in Hackney, east London, as 'Mick' and often employed locally as a bouncer, was having a quiet pint of bitter in the pub on the evening of 1 June 1993. A stranger wandered in and ordered a pint of Foster's lager, which he left on the counter. Then the man reached inside his jacket, pulled out a Webley .38 revolver and shot 'Mick' four times, cursing as he did so, before disappearing in a stolen Ford Fiesta parked outside.

'Mick' was, in fact, Jimmy Moody, the man who had helped wounded gang members escape from the Mr Smith's shoot-out back in 1966, the man who had stood trial with the Richardson gang, the man who had been a member of the 'Chainsaw Gang' of robbers, who broke into security vans in the seventies using chainsaws, the man who had escaped from Brixton prison with IRA man Gerard Tuite thirteen years earlier. Remarkably, he had been on the run ever since before surfacing under a pseudonym in east London. More significantly, some people believed he was now a hitman and the person behind the double murder in 1991, in another London pub, of a young man called David Brindle and a bystander.

The 'hitman' had re-emerged with a vengeance, sometimes literally, in the nineties. In January 1993, Robert Urquhart, the wealthy owner of the Elstree Golf Club, was walking in Marylebone with his Thai girlfriend when a man on a Yamaha motor cycle, dressed in black leather and wearing a crash helmet, shot him three times in the head. Urquhart's shocked family offered a £100 000 reward for information that would lead to the people behind his killing.

Coming as it did in the wake of a series of such anonymous and premeditated shootings, the killing rekindled the notion of the gangland hitman, the hired gun who had always been part of the scene in the United States and Italy without ever appearing as a major figure in the British underworld. But the hitman had in fact cast his shadow nearly twenty years earlier.

Terence 'Teddy Bear' Eve, a soft-toy manufacturer based in Dagenham, Essex, disappeared in November 1974. Two months later, not far away in Upminster, a transport contractor called George Brett and his ten-year-old son Terry also disappeared. Brett's wife, Mavis, told police that a man who called himself Jennings had visited and asked Brett to come and inspect some goods. Brett had gone to do so and taken his son along for the ride. His Mercedes was found in King's Cross but, despite a massive police hunt, neither father nor son were ever seen again. There were other puzzling disappearances:

of Robert Brown, a criminal and wrestler, in 1975; of Fred Sherwood, a nursing-home proprietor from Herne Bay in Kent, in 1978; of Robert Andrews, a roofing contractor from Barkingside in Essex, in 1978. But there was little indication that they were connected.

Then in June 1979 an armed robbery was committed on a Security Express van in Hertford. One of the robbers blundered and left his BMW car keys in the pocket of the uniform overalls used in the robbery and abandoned in a public toilet nearby. Identified and arrested, he told police the names of his associates. Three, including a man called John Childs, were speedily arrested. More ominous was the claim that the fifth robber, Henry 'Big H' MacKenny, who was still at large, had been involved in a number of unsolved murders. The names of Andrews, Eve and the Bretts were mentioned as victims and there were tales of a mincing-machine at the factory where the soft toys were manufactured. A major inquiry was launched.

MacKenny was a six-foot six-inches tall engineer. He was also a diver who had invented a new type of diving-jacket valve, a point he was to make much of at his later trial. His past included convictions for causing actual bodily harm, car and lorry theft and a couple of failed marriages. Childs, in contrast, was small and scruffy with a wispy beard and spectacles and was possessed of what MacKenny described as 'an inferiority complex to end all inferiority complexes'. Interviewed in Oxford prison, by Detective Chief Superintendent Frank Cater, Childs slowly embarked on a chilling series of confessions. 'Those hours were among the most horrific of my entire police career,' said Cater. The victims had either been strangled or shot in the head. The bodies had been burned in the fireplace at Childs' home in Poplar, east London, and the ashes thrown in the river at Wanstead Park.

It had all begun in 1972 after Childs had been released from prison. He had started a small business with MacKenny and former fellow-inmate Terence Pinfold at a factory in Dagenham, where they produced the MacKenny diving-jackets. Eve was sharing the premises and the others cold-bloodedly decided, for purely mercenary reasons, to get rid of him and take over the soft-toy business. According to Childs, Pinfold had said that, 'With all the unruly behaviour and muggings and stabbings that went on in London, what a great shame it was that someone couldn't mug and stab Mr Eve.' Eve was lured to the factory one night, beaten with a hammer by Childs and strangled with a rope by MacKenny. The men stripped to their underpants, cut up the body at Childs' flat and attempted to mangle it in an industrial mincer bought through *Exchange & Mart* for £25. This failed, as did

254

efforts to flush it in chunks down the lavatory. The remains were eventually burned in the fireplace, a process that took several days.

The bloody pattern continued. Childs claimed that Pinfold had offered to act as their agent, finding clients for them, while they carried out the executions.

The unfortunate George Brett was an early victim of a contract killing: £2000 was the price offered by a man with a grudge against him. Childs tricked Brett into coming to 'the factory' to discuss a possible deal. The killers had not anticipated that the boy would come along for the ride but his presence did not seem to deter them. MacKenny shot Brett through the head with a Sten gun while Childs held the boy. MacKenny then shot the boy, who was still holding a teddy bear he had been given on arrival.

The double killing presented a dilemma for MacKenny and Childs. The factory's handyman, Robert Brown, was on the run from prison and might suspect something. If caught he could implicate them. He was told that the authorities were on to him and offered a safe house as a hideaway. Thus lured to Childs' house, Brown was messily murdered with a diver's knife, a fireman's axe and a swordstick. He was sawn up, burned and his ashes scattered on Wanstead Flats.

A £4000 price had been offered for the killing of Fred Sherwood in 1978. Chillingly, by the time he confessed, Childs had even forgotten the actual motive. Sherwood had a Rover for sale and Childs pretended to be a potential buyer, asking Sherwood to drive him to his brother's house in Dagenham to pick up the money to pay for it. The house was MacKenny's bungalow, where 'Big H' was waiting to blow out Sherwood's brains with a silenced revolver. The first shot did not kill him and he was finally beaten to death with a hammer by Childs.

The Andrews killing was both personal and business. Mac-Kenny had fallen for Andrews' wife, Gwen, and saw killing her husband as a convenient solution to an old problem. Childs cautioned that 'Big H' would be an obvious suspect but agreed to take part when MacKenny offered him £500 for his trouble. Their plot was ingenious. They would send Andrews a postcard from Wisbech in Cambridgeshire with a woman's signature, hinting at an extramarital affair. Mrs Childs signed the card and also phoned the Andrews' home, giving the impression that she wanted to speak to Andrews. Andrews became suspicious, thinking that his wife might be up to something, and, fatally, asked MacKenny for advice. MacKenny blithely suggested hiring a 'private detective' – Childs.

At Childs' house the unsuspecting Andrews was offered vodka

from a bottle that had been wiped clean of fingerprints while Childs went through the pretence of taking details of the 'case'. MacKenny shot the victim through the back of the head. The pair then drove Andrews' car to a spot known as Foul Anchor on the River Nene near Wisbech, where MacKenny knew the river flowed strongly. The car was driven into the river by MacKenny, in a diver's suit, with the vodka bottle on the back seat. Andrews, so the theory would go, must have crashed the car while drunk and *en route* to his mysterious mistress. The body was disposed of in the now familiar manner.

After this amazing unburdening by Childs, who appears to have made a total of only £3180 for the killings, the hunt was on for 'Big H'. Although Scotland Yard hoped to keep his identity and the reasons for the hunt secret, a story surfaced in the *Daily Mirror*. It was decided on 29 July 1979 to release MacKenny's photograph as a wanted – and dangerous – man. A tip-off led police to a pub in Ilford but MacKenny managed to out-drive his pursuers. Further information led the police two months later to a maisonette in Plaistow, east London. The house was surrounded by armed police. When they telephoned, MacKenny answered the telephone himself and said he would give himself up, which he duly did in the glare of spotlights and under the gaze of the marksmen.

In October 1980 MacKenny stood trial. It was an ugly and emotional affair. MacKenny attacked the evidence of Childs, who had already pleaded guilty, calling him 'ill-mannered and crude in the extreme' and attacking his 'frightful' attitude to women. But his venom was reserved for the jury who convicted him of four of the six murders and whom he called 'mugs and mongols'. He was gaoled for life with a recommendation from Mr Justice May that he not be released for twenty-five years. Pinfold was gaoled for life for the murder of Eve. Relatives of the victims and the guilty screamed insults in the public gallery. Few cases involving professional criminals can have done more to deglamorize crime: the procession of killings had been both merciless and mercenary.

Another 'hit' that had attracted great attention was that carried out on model Barbara Gaul. She was the flamboyant and vivacious fourth wife of property millionaire John Gaul, who had made his fortune by renting his Soho flats out to prostitutes. In 1976 Mrs Gaul, who was in the process of divorcing her husband, was shot in the car park of the Black Lion hotel in Brighton by two brothers, Keith and Roy 'Micky' Edgeler. She died later in hospital. Gaul fled to Malta and successfully resisted extradition by Sussex police.

THE HOUSE OF HORROR

THIS is the death room at 13 Dolphin House, Poplar, where murder was a business. The £6-a-week flat was rented by self confessed mass murderer John Childs.

His fixation with vio'ence was shown by a macabre arsenal of weapons displayed on the walls of the room.

They included axes, daggers, knives, bayonets, a crossbow, speargun, machete, air rifle and Chinese flails.

But it was the fire that chilled ... Six bodies were des-...... tiny grate. Forensic scientists couldn't believe that the bodies could be disposed of in such a fashion.

So they cut up an 11½ stone pig and burned it in the same way as the bodies were said to have been cremated. It took 13 hours.

ILLUSTRATION: Bob Williams

John Childs (left) and Henry 'Big H' MacKenny, and a press reconstruction of the room in Child's home where the victims were dismembered.

The brothers were both gaoled for life. 'Micky' Edgeler admitted he had carried out the shooting for £5000 but resolutely declined to name his paymaster. However, there is little doubt that Gaul hired him, wanting to be rid of his wife either because she had potentially embarrassing information that she was threatening to disclose or because he wanted to avoid the expense of divorce. Gaul died of a heart attack in 1989 without ever standing trial.

But the hitman as a public figure did not really emerge until the nineties, most spectacularly with killings like those of Moody and Urquhart. These murders came in the wake of a series of shootings that involved men in motor-cycle gear blasting their victims on their doorsteps or in their local pubs, as though part of the purpose of the killing was to make a public statement. Police investigating these cases noticed the prevalence of guns adapted to take silencers, which they saw as a sign of hitmen at work.

One of the earlier victims was Ahmet 'Abbi' Abdullahi, a member of the Arif south London gangster family, who was shot dead in March 1991 in a betting-shop in Walworth, south London. Two brothers, Patrick and Tony Brindle, were cleared of his murder after a trial in which witnesses were allowed to give evidence from behind a screen. Earlier, the Brindles' brother, David, had been shot dead on 3 August 1991 in The Bell in Walworth by two men whose random blasting also killed a bystander, Stanley Silk. One of the hitmen shouted 'This is for Abbi' as they fired.

Another pub killing indicated the problems police faced in trying to find the perpetrators of such crimes. In July 1992 Kevin Fox, an east London criminal, got into an argument in the Memory Lane pub in Canning Town, east London, went out and returned with a gun. He opened fire, wounding the landlord's son, in a pub with around fifteen drinkers in it. Fox was set upon, beaten with a fire extinguisher and billiard cues, shot with his own gun and given a kicking outside the pub into the bargain. Despite so many witnesses, a year later no one had been charged with his killing.

Bumping off fellow members of the underworld has not been an entirely male pursuit. In 1990 Linda Calvey, nicknamed 'the Black Widow', was gaoled for the murder of her boyfriend, armed robber Ron Cook. He was supposedly killed because she had spent all his money while he was inside and was worried about his reaction. She had persuaded another criminal, Daniel Reece, who had become her lover while Cook was inside, to do the job when Cook was on a day release from Maidstone prison. But Reece panicked and Mrs Calvey fired the fatal shot herself. She was the widow of bank robber Micky Calvey, who had been shot dead by police during a robbery.

Although this sudden spate of shootings in the early nineties attracted the immediate public attention, in the underworld there were other, more far-reaching, developments.

In May 1993 around a hundred people deeply involved in organized crime, from the United States and Hong Kong, from Japan and Russia, gathered in a Hampshire mansion built in the seventeenth century by a man who had been a member of the commission for the trial of Mary Queen of Scots and a friend of the writer Ben Jonson. It was not a Mafia sharcholders' meeting convening to discuss another profitable year, but the first-ever conference on the subject of organized crime to be held in Britain, jointly sponsored by Britain's National Criminal Intelligence Service and the University of Illinois. It brought together detectives and justice officials from over twenty countries and took as its theme the notion of international organized crime.

While Canadian geese landed on the estate's lake and white deer strolled across the driveway of the Bramshill estate which the Home Office had bought as a police staff college in 1953, delegates heard of the movements of the new Russian and eastern European gangs, the Chinese Triads, the Italian and American Mafia and the Hell's Angels and motorcycle gangs, who were said to be one of the most active of the crime groups in the United Kingdom.

The theme was internationalism. Russian criminals were seeking co-operation with German gangs to move their Kalashnikovs and AK47s and launder their money in the West. English villains wanted to shift their stolen cars to the Far East. The Yakuza, the Japanese Mafia, were considering the new financial markets of the west and the Italians were looking for new drug markets to the north. Guns arriving in Britain came from Spain and Holland, from Germany and Russia. Increasingly, it appeared that firearms were being used as currency for buying drugs or added to drugs cargoes. The underworld is indeed now worldwide.

But how powerful are the new international criminal organizations? In Britain, the Triads were reckoned to be operating as long ago as the end of the nineteenth century in London's Limehouse area and in Liverpool. They were active almost solely within their own communities until the growth in the drugs trade from the sixties onwards offered opportunities they could not turn down. Martin Booth in *The Triads* suggests that by the start of the nineties they were importing large quantities of heroin into Britain, and that the

14K was still the most powerful of the groups, along with the Wo Shing Wo, in Manchester, London, Liverpool, Birmingham and Glasgow and the Shui Fong which has bases in Southampton and the capital. The Triads are believed to control much of the Chinese video and music market and to have fingers in the rich pies of labour contracting, gambling, protection and prostitution, but their activities impinge only minimally on major organized crime in Britain.

Far more prominent, on the surface at least, are the Yardies, a name derived from the Jamaican backyards. Although there was a tendency in the eighties to label every major crime committed by a black person as Yardie-inspired, the real Jamaican Yardies, loose-knit and small in number, had the same sort of reputation for unpredictable violence as the Glaswegians had in London in the fifties and sixties. Roy Ramm, the head of a short-lived Yardie Squad set up by Scotland Yard in the eighties, described it as 'disorganized organized crime'. Some Yardies had come to Britain after police action against them in Jamaica hotted up in the nineties, others arrived from New York with false passports and found London and Manchester wide open for heavily enforced crack dealing. By 1993, drug wars between rival groups were claiming bodies on the doorsteps of Brixton in London and Moss Side in Manchester. The Moss Side gangs – the Goochies from Gooch Close and the Doddies from Doddington Close – sport different-coloured bandanas and use hi-tech radio scanners to monitor local police activity as they go about their drug business.

When Chris 'Tuffy' Bourne was shot dead in south London in the summer of 1993 it highlighted the level of violence involving Yardies, although it received less coverage than more traditional 'gangland' deaths. The murders were just as numerous and frightening as those taking place in the Royal Hotel and The Bell, but the violence was black-on-black and the media was still without a map to this new territory. As Detective Superintendent John Jones put it: 'They [the Yardies] have a philosophy that it is a short life but a sweet one.'

But what the Bramshill delegates found most significant was the movement from eastern Europe to the west. In the late fifties, after the Hungarian uprising and suppression, a small number of refugees from Budapest took part in armed robberies in Britain. But the end of the Cold War has had a far more dramatic effect: as order has broken down in former communist countries, the selling of arms and the passage of drugs from the east has rocketed. Britain, where money can easily be laundered through property purchases and where there is a market for guns and drugs, is an obvious resting place.

In March 1993 two Russian brothers were found dead in London. The body of one had been wrapped in a carpet, put in a box and deposited in a garage in Pinner, north-west London. It had been found after delivery men became suspicious about the smell emanating from the box. The other brother was found shot dead in his luxury West End flat. Nearly a hundred years after Russians were accused of bringing arms and lawlessness to these islands, the same fears were being publicly expressed.

By the early nineties, too, there were hints that the Yakuza, were starting to eye their compatriots' activities in the City of London. The Yakuza have existed in Japan for 300 years and are best known to the outside world for tattooing their entire bodies and ritually amputating a finger. They can operate by buying company stock, digging up scandalous information and demanding hush money. They also blackmail senior businessmen who have filed false tax returns or have sexual secrets. Detective Inspector Graham Saltmarsh of NCIS suggested in 1992 that the Sokaiya, the white-collar wing of the Yakuza, was attempting to establish itself in London.

Internationalism was also obvious in the growth of the market for luxury cars in the nineties. Ferraris, Mercedes and Porsches were being stolen to order and shipped to Japan and the Middle East where they could be sold for as much as £250 000 each. One gangleader claimed to have made as much as £30 million in a year.

There were still the British-based gangs, but most people outside the all-night clubs of the Angel or Walworth or Clerkenwell would be hard put to name any 'families' that had been in operation since the early seventies. No one wanted to put their head above the parapet.

Bucking the trend were the Arifs, a family of Turkish-Cypriot origin who finally emerged from the shadows of the Old Kent Road in the nineties, when brothers Dennis and Mehmet were gaoled for the attempted armed robbery of a Securicor van in Reigate in Surrey.

Dogan Arif, the oldest of the six brothers, had already been gaoled for an £8.5 million cannabis-smuggling plot – he had dabbled in football, briefly owning the non-league Fisher Athletic club – and Dennis and Bekir had convictions for conspiracy to rob. But it was the Reigate shoot-out that was to lift the veil on the family, whom police had been pursuing for more than a decade.

The Arif brothers enjoyed the high life. A family wedding at the Savoy cost £30 000 and, as the court heard in the brothers' robbery trial, many other 'families' had attended including 'the Colemans, Frasers, Whites, Adams and Hiscocks'.

The team that did the job had an impressive array of fire power, enough 'to start a small war', as was said during their trial: a 12-bore Browning self-loading rifle, a Brazilian-made pistol, a 1922 Browning pistol and a US Army self-loading pistol. The robbers had disguised themselves in Ronald Reagan and 'old man' masks and were hoping for a haul of around £800 000 which police believed could have been used to finance drug dealing. But armed police were waiting for them and Kenny Baker, a veteran bank robber, was shot dead, his Reagan mask still covering his face.

In December 1991 Dennis and Mehmet Arif and their brother-in-law, Tony Downer, were gaoled for twenty-two, eighteen and eighteen years. Dennis ran the imaginative defence that Baker had forced him to take part because he owed him money from gambling debts but the jury were unconvinced. The judge, Heather Steel, whose looks and forthright manner had won her a reputation in the Old Bailey for making the hearts of barristers beat faster, was unimpressed by the defence's references to the Great Train Robbers: 'In comparison with this case, the train robbers seem like gentlemen.'

Crime in the United Kingdom was a business in a way that it never had been before. By the early nineties it could claim to be the country's fastest-growing industry with an annual turnover of around £14 billion and the active full-time involvement of at least half a million people, including police, prison staff, judiciary, lawyers and career criminals. Estimates are necessarily vague but, using Customs and Home Office figures, it is possible to suggest that the drugs trade alone was worth around £3 billion and rising. The Association of British Insurers estimated that £400 million was being lost in arson and the Association for Payment Clearing Services estimated a loss of £166 million on plastic-card fraud. Other crimes – robbery and theft from commercial property (£316 million), fraud (£5.3 billion), burglary (£591 million), shop theft (£3.2 billion) and car crime (£626 million) – all point to a criminal economy heading in the direction of that of the United States.

The body count remains remarkably low. The 1993 figures for London show that only 172 people were murdered, a drop of thirteen on the previous year and less than a tenth of the 2000 figure that New York, a city of a slightly smaller size, finds acceptable. The Metropolitan Police used their firearms only six times. Chicago it ain't.

A new development in the early years of the decade was kidnapping people with access to money – a crime that some criminals had previously regarded as 'unBritish'. Peter White and Carl Harrison were gaoled for twenty and sixteen years in October 1992 for the kidnap of the wife of an airline cargo supervisor. The plan had been to hold Ann Blake, and thus put pressure on her husband Ian to let the robbers have access to around £6 million of precious stones and jewellery held in the KLM high-security vault at Heathrow airport. Two members of the team were, in fact, undercover officers – Harrison claimed they had acted as *agents provocateurs* – and the plot was foiled. More common was the kidnapping of the relatives of bank or superstore officials who would be held until safes had been unlocked or money passed over. In November 1992 John Calton, a former paratrooper and explosives expert, was gaoled at Chelmsford Crown Court for twenty-five years for kidnapping the families of businessmen in Suffolk and Essex and holding them to ransom.

Another new crime was food contamination blackmail, whereby a blackmailer threatened to contaminate a major food product on supermarket shelves unless he was paid. In 1990 the police had to suffer the indignity of one of their recently retired detective sergeants, Rodney Whitchelo, being gaoled for an extraordinary plot. Whitchelo, from Hornchurch in Essex, had learnt about food contamination while training to combat it. A seed had been sown, and when he took early retirement on grounds of ill-health he put his plot into action: he contaminated Pedigree pet foods and Johnson baby foods and demanded that the firms concerned pay money into accounts that he had previously set up in bogus names and left dormant.

He got away with it for months and more than £30 000 was paid out as police sought to catch him. They believed a gang was involved and spent millions on round-the-clock surveillance of targeted cashpoints. Some 200 copycat contaminations complicated the investigation and Whitchelo, still friends with police officers, was able to pick up information on the investigation during casual drinks with old mates. He was finally caught when two officers noticed a man donning a crash helmet as he left a car and headed for a cashpoint; Whitchelo had realized that some cashpoints were now covered by video cameras. He fainted on arrest and fought the case by claiming he was the victim of a Masonic conspiracy. Gaoled for seventeen years in December 1990, he would at least have the time to complete a book he had been planning: how to commit the perfect crime.

The growth of some other modern crimes has perhaps been exaggerated. Certainly, there is computer crime, whereby people shift money from one account to another by access to bank computers. However, this is essentially an old-fashioned fraud or theft, using the modern equivalent of ledgers and bankbooks. There is computer blackmail, too, whereby a virus is placed in a company's computer and money is demanded to have it identified. But such crimes are still rare. Much more common are mortgage frauds and share-ramping, areas where some of the bright but dishonest young men who might have gone into long firm frauds or black marketeering in a different era now see a bloodless way of making illegal money.

There is always a tendency to look back at a 'golden era' of crime, a magical time when the 'unwritten rules' were always observed, when crooks only attacked other crooks and a code of honour ruled. The theme of the Krays and Richardsons has always been that they did not injure any 'civilians', their victims were other members of the underworld who knew the game and had broken the rules. There was also a notion that a number of the older criminals were less acquisitive and spread their largesse around. But as Dick Hobbs observed in *Doing The Business*, the only Robin Hoods in the East End were pubs.

Bill Gardner, the Mr Smith's veteran, looks back nostalgically to a time when 'we always wore suits, ties, collars. Today they're walking about with designer stubbles and dirty old shoes and you think – where's the pride gone?'

Great Train Robber Tommy Wisbey agrees: 'Years ago we could go out on blags as you would call them and you would be able to go home to sleep and you wouldn't worry about who you told because you were all united. There was more camaraderie than there is today. All the principles have gone by the wayside.' As for the underworld: 'There's not such a thing as the underworld, they're just criminals, aren't they, known criminals.'

Certainly, little respect was shown for the elder statesmen of the underworld in August 1992 when 'Mad' Frankie Fraser, the Little Big Man of British crime, was shot in the head outside Turnmills night club in Clerkenwell. He survived, famously giving his name as 'Tutankhamen – I'm keeping mum' when he was taken to hospital, and gave the police no help as to his likely attacker.

In July 1993 three armed men in baseball caps and a hurry let themselves into a jewellery store in Hatton Garden, handcuffed the staff and made off with around £7 million worth of jewellery. The shooting of 'Mad' Frankie and the robbery both took place just round the corner from where Dickens' Fagin sent his fictional tearaways into action, and where Darby Sabini organized his protection rackets in the thirties. In many ways the underworld, for all its computerized internationalism, is still a small, small world indeed.

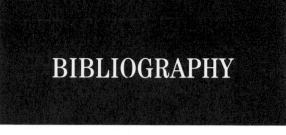

BIBLIOGRAPHY

Anon, *Lives of Robbers and Murderers*, Milner and Co., Undated
Ball, John, Chester, Lewis and Perrott, Roy, *Cops and Robbers*, André Deutsch, 1978
Bean, J. P., *The Sheffield Gang Wars*, D & D Publications, 1981
Beltrami, Joseph, *The Defender*, M & A Thomson, 1988
Booth, Martin, *The Triads*, Grafton Books, 1990
Boyle, Jimmy, *A Sense of Freedom*, Pan, 1977
Burt, Leonard, *Commander Burt of Scotland Yard*, Heineman, 1959
Byrne, Richard, *Safecracking*, Grafton 1991
Campbell, Duncan, *That Was Business, This Is Personal*, Secker and Warburg, 1990
Cannon, Joe, *Tough Guys Don't Cry*, Magnus, 1983
Cater, Frank and Tullett, Tom, *The Sharp End*, Grafton, 1990
Challenor, Harold, with Alfred Draper, *Tanky Challenor*, Leo Cooper, 1990
Cox, Barry, Shirley, John and Short, Martin, *The Fall of Scotland Yard*, Penguin, 1977
Darbyshire, Neil and Hilliard, Brian *The Flying Squad*, Headline, 1993
Dickson, John, *Murder Without Conviction*, Sphere 1988
Du Rose, John, *Murder Was My Business*, Mayflower, 1973
Eddy, Paul, Walden, Sarah and Sabogal, Hugo, *The Cocaine Wars*, Arrow, 1989
Fabian, Robert, *Fabian of the Yard*, Cedar Books, 1956
Fabian, Robert, *London After Dark*, Naldrett Press, 1954
Finmore, Rhoda Lee, *Immoral Earnings*, MH Publications, 1951
Firmin, Stanley, *Scotland Yard*, Hutchinson, 1948
Firmin, Stanley, *Crime Man*, Hutchinson, 1950
Forbes, George and Mehan, Paddy, *Such Bad Company*, Paul Harris Publishing, 1982
Fordham, John *Let's Join Hands and Contact the Living*, Elm Tree, 1986
Fordham, Peta, *The Robbers' Tale*, Hodder and Stoughton, 1965
Fordham, Peta, *Inside the Underworld*, Allen and Unwin, 1972
Fry, Colin, with Charlie Kray, *Doing the Business*, Smith Gryphon, 1993
Goodman, Jonathan and Will, Ian, *Underworld*, Harrap, 1985
Gosling, John, *The Ghost Squad*, W. H. Allen, 1959
Grant, Douglas, *The Thin Blue Line*, John Long 1973
Greeno, Edward, *War on the Underworld*, John Long, 1960
Hercules, Trevor, *Labelled a Black Villain*, Fourth Estate, 1989
Higgins, Robert, *In the Name of the Law*, John Long, 1958
Hobbs, Dick, *Doing the Business*, Oxford University Press, 1988
Hobsbawm, E. J., *Bandits*, Pelican, 1969
Howe, Sir Ronald, *The Pursuit of Crime*, Arthur Barker, 1961
Hutchinson, Roger, *High Sixties*, Mainstream Publishing, 1992
Kelland, Gilbert, *Crime in London*, Grafton, 1987
Kohn, Marek, *Dope Girls*, Lawrence and Wishart, 1992
Kohn, Marek, *Narcomania*, Faber and Faber, 1987

Knight, Ronnie, with Barrie Tracey, *Black Knight*, Century 1990

Kray, Kate, *Married to the Krays*, Atlantic Publishing, 1988

Kray, Kate *Murder, Madness and Marriage*, Blake, 1993

Kray, Reg, *Born Fighter*, Arrow, 1991

Kray, Reg, *Thoughts*, River First, 1991

Kray, Reg and Ron Kray, with Fred Dineage, *Our Story*, Sidgwick and Jackson, 1988

Kray, Charlie with Robin McGibbon, *Me and My Brothers*, Grafton, 1988

Lambrianou, Tony, *Inside the Firm*, Smith Gryphon, 1991

Lee, Dick and Pratt, Colin, *Operation Julie*, W. H. Allen, 1978

Lock, Joan, *Scotland Yard Casebook*, Robert Hale, 1983

Lucas, Norman, *Britain's Gangland*, W. H. Allen, 1969

McArthur, A. and Long, H. Kingsley, *No Mean City*, Neville Spearman, 1956

McNee, Sir David, *McNee's Law*, Collins, 1983

McVicar, John, *McVicar By Himself*, Arrow, 1979

Mark, Sir Robert, *In the Office of Constable*, Collins, 1978

Martienssen, Anthony, *Crime and the Police*, Penguin, 1953

Morton, James, *Gangland*, Little Brown, 1992

Morton, James, *Bent Coppers*, Little Brown, 1993

Murphy, Robert, *Smash and Grab*, Faber and Faber, 1993

O'Mahoney, Maurice, *King Squealer*, W. H. Allen, 1978

Parker, Robert, *Rough Justice*, Fontana, 1981

Patrick, James, *A Glasgow Gang Observed*, Eyre Methuen, 1973

Payne, Leslie, *The Brotherhood*, Michael Joseph, 1973

Progl, Zoe, *Woman of the Underworld*, Arthur Barker, 1964

Read, Piers Paul, *The Train Robbers*, Coronet, 1986

Richardson, Charles, *My Manor*, Sidgwick and Jackson, 1991

Samuel, Raphael, *East End Underworld*, Routledge and Keegan Paul, 1981

Scott, Sir Harold, *Scotland Yard*, Penguin, 1954

Sharpe, F. D., *Sharpe of the Flying Squad*, John Long, 1938

Short, Martin, *Crime Inc*, Thames Methuen, 1984

Short, Martin, *Lundy*, Grafton Books, 1991

Sillitoe, Percy, *Cloak Without Dagger*, Cassell and Co., 1955

Slipper, Jack, *Slipper of the Yard*, Sidgwick and Jackson, 1981

Sparks, Ruby, with Norman Price, *Burglar to the Nobility*, Arthur Barker, 1961

Stedman Jones, Gareth, *Outcast London*, Oxford University Press, 1971

Taylor, Laurie, *In the Underworld*, Basil Blackwell, 1984

Tullett, Tom, *Murder Squad*, Triad Grafton, 1981

Van Den Berg, Tony, *Who Killed Freddy Mills?* Penguin, 1993

Webb, Duncan, *Dead Line for Crime*, Frederick Muller, 1955

Wheen, Francis, *Tom Driberg*, Chatto and Windus, 1990

Wickstead, Bert, *Gangbuster*, Futura, 1985

Woodhall, Edwin T., *Secrets of Scotland Yard*, Bodley Head, 1936

INDEX

267